A Case Study in Contextualization

A Case Study in Contextualization

The History of the German Church Growth Association 1985–2003

FRED W. MCRAE

With a Foreword by William Wagner

WIPF & STOCK · Eugene, Oregon

A CASE STUDY IN CONTEXTUALIZATION
The History of the German Church Growth Association 1985–2003

Copyright © 2014 Fred W. McRae. All rights reserved. Except for brief quotations in critical publications or reviews, no part of this book may be reproduced in any manner without prior written permission from the publisher. Write: Permissions, Wipf and Stock Publishers, 199 W. 8th Ave., Suite 3, Eugene, OR 97401.

Wipf & Stock
An Imprint of Wipf and Stock Publishers
199 W. 8th Ave., Suite 3
Eugene, OR 97401

www.wipfandstock.com

ISBN 13: 978-1-62032-850-7

Manufactured in the U.S.A.

Trademark Office by Biblica, Inc.™

Scriptures taken from the Holy Bible, New International Version®, NIV®. Copyright © 1973, 1978, 1984, 2011 by Biblica, Inc.™ Used by permission of Zondervan. All rights reserved worldwide. www.zondervan.com The "NIV" and "New International Version" are trademarks registered in the United States Patent and Trademark Office by Biblica, Inc.™

Contents

	Foreword by William Wagner	vii
	Preface	xi
	Introduction	xv
1	Defeat and Disgrace: Germany in Context	1
2	The Formative Years of German Church Growth 1967–1979	31
3	The Foundational Years of German Church Growth 1980–1985	64
4	German Church Growth Takes Root 1986–1990	97
5	The Zenith of German Church Growth 1991–1995	131
6	The Decline of German Church Growth 1996–2003	155
7	Analysis: German Church Growth and Missiology	184
	Further Readings	217
	Glossary	219
	Important Events in the Development of the GCGA	223
	Bibliography	225
	Index	233

Foreword

Since the end of World War II there have been many very important changes in the religious landscape of Germany as well as all of Europe. Prior to the great war most Germans believed that the church played an important part in their lives, but the war was so disastrous that their beloved "Heimat" lay in ruins and some even doubted that the church could rise again to its same high level of acceptance. Starting in 1945 and extending for five years there was a real revival of Christianity; but soon due to the rise of secularism and other forces, the church began its slow decline in both membership and influence.

Many church leaders tried to stem the tide or at least they sought to understand the reasons for the church's demise. It was from this situation that many began to look to other countries where the churches were vibrant, alive and growing. During the second half of the twentieth century the church in the United States was at the forefront of developing new tools that could lead to growth. For example, some rather normal churches had spectacular growth and gave rise to the creation of the term "Mega Churches."

At the same time another movement called the Church Growth Movement was founded by Dr. Donald McGavran, a professor at Fuller Theological Seminary. He sought to discover the underlying reasons for growth in the church by discarding the usual reasons and doing a much deeper study using such tools as anthropology, sociology and other areas of study. He was mostly interested in helping the churches in the developing countries but many of his students took the new information and began to apply it to the western church. As the movement began to show success, some in Europe took notice and wondered if they too could use the works of McGavran and his students to help stop the decline and aid in growing the church in their part of the world.

It is at this point in the history of the movement that Dr. Fred McRae takes up the story. Many European church leaders felt that they had much to learn from what was taking place in the United States of America. It was in 1985 that some laymen and a few pastors created the German Church Growth Association in the hopes that the German church might turn around and been to grow once again.

I first met Fred at several church growth meetings but I really got to know of his talents when he became one of my PhD students at the Evangelical Theological Faculty in Leuven, Belgium. His credentials were solid and he also was interested in seeing the church grow in Europe. Fred was an American missionary working in Germany who was successful in understanding the German culture and in finding ways for him and his family to become a part of it. When some of my German colleagues learned that Fred wanted to write on the German Church Growth Association they were skeptical that such a study could be accomplished by an American—whom they saw as an outsider. This book has proven them wrong. In fact one of the great advantages of the book is that the author is well versed in both cultures and has some gifts that a person living in only one culture does not possess. He has produced an outstanding book showing the two elements of the study, the American movement and the German Church.

Again some doubted that a satisfactory study could be written so soon after the events had taken place. Generally a longer time period is needed so that the historian can better evaluate what really took place. However Fred was fortunate in that the German Church Growth Association had a very well defined beginning and end and only had a real life of eighteen years. This made it much easier to define the events during the period of its existence.

Fred not only wanted to write a history but more importantly, he desired to study and analyze the process of contextualization of an American movement into a German context. A major question that the book seeks to answer is, "Was the German Church Growth Association successful in taking an American model and placing it into a German situation?" The answer will surprise you.

This book provides the reader with both a big picture perspective on the growing church in general together with a very personal application. Fred was not interested only in reporting facts, but because he and his family have spent so much of their lives in mission work, he wanted to write a book that would help others in their task of attempting to win the world to a saving knowledge of Jesus Christ. Although he has needed to approach the subject with a critical mindset it is apparent that his end goal is to help the church find better ways to present the Gospel.

The book has some limitations in that it is written at a high academic level. It will be most useful in the hands of those who are working in the area of church growth and contextualization. But at the same time the style and flow are such that the average reader will find it refreshing and enjoyable. This book is one of the first to be written that makes a full appraisal of a church growth association in a country. Many others will follow in the author's footsteps and will undoubtedly benefit from the research done by Dr. Fred McRae.

Dr. William Wagner
Director PhD Program
Olivet University, San Francisco

Preface

Contextualization is the most important aspect of doing missionary work. The purpose of this book is to introduce missionaries, students of missions, and local churches' mission committees to this topic. The gospel message that Jesus Christ paid the penalty for the sins of the world never changes. However, communicating it in such a way that the hearer understands and responds to the good news may take different avenues and forms, depending on the situation. Explaining the gospel to a young man who has never held a Bible is very different than communicating it to a nominal Christian caught cheating on his wife.

Contextualization means tailoring the gospel presentation for a particular context or culture. The most elementary aspect of contextualization is obvious; a missionary sent to Japan must first learn Japanese. However, understanding culture involves much more than learning the language. Our culture forms the common ideas, feelings, and values that guide us. It organizes and regulates what we think about God, the world, and humanity. Culture explains why Germans use first names only when addressing family and friends, and why Americans use first names to address almost everyone. It explains why Americans view Germans as unfriendly and aloof, while Germans find Americans arrogant and loudmouthed. For me, learning German was only the first step in understanding the culture. It took time to understand the intricate nuances of the culture. However, I quickly learned not to address my son's kindergarten teacher by her first name. That was taboo.

This book is a case study of contextualization on a massive scale, encompassing the entire country of Germany. It traces the history of the German Church Growth Association and shows how this indigenous or native organization contextualized an American evangelistic endeavor, the Church Growth Movement.

After ten years of pastoring in the United States and twenty-five years working as an American missionary, I realized that there is a scarcity of basic knowledge concerning how the gospel spreads in a culture.

Preface

While there is much literature on the topic of missions, few Christians read literature that concentrates on how missions function. It is not because Christians are not interested in missions, but because this literature is difficult to understand. The most important book on missions written in the past fifty years is David Bosch's *Transforming Mission* (1991). It is the most widely used textbook on missions in the world. However, it is so complicated that a reader's guide was published so students could understand it.

Many churches and many Christians financially support foreign missions. On the other hand, there is little understanding of how the gospel is disseminated and subsequently Christians may be ill prepared to judge how their missionaries carry out their ministries. My hope is that this study will encourage Christians to be more knowledgeable of how the Great Commission is carried out. I hope this book pushes the reader to begin to seek more understanding of missions and what goes on in the field, so he will read more, study more, and pray more. In order to do this I have concentrated on what I consider the most important and all-encompassing aspect of missions: the contextualization of the gospel.

This study is a history of how the German Church Growth Association (GCGA) contextualized the gospel using church growth methodology. Chapter 1 introduces the reader to those factors influencing the German culture and to the German Protestant Church, which plays the central role in the contextualization process. Chapters 2 to 4 show that, following its founding in 1985, the GCGA went through a phase of rapid development where it implemented its plan for contextualization. Chapter 5 explains how the organization advanced until it reached the peak of influence in the 1990s. After this period, the movement slowly declined until ceasing to exist. Chapter 6 records the negative trends that eventually led to the closure of the organization in 2003. Finally, chapter 7 analyzes the contextualization strategy of the GCGA, judges how well the organization met its goals, and its contribution to the field of missiology.

There are discussion questions at the end of each chapter. These questions are not exhaustive and are not meant to correspond to every contextual issue in the chapter. The questions should evoke discussion on the major issues pertaining to the contextualization process and lead the reader to discover other factors in the chapter influencing how church growth and the gospel were communicated to the German culture. For the purpose of this study a glossary is included in the appendix. A time line of important events in the life cycle of the GCGA is also included. Transcripts of interviews and personal communications are available in English from the author.

From 1986 to 1993, I was a missionary with OC International serving in Germany as a church growth consultant with the Campaign for Church Growth (*Aktion Gemeindeaufbau*), the German branch of Overseas Crusades, and a founding member of the GCGA. I became acquainted with most of the personalities involved in developing and promoting church growth in Germany, and helped promote church growth principles in both West Germany and East Germany. My work involved consultations with the German Protestant Church, the Free Churches, and the Catholic Church. Although a latecomer in the development of the GCGA, I was able to observe the organization at its zenith and to experience opposition to the movement, as well as its relative success in contextualizing church growth within the German culture. While this vantage point was beneficial in analyzing the movement, close association potentially could impede a critical examination of the association. From 1993 until the present, I have worked with the German Baptists and Brethren Church as a church planting and church growth consultant. The long period working independently of the GCGA has provided not only more experience but also ensured a healthy distance to critically evaluate its impact.

I am extremely grateful to the founding fathers of the German Church Growth Association. I was granted unfettered access to all archival material and personal libraries tracing the development of German church growth. The translations from German to English for the purpose of this study are entirely my own.

Introduction

The German Church Growth Association (GCGA) was an attempt to contextualize the worldwide Church Growth Movement (CGM) within the framework of the German Protestant Church. Donald A. McGavran (1897–1990) is the Father of the CGM. While a missionary in India, McGavran began to wonder why some churches grew and others did not. This led him to discover the factors that both facilitated and inhibited the growth of the church. In 1957, he returned to the States and founded the Institute for Church Growth in Eugene, Oregon. In 1965, he became the founding dean of the School of World Mission at Fuller Theological Seminary. While at Fuller, his church growth ideas were popularized and distributed internationally through literature and by Fuller graduates.

The amount of church growth literature multiplied and is now massive, but McGavran's primary work, *Understanding Church Growth*, remains the bible of the CGM. It was one of the first church growth books translated into German. McGavran advocated a return to the classical mission principles of emphasizing evangelism and church planting. He also encouraged the use of both the social and behavioral sciences as missionary tools to determine how best to contextualize the gospel in a particular culture. McGavran's most significant contribution to contextualization was his belief that a person should not have to leave their home culture in order to hear the gospel and become a Christian. McGavran's influence on the GCGA, as well as that of other American church growth specialists, is documented in this study.

This German Church Growth Association sought to contextualize church growth principles within the German Protestant Church (GPC) at a time when the GPC was in rapid decline. Thousands of church members were leaving the church each year. This offers an intriguing situation seldom available to be observed. When the GCGA offered to help bolster the failing GPC using church growth methods, the Church Growth Movement was at the height of its world influence. This offered an unparalleled opportunity to observe how American church growth principles would work in such a complex environment as the GPC. The possibility to research this situation was the motivation behind this case study. It provided an opportunity to learn from the successes and failures of a mission-oriented indigenous movement, the GCGA, which strived to revive a dying German church through an imported American evangelistic model.

This situation raised three important questions. First, how successful was the GCGA in contextualizing an American program in Germany? Second, what can be learned about contextualizing the gospel in other countries? Third, is it wise for missionaries to try to contextualize an American method of evangelism into a foreign culture? It is the goal of this study to answer these and other questions related to missions. In addition, I hope that this study will provide insights into the ways to contextualize the gospel in Germany, as well as other countries. Most importantly, I hope this case study will encourage Christians to understand not only the importance of how the gospel is spread on the mission field, but to see that God is the true missionary. He is the one who continues to seek out the lost wherever they are, and reaches them regardless of cultural obstacles and the mistakes made by his servants.

1

Defeat and Disgrace

Germany in Context

> Proclamation No. 1
>
> To the People of Germany:
>
> I, general Dwight D. Eisenhower, Supreme Commander of the Allied Expeditionary Force, do hereby proclaim as follows: The Allied Forces serving under my command have now entered Germany. We come as conquerors, but not as oppressors. In the area of Germany occupied by the forces under my command, we shall obliterate Nazism and German militarism. We shall overthrow the Nazi rule, dissolve the Nazi party and abolish the cruel, oppressive and discriminatory laws and institutions, which the party has created . . . Issued, March 1945.[1]

History in Germany is the national pastime. Everything centers on it whether it be familial, parochial, or political. This is something many Americans have failed to learn. According to Germans Americans have no history, relatively speaking, so they ignore it. Germans have a point, especially when you realize the doors of the local German bakery are older than our country. American missionaries and business people ignore this fact to their peril. Why does it take Germans so long to make a decision about anything? Why do they think Americans are rude and pushy? Why do Americans think Germans are so unfriendly? Why have so few Germans accepted Christ as their personal Savior? These problems are solvable, but not without contextualization.

---

1. Hartrich, *The Fourth and Richest Reich*, 44.

I want to introduce you, the reader, to the German culture. This is the first and most important step in contextualizing the good news about Jesus, and will take some effort on your part. To understand Germans, you have to understand the aftermath of World War II. Yes, you can skip the entire story of WWII, but you have to know what happened to Germans after their defeat. This is what still haunts them today and is key to understanding the German psyche and the contextualization process. Most importantly, Germany is a mission field. There are 82 million Germans, making it the most populated country in Europe, but only 2.5 percent of Germans have trusted Christ as Savior. Understanding how the postwar period affected the German mind and heart is the key to contextualizing the gospel in this very complex and needy mission field. Finally, the postwar period serves as a direct link to the founding of the German Church Growth Association.

The Effects of the War on Germany

In 1937, the German Reich extended over 470,662 square kilometers. During the course of World War II more land was added through the acquisition of Czechoslovakia, Austria, Poland, and Russia. Following the May 8, 1945 unconditional surrender to the Allied Forces Germany lost 24.20 percent of its original area.[2] It no longer included the lands of the former Reich east of the Oder-Neisse Line such as parts of Pomerania, West Prussia, Silesia, and East Prussia. These former German areas were then integrated into Poland and Russia.[3] Since the Russians had insisted on holding on to all the parts of Poland they had annexed in 1939 (the Curzon Line), the Poles were compensated with the lands of the former German Reich.

The Allies were divided on administrating postwar Germany. The Russians' idea of democracy was a Bolshevized Germany, a people's republic subservient to Moscow. In October of 1945, it became apparent this problem with the Russians was not going to be resolved. In April of 1949, the western Allies agreed to replace the military government with a civilian government. In May, the Constituent Parliament adopted the Basic Law (*Grundgesetz*) of the future Federal Republic of Germany. In the Russian zone, a constitution for the Democratic Republic of Germany

2. Grosser, *The Federal Republic of Germany*, 4–5.
3. Bramsted, *Germany*, 6.

was adopted, and by August, the institutions of the new country were in place. Politically and ideologically, the division of Germany was initiated. With the building of the Berlin Wall in 1961, the division of the two states of Germany was complete.[4]

The Effects of the War on the German People

The German problems of 1945 were immeasurable. Beyond the fact that they were a conquered people, their immediate needs were food, shelter, clothing, purging (of Nazis), and disarmament. Refugees and displaced persons numbered in the millions. Almost 4.5 million Germans were expelled from the land annexed by Poland and poured into western Germany. Hundreds of thousands of these refugees, mostly the elderly, women, and children never arrived at their intended destination. All central and state governments had collapsed; county and city governments no longer existed. People searched for shelter, clothing, loved ones, and food.[5] By the end of the war, few Germans were living in their homes. Millions of city dwellers had sought safety in the countryside, and millions fled from the east to the west, fearing the hordes of Russians.

Two and a half million German civilians died in the war. Every major German city was a pile of rubble. For example, in Berlin, a city of four million, there were more houses destroyed than ever had existed in Munich. The historian Friedrich Meincke wrote that in 1945 "Germany was a burned out crater of power politics."[6] Everywhere there was hunger and despair. The end of the war created more hardships instead of less. Three million German soldiers had died in the war. Nearly a million German prisoners of war died in captivity in Siberian prisons. According to the official calculation in 1959 of the West German government, 7,032,800 Germans perished in Hitler's war. War tribunals tried 22,000 Germans for war crimes. Fifteen hundred of these were executed and 15,000 imprisoned.[7]

The Allies' desire to rehabilitate the Germans was applied to a demoralized and wretched people. One hundred thousand people were dying of hunger in Hamburg at the end of 1946. In Cologne, only 12

4. Birke, *Nation ohne Haus*, 313.
5. Clay, *Decision in Germany*, 15–16.
6. Elliott, *Hitler and Germany*, 108.
7. Ibid.

percent of the children were of normal weight. Millions of Germans were without the basic needs to exist. The misery endured by the Germans is hard to imagine. Refugees had nothing but the clothes on their backs and no hope. They wandered from place to place, barred from every form of shelter, simply because there was nothing left to share. The death statistics of the German military and civilian war do not include the number of German refugees who died. The humiliation, physical and psychological damage to German women has yet to be fully comprehended. As the Red Army "freed" Germans from National Socialism, they raped over a million German girls and women.

Every aspect of German life felt the influence of the occupational forces. All four powers carried out de-Nazification efforts. However, in the West-Zone the Americans were especially fervent in carrying out this aspect of the occupation. Where the British and the French were somewhat liberal in how they carried out investigations, and willingly compromised on some issues, the Americans had no interest in compromise. They fired school teachers, university professors, public officials, and business leaders. Everyone having any dealings with the old regime, and any directly affiliated or even remotely involved with the administration of the Nazis was arrested. By the end of 1945, approximately one hundred thousand Germans had been detained. The Americans tried to sift through the population and found themselves inundated with over 13 million dossiers. This de-Nazification and re-education program continued until 1947 when it was obvious the program not only had failed, but actually hindered the rebuilding of the country. The Germans felt that "only the stupid and small fish get caught, the big ones get away."[8]

The loss and devastation of the war not only left terrible scars on the German self-confidence, but this hated re-education campaign also served to destroy whatever self-confidence may have existed prior to the war. Further, the occupying forces were not content to focus on rooting out Nazis and re-education of the populous. They sought to change all aspects of German life by controlling the press and radio. In addition, Germany was to pay war reparations. The Russians' price tag was $20 billion. The Russians also wanted to crush Germany economically. Complete factories were dismantled and taken to Russia.[9] It would not be until

---

8. Birke, *Nation ohne Haus*, 66.
9. Balfour, *West Germany*, 138–39.

the 1960s that Germany's economy would emerge as the *Wirtschaftswunder*, becoming an economic world power.

In 1945, there was a national sense of bearing guilt for the atrocities of the war. Politicians and theologians did their best to communicate this to the populous. The message was that each German bore guilt for war atrocities. The fledgling political parties quickly recognized this collective guilt. For example, the Christian Democratic Union's founders voiced the shame of the German nation: "Out of the chaos of guilt and shame that the idolizing of a criminal brought us, a new order of democracy and freedom can be founded, if we always use as our source the spiritual power of Christianity."[10]

Although the political parties were quick to recognize collective guilt, this process was slow in the nation as a whole. In addition to dealing with the loss and destruction of the war, the German culture had not escaped the ramifications of having four different forms of government in less than a generation; before 1918 there was the constitutional monarchy, from 1918 to 1933 there was a parliamentary democracy, from 1933 to 1945 a dictatorship, and after 1945 the divided Germany. The great majority of teachers avoided mentioning the dark aspects of the nation's past and taught no history after the nineteenth century. The older generation of teachers were reluctant to discuss these things, because they had already been through several purges. The younger people learned little or nothing at the universities of Germany's role in the war.[11] This lack of dealing directly with the issues left an entire generation of Germans wondering what it meant to be a German. If any clear meaning emerged, it was that it was bad to be German.

The lack of self-esteem for Germans continues to have repercussions for German Christianity. It is difficult for German Christians to speak assertively of the uniqueness of Jesus Christ and Christianity in reference to other religions and the need for Christian faith. Although they believe this, they find it very difficult to speak dogmatically of Christianity as the only true religion. Some German Christians believe that the current pitiful state of German Christianity is the direct result of God's punishment on the German nation.

The postwar period brought a desire to try new things, especially if it came from America. One of the first things introduced into the German

---

10. Birke, *Nation ohne Haus*, 106.
11. Grosser, *The Federal Republic of Germany*, 108–9.

economy as it began to recover was canned beer. The American model of the supermarket also was introduced and was viewed as very progressive. Although the German identity was never lost, seen in the continued bent toward provincialism and conservatism, there was a desire to modernize, using America as a model. This meant going beyond what was typically German and opening up to new ideas of modernization. This resulted in a change in all areas of German life from its very foundations.[12]

The Effects of the War on the German Church

There were some positive effects on the church in that there was a sense of solidarity and unity after having survived the onslaught of the war. There were also church leaders who wanted to reorganize the church so that it could function in the chaos of postwar Germany. This resulted in the formal founding of the German Protestant Church in Eisenach in 1948. Unfortunately, Americans refer to the German Protestant Church as the "German State Church." This is incorrect, since in 1918 the German Kaiser abdicated the throne and simultaneously ended the German State Church. Thus, Germany has no "state church." The correct title is "German Protestant Church," "German National Church," "*Volkskirche*," or "*Landeskirche*."

Although the government subsidizes the German Protestant Church through income taxation, there is no state control over the churches. The subsequent federation and constitution allowed for formal unity while guaranteeing the autonomy of the different confessions. This constitution unified the German Protestant Church, both in East and West Germany. Although this was established in 1948, a common union between the twenty *Landeskirchen* or regional churches already existed. In 1948, they simply agreed on a common ground for fellowship and ministry. Three confessions were recognized: Lutheran, Reformed, and United. They were autonomous denominations sharing a wider fellowship.[13] Thus, the German Protestant Church (GPC) is the officially recognized and subsidized national church consisting of three confessions (Lutheran, Reformed, and United) spread out over twenty districts or regions in Germany. This church is distinct from the German Free Churches, discussed below.

---

12. Ibid., 397–406.
13. Drummond, *German Protestantism*, 276.

Defeat and Disgrace

The German Baptists, one of the so-called Free Churches, experienced a time of revival in the years immediately after the war. In 1946, the Baptists had 81,796 members. At the end of 1949, they had grown to over one hundred thousand.[14] The Baptists, along with the Methodists, Pentecostals, and others are the German Free Churches, because their members are free of (not subject to) the church income tax. The German Protestant Church also experienced a time of renewal.

Churches were full. The church was the only German institution left intact and, to some extent, had stood its ground against the Third Reich. The *Volkskirche* also provided much needed social and material assistances to the populous. "The masses, in looking for hope, rediscovered the Bible, and found that its redemptive, healing message had behind it the ultimate authority of God."[15] In spite of full church services during that time, a real national spiritual revival never came about. It was not that the Germans were irreligious, but other things occupied their minds. The misery that Germans endured took precedence over religious duty. The very act of existing became the typical German's religion. Time was spent finding ways to avoid death by starvation or exposure, rather than expanding one's spiritual life.[16] The church was not able to speak to the problems of postwar Germany, because the church was not aware of the actual nature of the problems. Instead of revising its position to meet the special needs of the time, the GPC continued with its traditional activities and subsequently lapsed into stagnation.

In 1945, those prominent church leaders who had identified with the Nazis were publicly disgraced, and never again held church office. Others were given minor pastoral responsibilities in some church district other than their own. The provincial structure of the church was reorganized coinciding with the new civil administrations. A central council and synod were founded that unified all of the ecclesiastical provinces in both East and West Germany. The single most significant postwar ecclesiastical event was the signing of the Stuttgart Confession of Guilt. The confession was an admission of guilt by the German church leaders for "not having done enough with greater courage, prayed with greater faith, believed with greater joy and loved with greater zeal." This was a

---

14. Wagner, *New Move Forward in Europe*, 59.
15. Ibid., 193–95.
16. Greschat, *Die evangelische Christenheit*, 70–73.

statement made to the ecumenical movement outside of Germany. Many of those who signed themselves had suffered under Hitler.[17]

The first contact with the German Protestant Church directly after the war was Great Britain. Britain's desire was to use the *Volkskirche* as another avenue to indoctrinate Germany with western values, especially democracy. By transforming the German society into a democracy, the West could insure that Germany never again would threaten world peace. The British saw close ties with the church and state as normal, because they also had a similar relationship between the Anglican Church and the British government. Great Britain viewed the church and democracy as mutual partners, because they had the same goals of seeking a lasting peace and the welfare of man. This was also the position of the Americans, who supported fully using the German church as a way to rid Germany of Nazis and their sympathizers. Democracy would only grow in soil rid of National Socialism.[18] Much exchange resulted between Germany and England, as well as the United States.

The United States sought to promote cultural exchange, especially among the youth. Interdenominational congresses promoted German and American theologians. The Office of Education and Religious Affairs, an arm of the American military government, controlled this exchange program. Even before the military began to organize and promote religion as a means of re-inventing German culture, Christians in the States had already made contact with Christians in Germany. The Federal Council of Churches of Christ in America (FCC), which represented thirty-two protestant denominations, formed a network between member churches in the States and German Protestants. Study trips for American theologians and church leaders were already taking place in 1945. The FCC coordinated this exchange with the American military. The Germans felt this step was not necessary since they were more than willing to correspond with American Christians. The Lutheran Church–Missouri Synod had maintained ties to Lutherans in the Old Country. After the First World War physical relief for fellow Lutherans was a prime consideration; this concern continued after the Second World War. The American Lutherans not only sent tons of food and other relief to Europe after the war, but they also provided theological literature for German Lutheran pastors. In 1948, the Missouri Synod launched a series of seminars

---

17. Gollwitzer, *The Demands of Freedom*, 17.
18. Greschat, *Die evangelische Christenheit*, 31–37.

at Bad Boll. These seminars were "meant to apprise of and reappraise the principles of Lutheran confessionalism."[19]

In spite of the positive developments for Christians in Germany and America, the war destroyed German trust in the church. The Nazis' intervention into the life of the church had a lasting negative effect. The reorganization of the GPC in 1945 had no effect in undoing the damage. The independence of the GPC and the lack of respect for any centralization of church leadership became the chief characteristic of the postwar German Protestant Church.[20]

In 1949, West Germany's constitution recognized the GPC's status as a legal corporation, guaranteeing the church's freedom and governmental financial support subsidized by an income tax levied on all church members. This was not the case in East Germany, the German Democratic Republic (GDR). The relationship between the church and the communists went through several phases. At first, the Soviets were friendly toward the church. The reason for this was the opposition to the National Socialists by many church leaders during the war. After the war, the church continued to take a stand against the arms race and the nuclear build-up. This coincided with the communists' ideas. This kept the church in relatively good relationship with the communist regime, at least for a while. However, this soon changed. The second phase ushered in the state's desire to coordinate the church's activities with its own goals. There was an attempt by certain pro-communist pastors to wrestle control of the church from the more skeptical pastors, but this failed. The communist sympathizers among the pastors never numbered more than 2 percent.[21]

In spite of the tension between the occupying powers, as well as the ever-increasing political division, the German church continued to organize meetings between the East and the West. These meetings became a symbol for what Germans wanted; total unification.[22] The last such meeting was the Church Day at Leipzig in 1954, with half a million people attending this national church conference. Because Leipzig is in the GDR, this made a religious, as well as a political, statement to the Marxist regime. There was a rally on the last day of the conference that

19. Ibid., 428–29.
20. Ibid., 49.
21. Ulrich, "Evangelism in Germany," 8–9.
22. Chadwick, *Christian Church*, 11.

was clearly anti-communism. This did not sit well with GDR officials. These types of actions, along with the steady stream of the populous fleeing to the West, eventually led to the construction of the Berlin Wall.

Marxism was determined to rid East Germany of the vestiges of Christianity. Schools and universities were seed grounds for the communist ideology. Written and spoken propaganda swayed minds away from "the harmfulness of religious superstition." By the early 1950s, the communists had failed to gain German followers. Only 10 to 15 percent of East Germans were party faithful, while 70 percent of Unity Party members were church members and sent their children to church for religious instruction. This, however, would soon change.

The third phase brought severe pressure on the church. The Soviet-backed Socialist Unity Party of Germany sought to isolate the church from public affairs. The state withdrew subsidies and the scope of the church was strictly limited. Gospel preaching and evangelism, especially among the youth, was prohibited. By June of 1953, the East German state arrested more than five hundred pastors, and over three thousand youths were expelled from school or penalized in other ways. The following months brought some reprieve. The government desired to patch the relationship with the church by reversing some of its most draconian measures. This period was short-lived.

The fourth phase came in 1954. East Germany expelled all pastors and deaconesses from the West who had volunteered for an exchange program in the East and the program stopped. This was an attempt to secularize institutions previously supported by the church. The state barred the church from any institution having state ties. For example, East Germany banned chaplaincies in police stations, made hospital work difficult, and kept prison ministry to a minimum. The state instituted the Youth Dedication (*Jugendweihe*) for those fourteen years of age, in order to compete directly with confirmation. The goal was to alienate young people from the church and indoctrinate them with the Marxist-Leninist philosophy.[23] In 1955, in spite of governmental efforts, only 15 percent of the youth participated in the Youth Dedication. Two years later participation was at 32 percent, and by 1958, it reached 47 percent. Surveys in 1964 indicated that at least 90 percent of the youth opted for the state sanctioned Youth Dedication, instead of confirmation.[24]

23. Ibid., 43–44.
24. Kuen, *I Will Build My Church*, 288–89.

In East Germany, there was no church tax and religious people held no high public office. Action by the state put much pressure on the families of Christian pastors. Those pastors I worked with said that their children were ostracized in school for not joining the Young Pioneers, and therefore never able to attend college. The Young Pioneers was a communist youth organization for children six to fourteen years of age. In addition, while West German school children were learning English and French, those in East Germany were taught Russian. Also, the church tax system made it easy to count members in the West. If you paid the tax, you were a member. In East Germany, counting members was much more of a challenge. The conditions in the GDR caused church leaders to rethink traditional church membership. For example, many parents did not have their infants baptized because it could hurt the child in both school and vocation. The number of baptisms in the GDR sank to only 20 percent of the population in the 1970s. Many un-baptized Germans took part in church activities without formal church membership. As a result, church leaders believed the number of "real" church members outnumbered the formal members.[25]

Marxism's attack on the church was relentless and, after years of pressure, had devastating effects. In 1950, 81 percent of East Germans considered themselves Protestant. By 1964 the number fell to 59 percent, and by 1982, the percentage fell further to around 46 percent, with 45 percent registering no confession. In 1990, 32 percent of East Germans stated that they believed in God, 54 percent indicated they were atheists, and 14 percent said they could not say whether they believed in God.[26] In 2012, 75 percent of East Germans have no church affiliation, while 70 percent of West Germans are church members. However, the true indicator of just how successful the communist regime was in inoculating the populous against the church is in another figure. In West Germany, for example, only 24 percent of those belonging to no confession have never belonged to a church. That means that the vast majority of West Germans *leave* the church, because of a personal decision. In East Germany, 60 percent of those not claiming church membership have *never been* in the church. They are the third or fourth generation of East Germans who, because of their upbringing, view the church with ambivalence or suspi-

25. Chadwick, *Christian Church*, 189–90.
26. Ulrich, "Evangelism in Germany"; Hild et al., *Was Wird Aus Der Kirche?*, 60–61.

cion.[27] At the very least, the church is irrelevant. The communists were very successful in contextualizing their philosophy.

The Effects of the War on German Evangelism

The positive exchange between the German church with British and American Christians, coupled with the western leanings of the Germans, resulted in an unprecedented openness of Germans toward Americans, as well as toward the rest of the world. This brought about a stronger German church because of ties with Christians from other countries. It also exposed Germany to new methods of evangelism.

That not all welcomed the wave of evangelistic activity after World War II was not because it exposed deficits in the church and accentuated the need for change. Following the war, the GPC simply was not able to meet the evangelistic needs of Germany because it was dealing with its own internal problems.[28] Further, this evangelistic thrust reveals that the German Church Growth Association (GCGA) by far would not be the first and only movement emphasizing evangelism in Germany. Numerous groups desirous of evangelizing Germans filled the postwar years. Evangelistic crusades in the late 1950s through the late 1970s formed a direct link between postwar evangelism and the foundational years of the GCGA.

Germany is, relatively speaking, a young nation. If you consider the reunification, the Germany of today is even younger. The postwar period opened Germany up to the western way of life. Modernization came, bringing with it everything from Elvis Presley to Billy Graham. German life turned upside down. This turmoil also exposed the German church to outside influences. Exchanges began early on, and continue to this day. The importing of American church growth that began in the 1970s was not an anomaly. It simply continued a long tradition of American-German exchange resulting from the tumultuous postwar years. In 1946, Karl Barth's remarks concerning Germany's relationship with America reflected the shame and consternation with which the German culture was now confronted:

> Europe did not free itself, it was freed. A German writer recently wrote that it was a disgrace that they had to come here by land

27. Knepper, "Konfessionslosigkeit."
28. Thadden, "Church Under The Cross," 46–47.

and by sea, thousands of kilometers away, to free Germans from certain Germans, and Europeans from certain Europeans. Are we now going to be revived by America? Imagine if someone had asked this question at the end of the fifteenth century, when America was discovered! Today this is a very serious question. Does this now mean that American democracy, American economics, psychology, sociology, American morality and American Christianity is definitive for us?[29]

As stated above, there was a concerted effort by the West after the war to render spiritual aid to Germany. First, waves of postwar evangelism came from Great Britain, and especially from the United States. As early as 1947 Youth for Christ (YFC) was holding evangelistic rallies in Germany and providing relief material, thousands of Bibles and tracts, as well as "much relief and encouragement to the people of Germany."[30] The Union of Evangelical Free Churches appointed Pastor Willi Sauer to head the German YFC. He coordinated these rallies with John Young, chief of army chaplains. The rallies were of three types. First, there were strictly English-speaking rallies for military personnel and military government employees. Second, there were rallies in English and German for both German and American leadership. Third, there were meetings where only German was spoken. These evangelistic rallies were considered a transitional period with a view to conducting rallies exclusively in German. Some suggested that it would be less expensive and more culturally relevant if Germans came to America for training. This idea failed because, "experience has proven that Americans must enter a country and the work be done in the American style."[31]

In August of 1948, YFC held an international conference at Beatenberg Bible Institute in Beatenberg, Switzerland, to forge plans for a systematic re-evangelization of Europe, and particularly of Germany. Leading American evangelicals such as Billy Graham, Oswald Smith, Harold J. Ockenga, Ralph Freed, Robert Cook, and Bob Jones, II took part in the conference. Participants studied proposals on how "radio, airplanes, evangelistic campaigns, publications, etc." could play a role in reaching the continent. Six hundred participants united to "utilize the ministries of several hundred evangelists, pastors, youth leaders, musicians, contact men and others to reach the major cities of Europe with the

29. Barth, "Zwei Vorträge," 13–14.
30. *Letter from Torrey M. Johnson.*
31. Ibid.

gospel." The Beatenberg Conference resulted in specific plans for evangelistic crusades in Germany under the auspices of the German Evangelical Alliance.[32] The German Evangelical Alliance is a member of the World Evangelical Alliance formed in London in 1846. The purpose of the Alliance is to promote unity among denominations and mission agencies that hold to a belief in the Bible as the inspired word of God and the necessity of faith in Jesus Christ for salvation.[33]

The German Evangelical Alliance invited Billy Graham for a series of evangelistic meetings in the 1950s and 1960s. This was Germany's first exposure to American style evangelism, and it created a mixed reaction. Many criticized Graham's inability to appreciate Germany's postwar problems and his aggressive preaching style. The East German state-controlled press was especially critical of his evangelistic efforts. The *Berlin Sunday News* (*Berliner Sonntagsblatt*) called Graham, much to his chagrin, "God's machinegun."[34] If not for the support and effort of one of Germany's most respected pastors and evangelists, Wilhelm Busch, Graham would have had more difficulties. Busch put his stellar reputation fully behind Graham. In total, Graham led crusades in Germany in 1954, 1955, 1960, 1963, 1966, and 1970.[35]

Graham was not the only evangelist in Germany. The official branch for evangelistic outreach in the GPC, the Office for Evangelism, was vastly expanded and the laity was encouraged to use this opportunity for the gospel. The leaders of the GPC understood that many Germans would be seeking God after the turbulent war years, and in the fall of 1951 in Oldenburg they held various evangelistic outreaches. From 1950 to 1952 there were several other evangelistic campaigns supported by pastors, missionaries, and the laity. In 1952 in Hamburg-Altona, after five months of intensive training, 130 laity visited 2,320 families. Under the leadership of Wilhelm Busch, 400 trained lay workers visited 30,000 homes in Essen in October of 1955. These are a few examples of the extensive efforts of evangelistic campaigns introduced in Germany in the years following the war.[36]

32. *Letter from S. Wasserzug.*
33. "Geschichte."
34. Dr. Billy Graham kommt nach Berlin; Das 'Maschinengewehr Gottes'.
35. Geldbach and Schneider, "Graham," 814.
36. Scharpff, *Geschichte der Evangelisation*, 318–21.

The Graham crusades culminated with the evangelistic campaign, Euro 70, in April of 1970. Transworld Radio transmitted the televised crusade to thirty-five German and twenty other European cities.[37] Euro 70 was sponsored by the German Evangelical Alliance headed by Peter Schneider, who also served as Graham's translator. Over one hundred thousand Europeans simultaneously saw the broadcast, making it the largest evangelistic event in German history. Similar to earlier crusades, there was opposition to Graham's evangelistic methods. Critics viewed his methods as too controversial exemplified by the "call to come forward." The Protestant Student Organizations of North Rhine Westphalia opposed Graham's preaching methods and specifically his over-emphasis of the need for salvation at the expense of social concerns. According to the Student Organizations, Graham "closed the eyes of hearers to social needs."[38]

Although Billy Graham never maintained a permanent presence in Germany, his organization, Youth for Christ, remained. Youth for Christ held its first meeting in Germany at the Bible School in Wiedenest, Germany in 1951. This was a pivotal meeting for German evangelistic ministry. Anton Schulte, who later became one of the most prominent evangelists in Germany, as well as the founder of the New Life Mission and the New Life Bible School, attended this meeting. Hans-Rudolf Wever, the director of German Youth for Christ at that time, provided a tent, as well as evangelists from America. Schulte organized the crusades, worked as tent master, and translated for the Americans. In his organizational role, Schulte encountered the Janz Team. Youth for Christ invited this German-speaking quartet from Canada to hold evangelistic crusades for three months in Germany. Leo Janz, the lead evangelist of the group, encouraged Schulte to begin his own crusade ministry.[39]

The German Tent Mission also carried on a prolific evangelistic tent ministry and arrived much earlier on the scene than Billy Graham, the Janz Quartet or Anton Schulte. The German Tent Mission had a history of holding evangelistic tent meetings well before crusade ministries gained popularity. Jakob Vetter founded the German Tent Mission (GTM) in April 1902, and the ministry continues to this day.[40] The GTM is directly

---

37. *Evangelisationsfernsehen.*
38. *Der Showmaster Gottes.*
39. Schulte, *Nur ein kleiner Dicker,* 75–83.
40. Schmidt-Schell, *Meine Gnade,* 10.

linked to one of the most famous revivals in Germany that occurred in Mülheim in 1905. The GTM provided the tent for a series of prayer meetings that eventually led to the conversion of several thousand Germans. Although the GTM, Anton Schulte, and the Janz Team had similar goals, they worked independently from one another. Even though a German evangelist who had once been employed by the GTM served with the Janz Team, the two organizations had no formal contact.[41]

The German Tent Mission remained dormant during the war years, but evangelistic meetings were welcomed after the war, and the tents were full. The GTM experienced unparalleled openness to the gospel.[42] They were not alone in using tents for evangelism. The Office for Evangelistic Outreach for the GPC in Westphalia, and Youth for Christ made use of tents. There were also independent tent missions that sprang up in several states, including Bavaria and the Rhineland. The Liebenzell Mission and Free Churches also made use of tents to evangelize. By 1960, sixteen tent missions had held 235 evangelistic campaigns. As stated above, Germany had a long history of evangelistic crusades well before the arrival of North American evangelists. However, it was the North Americans who played a prominent role in influencing the formative years of the GCGA.

The Janz Team and Billy Graham formed a direct link to the foundational years of the GCGA. They had a great influence on Bernd Schlottoff, the first chairman of the organization and one of its founders. This connection is explained in chapter two. As Billy Graham's, Schulte's, and the Janz Team's evangelistic ministries peaked and then began to decline, the foundation of the GCGA began to take shape. In fact, the organization saw itself as the third stage of German evangelism. The first stage consisted of the evangelistic crusades in the 1950s and 1960s. The second stage stressed personal evangelism, where Christians shared their faith on an individual and personal level. The third stage implemented church growth.[43] Although the GCGA held no evangelistic crusades, it implemented the methodology of individuals needing a personal conversion experience. The implementation of a call for personal conversion would be the basis for its German church growth strategy. This is crucial for understanding the ecclesiology (what the church is) and practical theology (what the church does) of the new group. As church growth gained

41. Braaten, personal communication with author, 11 March 2005.
42. Scharpff, *Geschichte der Evangelisation*, 303–4.
43. Maier, "Gemeindeaufbau," 181.

momentum in Germany in the 1980s, other indigenous church growth paradigms emerged. These paradigms arose from differing views of the church. The GCGA's emphasis on personal salvation will distinguish it from other church renewal strategies.

Contemporary Renewal Movements

The GCGA and other contemporary renewal movements recognized that the German Protestant Church was losing thousands of church members each year. Each organization had its own interpretations of the reasons for the church's problems, and used church decline to bolster claims for change and to legitimize its own existence. Before the 1960s, there was little concern regarding how many left the church, because the number of those entering the church balanced out those leaving. In the late 1960s, however, the number leaving the church began to far exceed those joining the church. The year 1969 was a low point for the membership of the GPC and marked the beginning of real concern. The number of people leaving the church broke all records, and the number of those attending worship services hit a record low. The number of losses began to increase from 44,000 in 1967 to 61,000 in 1968. In 1969, 112,000 left the church. In 1970, the number jumped to 203,000.[44] The Protestant Church in East Germany also lost members. In 1949, at the time of the founding of East Germany, over 15 million East Germans were members of the Protestant Church. By 1989, little more than 4 million East Germans held ties to the church.[45]

This trend of church losses continued into the 1970s and beyond. The situation led the church to study the sociological, cultural, and economic reasons behind the loss of interest in church membership. The study began in 1972 and the results were published in 1974, under the title, *How Stable is the Church?* (*Wie Stabil ist die Kirche?*). Since the initial investigation, a membership analysis is undertaken every ten years. This analysis of the state of the church coincides with the beginning of the Church Growth Movement in Germany and the establishment of the GCGA. The 1970s proved to be the incubation period for the organization.

---

44. Hild et al., *Wie stabil ist die Kirche?* 1.
45. Pollack, *Change in Religion and Church*, 9, 19.

Restoring the GPC by evangelizing church members started early with the Pietists. Latent Pietism formed fertile ground for discontent with the status quo of the church, and led to the foundation of several organizations desirous of change. The following three contemporary renewal movements were based on certain ecclesiological paradigms. The understanding of the nature and purpose of the church gave rise to each organization having a particular nuance and subsequently spawned their particular renewal strategies for the church. Exploring these major movements will help in understanding why the GCGA was established.

The Fellowship Movement

The Fellowship Movement (*Gemeinschaftsbewegung*) is at its core an evangelistic movement. The parable of the wheat and the tares in Matt 13:24–30 is the basis for the ecclesiology of the Fellowship Movement. According to the movement, the church is a mixture of believers and non-believers. *Corpus permixtum* is not the will of God, but is simply a reality until the Lord's return. The organization sees this condition as an opportunity for evangelism. It is not its mission to root out the tares, but to evangelize them. Their course for church restoration lies in maturing true believers so they are able to evangelize church members not considered true believers.[46]

The Fellowship Movement traces its roots to the German Christian Society, founded in 1780 by the Augsburg preacher, Johann A. Urlsperger. The society drew together those who were concerned about the negative influences of European philosophy and rationalism on German Protestantism. As the movement gained momentum, branch works sprang up throughout Germany and Switzerland. These included groups formed to evangelize the lost, especially Jews and Turks; other branches supported the poor and distributed Christian literature.[47] In 1808, Christian F. Spittler became secretary of the German Christian Society in Switzerland. One of Spittler's greatest achievements was founding the Pilgrim Mission St. Chrischona in 1840. His vision was that St. Chrischona would become a center for the training of evangelists. After Spittler's death in 1867, Carl H. Rappard assumed leadership of the center. Rappard was strongly influenced by the Oxford Movement. The English Oxford Movement

---

46. Drechsel, *Das Gemeindeverständnis*, 35–37.
47. Scharpff, *Geschichte der Evangelisation*, 124–25.

appealed to both the Anglican Church and Catholic Church to return to their former emphasis of personal piety and to reawaken traditions described in the writings of the Church Fathers.[48] Rappard led the school to become the first in German-speaking Europe to train evangelists. Among the later graduates of the school was Jakob Vetter, the founder of the German Tent Mission.[49]

The Oxford Movement in England provided the impetus for the subsequent Sanctification-Evangelization Movement in Germany. These movements ultimately led to the founding of the Fellowship Movement. It was the revival of German Pietism, however, that was the harbinger for these movements.[50] Johann H. Wichern was one of the earliest preachers reviving pietistic theology. His speech on the importance of evangelism in 1848 in Wittenberg led to the founding of the Interior Mission. Wichern's evangelistic enthusiasm is traced to the influence of the Baptist, Johann G. Oncken. Oncken, working for the Tract Society of Lower Saxony, founded in Hamburg the first German Sunday school. The Sunday school, modeled after those in England, taught the Bible, as well as reading and writing to illiterate children. When Oncken resigned from the Sunday school leadership, Wichern then led the school. He carried on the tradition of linking evangelism and social concern with the founding of the Interior Mission. The subsequent popularity and expansion of the mission influenced the future Fellowship Movement. When local Interior Mission groups formed, these drew those with pietistic leanings. These gatherings sparked interest among the neo-Pietists for more formal meetings in order to strengthen the resistance against the growing European secularism.

The secularization and growing atheism of nineteenth-century Germany formed the background for the official founding of the Fellowship Movement. In 1882, Theodor Christlieb explained the basis of the Movement, "We are in the church, we work whenever possible with the church, but we are not under the church."[51] In 1888, the German Protestant Society for Church Revival (GPSCR) held a conference in Gnadau, a small enclave of Moravians near Magdeburg. The conference emphasized the fundamentals that would guide the organization in

48. Latourette, *A History of the Christian Church*, 1116–17.
49. Lange, "Zur Geschichte," 15–16.
50. Fleisch, *Die moderne Gemeinschaftsbewegung*, 10–14.
51. Heimbucher, "Ein missionarischer Unruheherd," 5–8.

the future. Personal salvation and holiness, the second coming of Christ, as well as understanding the church as being the body of Christ, were the fundamentals forming and guiding the Fellowship Movement. The GPSCR, officially organized the following year, incorporated the ideals of the Fellowship Movement. Today it is known as the Gnadau Society (*Gnadauer Verband*).

Theodor Haarbeck and Elias Schrenk gave further profile to the movement with their emphasis on evangelism and the encouragement of a strong laity involvement. Schrenk became one of the most influential Bible teachers in the Fellowship Movement and was prominent as being the first fulltime German evangelist. The involvement of the laity, or the "priesthood of all believers," formed the fundamental ecclesiology of the movement. Church renewal meant allowing the laity to fulfill this scriptural mandate. The theologian, Friedrich Fabri, explained in 1887 that the church sinned if it did not equip believers to use the gifts that God had given them.[52] The Gnadau Society, influenced by the Sanctification-Evangelism Movement, emphasized the need for a personal salvation through Christ. The true church was composed of those having experienced a personal conversion. Personal conversion must precede the maturation of the inner spiritual life or progression in sanctification. As a result, evangelism, with a view to personal conversion and sanctification, were pre-requisites for the restoration of the church. This rubric defines church renewal as an ecclesiastical return to the basic tenants of the Christian faith, which includes a biblical view of evangelism and sanctification. The GCGA also held this view of church renewal.

In November of 1918, the German Kaiser abdicated the throne. This ended the German State Church. The Gnadau Society saw the demise of the German State Church as an opportunity to further their renewal efforts. The vision of a new church, guided by the laity under the preamble of "the priesthood of all believers," could be achieved. How this would practically function within the confines of a well-established parochial and pastoral-centered system would continually be re-examined and discussed for years within the organization.[53] However, the ministries of the Gnadau Society would remain within the GPC. There was no desire to break away from the church, but to remain in the church and work

---

52. Drechsel, *Das Gemeindeverständnis*, 9–12.
53. Ibid., 14–16.

towards evangelism and church renewal.[54] The work of the Society resulted in the establishment of Bible schools, retreat and rehabilitation centers, hospitals, homes for the aged, children's homes, and foreign mission work. Today there are Societies in Holland, Switzerland, Austria, and Scandinavia, as well as in many Eastern European countries.

The Gnadau Society had success in many areas. However, it was never able to fully penetrate the GPC and bring about renewal. Church leadership understood the movement to be anti-church and mistrusted attempts by the group to lead the church back to its biblical roots. As a result, the Society developed a mistrust of the church institutional structure and formed fellowships outside the parochial structure.[55] Nevertheless, they did not break from the church. The inability of the Gnadau Society to integrate its ecclesiology into the GPC left a vacuum in the renewal movement. This need to mature believers and evangelize church members was not lost when the GCGA emerged. The Association developed new methods derived from church growth principles to promote "the priesthood of all believers" in the *Volkskirche*. Likewise, the organization reflected the Society's emphasis on the need for personal conversion and adopted their predecessor's vision of evangelizing church members. The GCGA re-shaped the importance of personal conversion to focus on the growth of the church and couched traditional evangelistic ideas in church growth terminology. Thus, with the introduction of church growth, a new renewal tradition emerged in Germany.

The Confessional Movement

Like the Gnadau Society, the roots of the Confessional Movement (*Bekenntnisbewegung*) continue back to Pietism, as well as the Sanctification-Evangelism Movement. However, the Confessional Movement has a different understanding of the foremost problem of the GPC and the remedy for renewal. Whereas the Gnadau Society understands its role as *missional*, the Confessional Movement views its role as *prophetic*. Whereas the Society's ecclesiology emphasized that it was not the mission of true believers to root out the tares, the Confessional Movement

---

54. Lange, "Zur Geschichte," 25.
55. Heimbucher, "Kirche und Gemeinschaft," 419–27.

takes a more radical approach in adopting Gal 1:6 as their ecclesiological preamble.⁵⁶

The Movement stands against the modernization and liberalization of GPC theology, especially that propagated by Rudolf Bultmann.⁵⁷ Its mission is to magnify and publicize the fact that liberal theology is destroying the traditional GPC, as well as the very fabric of the Christian faith. According to the Movement, the rationalistic erosion of Scripture began in the 1940s. There was concern at that time about the direction of modern theology, but it posed no imminent danger for the parishes, because it was confined to theologians at the university. This changed with the pronouncements of Prof. Dr. Bartsch in Frankfurt in 1941. He argued for the abandonment of Christmas, since it was based on a mere legend in Luke. In addition, on April 21, Rudolf Bultmann gave a lecture in Frankfurt where he stated that the worldview of New Testament writers was one based on mythology. Images such as heaven, hell, angels, demons, and miracles should be understood through the worldview of myth and not reality. This method of interpreting the Bible became known as "de-mythologizing the Scriptures." Bultmann's lecture resulted in a series of protests, since his thesis questioned the veracity of the Bible and the foundations of the Christian faith.⁵⁸ Initially, Bultmann's critics were found only at the universities. Julius Schniewind, Helmut Thielicke, and Felix Flückiger all criticized aspects of Bultmann's findings. Schniewind and Thielicke criticized his denial of the historicity of the Resurrection. Flückiger disputed his dependency on Martin Heidegger's ontology. However, these theologians agreed with the application of the historical-critical method in Bultmann's methodology. The polemic against Bultmann gained momentum in 1948 with the publishing of his 1941 lecture, *New Testament and Mythology*. The protest against his teachings continued into the 1960s with the formal development of the Confessional Movement.⁵⁹

The calling of Willi Marxsen, theology professor at Munster, to the Exam Commission of the Protestant Church in Westphalia in 1961, not only brought the controversy to a head, but also resulted in the dispute finding its way to the parochial level. Two GPC pastors, Rudolf Bäumer

---

56. Bäumer, "Vom ersten zum zweiten Kirchenkampf," 15–22.
57. Stratmann, *Kein anderes Evangelium*, 14–15.
58. Ibid.
59. Schmithals, *Die Theologie*, 254–55.

and Paul Deitenbeck, opposed Marxen's appointment on the grounds he denied the basic tenants of Christianity. After their concerns were ignored, the two pastors called together other pastors and theologians who had similar reactions against Bultmann's de-mythologizing of Scripture. In 1961, these concerned leaders formed the Bethel-Group.[60] On January 12, 1966, the Bethel-Group in the state of North Rhine-Westphalia held a meeting in the city of Hamm to protest the continuing bent of the GPC toward a modern understanding of Scripture that cast doubt on the Christian faith. This meeting resulted in the founding of the Confessional Movement "No Other Gospel" (*Bekenntnisbewegung "Kein anderes Evangelium"*).[61] On March 6, the newly formed organization held its first public conference in Dortmund where approximately 22,000 people attended.

The conflict between the Confessional Movement and the GPC was also evident during the Church Days (*Kirchentage*) in the late 1960s. Church Days were national GPC conferences held every two years, drawing thousands of people and serving as a forum for various religious, political, and social agendas. Unable to condone the theological pluralism represented at the annual event, the Movement not only urged its associates to boycott the Church Days conference, but also inaugurated its own conservative convention called Church Day Under the Word (*Gemeindetag unter dem Wort*). The first conference was held in May of 1973 in Dortmund and 24,000 attended. The second conference in 1975 in Stuttgart had 40,000 in attendance. Subsequent conferences also drew thousands of participants.[62]

Soon after the founding of GCGA in 1985, it attempted to send representatives to these conservative congresses. At least three representatives went to man a booth at the conferences offering church growth literature and information on future regional meetings and study trips. The GCGA hoped to introduce the participants, especially conservative pastors, to church growth by offering free copies of the magazine *Church Growth* (*Gemeindewachstum*) and dialoguing about church growth. It was not easy to gain permission to send representatives, because the congress leadership was skeptical of the GCGA's motives, since they also participated in the theologically liberal Church Days conferences.

60. Bäumer, "Die Bekenntnisbewegung," 36–37.
61. Büchner, "Kein anderes Evangelium," 34.
62. Bäumer, "Die Gemeindetage," 94–95.

The constant theological conflict with the GPC led to a new phase in the development of the Confessional Movement with the establishment of the Theological Society in March of 1969 and the Conference of Confessing Fellowships in October of 1970. The latter served as a union of the organizations in Germany that stood against modern theological trends. This allowed groups such as the Confessional Movement "No Other Gospel," the Church Society, and the Protestant Fellowship for Church Revival to band together. These organizations protested not only biblical criticism, but also the involvement of the church in what they labeled left-wing politics. These groups blamed religious pluralism for the current condition of the church and stood against the teaching that psychology, sociology, or government can meet an individual's needs rather than the gospel. Further, the Conference served as a platform for conservative scholars, leading to the forging of the Frankfurt Declaration in March of 1970. The single goal of the Declaration was to reaffirm the biblical basis of missions.[63]

The Confessional Movement understood that the source of the theological crisis in the GPC was in the universities. In order to help students develop or maintain a conservative approach to Scriptures, the organization was instrumental in founding several student houses at major universities where theological students could live and receive instruction from conservative theologians. This would help ensure a steady source of pastors opposing the historical-critical view of the Bible and prevent conservative students from losing their biblical principles while under the influence of liberal professors who dominated the universities. The hope was that providing a steady input of biblically conservative pastors would subsequently reverse the liberal trend and eventually form the basis for authentic church renewal. The GCGA supported this process by offering personnel to mentor students at the Friedrich Hauss Student Center in Schrieshiem (Heidelberg) from 1988 to 1991. This was an attempt by the GCGA to introduce conservative theological students to church growth principles. The GPC, on the other hand, ignored the concerns of the Confessional Movement, just as it did with the Gnadau Society.

Although both the Movement and the Society shared common ground in their opposition to existential theology, they had different understandings of their role in the church. Whereas the Society works as a mission and renewal effort within the GPC institutional structure, the

---

63. Tlach, "Von den wichtigsten Aufgaben," 54.

Movement views itself as a sentry. The Movement does not view itself as *ecclesiolae in ecclesia* (little churches in the church), because it does not see itself as apart from the church, but sees its opponents as those apart from the church (Gal 1:6–9). The goal is to warn the whole church of pernicious theology and set scholarly standards for the exegesis of the Bible.[64] Church renewal will occur when the church leadership rejects liberal theology and requires universities to base its theological curriculum on the veracity of the Scriptures. The Confessional Movement failed to bring this type of renewal to the GPC. Church leadership maintains a monopoly on university theology departments. The universities transmit liberal theology to the parishes via the students, and church leaders persist in viewing the Movement as a movement promoting a dogmatic theology resulting in church divisiveness.

As previously stated, the GCGA, employing a church growth paradigm, adopted the missional perspective of the Gnadau Society. However, it did not take on the prophetic-sentry role exemplified in the Confessional Movement. In the future, not taking the concerns of the movement seriously had a negative effect on the German church growth movement. But the GCGA did not completely ignore the problem of liberal theology and the resulting erosion of the church. The GCGA eventually responded to this difficulty within the ecclesiological model of church growth.

The Charismatic Church Renewal Movement

Like the Gnadau Society and the Confessional Movement, the Charismatic Church Renewal Movement (*Geistliche-Gemeinde Erneuerung*) emphasized its own reasons for the demise of the GPC. According to this new charismatic initiative, the crisis in the *Volkskirche* was the result of the prevailing ecclesiology that allowed no room for free expression or exhibition of spiritual gifts within the church. The Charismatic Church Renewal Movement has no evangelistic priority as with the Society, and fighting theological battles is not an emphasis. Its priorities lie in promoting an ecclesiology reflected by the worldwide charismatic movement.

The roots of The Charismatic Church Renewal Movement, founded in 1984, go back decades earlier to the forerunners of the European Pentecostal Movement of the late nineteenth century. This proto-Pentecostal theology and subsequent rise of Pentecostalism also influenced

---

64. Büchner, "Kein anderes Evangelium," 39–40.

the Fellowship Movement. Both groups stressed the need for personal holiness. The introduction of Pentecostalism into Germany began with controversy. The issue of sanctification was the catalyst for the problem. A second blessing, punctuated by speaking in tongues, was required to insure a life of holiness and advancement in sanctification. Without this specific sign, the Christian could not advance to the level of sanctification required by God and reflected in the Bible. This teaching was the harbinger of future division within the Fellowship Movement.[65] The GCGA would later become involved in this dispute.

In the fall of 1962, Arnold Bittlinger, Director of the Office for Evangelism in the GPC in the German state Rheinland Palatinate, participated in a study trip to the United States.[66] He visited a charismatic Lutheran church led by Larry Christenson, along with Anglican churches influenced by the charismatic movement. He was impressed with the orderliness of the charismatic services and the involvement of the laity. In August of 1963, Bittlinger invited Christenson to speak at a retreat in Enkenbauch at the Protestant Academy. The eighty participants were at first skeptical about the American, however, they were desirous of spiritual renewal in their churches. This relatively small group of participants from the GPC represented a wider group of church members who were open to new ideas of church renewal. The next year, the Ecumenical Church Days were founded as a forum to exchange ideas, experiences, and develop a biblical theology to support the movement.

Ten years later, on the heels of the German Jesus-People Movement, the charismatic movement began to influence the GPC. The American Jesus-People or "Jesus Freaks," stemming from the counterculture revolution in the 1960s, gave rise to the thoroughly charismatic German Jesus-People Movement.[67] In 1978, a newly established coordination team offered advice and planning to the charismatics within the church. Wolfram Kopfermann, a GPC pastor, led this initiative. In 1980, the Working Group for the Spiritual Renewal of the Church was founded and Kopfermann was elected director. In 1984, "Working Group" was dropped, and the official name became Charismatic Church Renewal Movement (*Geistliche Gemeinde-Erneuerung*). The goal of this

---

65. Beyreuther, *Kirche in Bewegung*, 184–88.
66. Böckel, *Gemeindeaufbau im Kontext*, 102–3, 456–58.
67. Adler, "Wird die Jesus-Bewegung?," 2–12.

organization was spiritual renewal within the confines of the GPC.[68] According to this charismatic movement, church renewal will occur when the *Volkskirche* recognizes the authenticity of the *charisma* and promotes their free exercise in the churches. In 1999, there were approximately 75,000 sympathizers of the movement, with 3 to 5 percent of the GPC pastors subscribing to the movement's charismatic publications. In 2005, charismatics from all denominations numbered approximately 250,000.[69] The importance of the movement was not the number of adherents, but that it was charismatic. This carried with it the label of Pentecostalism and led to conflicts stemming from the Berlin Declaration which stated that Pentecostal teaching is demonic. Chapter 4 will detail the events that led to the creation of the Berlin Declaration in 1909.

Whereas the GCGA had no formal alliances with the Gnadau Society or the Confessional Movement, it did with the newly formed German Charismatic Renewal Movement. From its inception, the GCGA embraced the ecclesiological paradigm of the German charismatics and the worldwide charismatic movement. In 1986, the GCGA invited Wolfram Kopfermann to join its board.[70] The sign gifts of healing, prophesying, and speaking in tongues were all encouraged. The fundamental reason for this was the close ties with the American church growth movement, popularized by Donald McGavran, Peter Wagner, and the School of World Mission at Fuller Theological Seminary in California. History will show the results of the GCGA's choice to align itself with the German charismatics and the effects this alliance had on contextualizing the German church growth movement.

Summary: Contextualization or Compromise?

As already stated, the GCGA came into existence in an already crowded field of participants desirous for change in the GPC. Several contextualization questions arise. Why did the founders desire a new organization? What did the founders hope to contribute to these contemporary renewal efforts? Did the Association contribute anything, or did it simply duplicate the previous options offered by their predecessors? The presence

68. Reimer, "Die Geistliche Gemeinde-Erneuerung," 310–16.
69. Böckel, *Gemeindeaufbau im Kontext*, 298; Simson, *Wie christlich ist Deutschland?*, 67.
70. "AGGA betont Zusammenarbeit," 17.

of these other parachurch renewal movements, untainted by suspicious American baggage, begs the question if there was indeed room for one more renewal movement. The very founding of the GCGA was provocative, because it called into question the renewal efforts of the other organizations. On the other hand, the German Church Growth Association took on the most fundamental philosophy of its contemporaries; it chose to work in the confines of the GPC.

In 1988, Hans-Martin Wilhelm completed his Fuller Theological Seminary dissertation, "Church Renewal in Germany: Is it Possible? A Study of the Established Protestant Church." He writes specifically for North American missionaries who desire to come to Europe to work. Wilhelm offers a basic overview of the GPC, outlining its structure and some of the reasons for its decline. He lays the blame of church decline on nominal Christianity. He defines a nominal Christian as someone who considers himself a church member, but has no commitment to Christ. Wilhelm finds a solution to the church's ills in the German Church Growth Movement. His fundamental premise of missions is that the best avenue for reaching Germany is through the GPC. He stresses that ". . . any ministry outside this body is only peripheral in reaching the nation as a whole." He is especially critical of American missionaries working in Germany who refuse to acknowledge the importance of the GPC in their mission work. In his estimation, this is the reason American missions have failed in Germany.[71] His thesis resulted in a backlash from the American missionary community. American mission organizations viewed the GPC as hopelessly skewed by biblical liberalism and avoided any connection with it. When an American pastor discovered I was working with an organization tied directly with the National Church, he asked me, "When did you give up your faith?"

Soon after the founding of the GCGA, various corners of German evangelicalism criticized the new group. This criticism gained momentum and continued throughout the history of the organization. What were the sources and the grounds for this persistent criticism? The GCGA made no excuses for importing church growth to Germany. It also made no secret of the fact that most of its renewal strategies came directly from church growth practitioners in the United States. It is important to understand how the organization attempted to contextualize these foreign principles for the GPC. Missionaries, missiologists, and students concerned with

71. Wilhelm, "Germany," 8–12; "Church Renewal?," 124–25; "Europe," 21–22, 34.

reaching those in another culture with the gospel, must consider this. It goes to the very heart of mission activity that seeks to transmit the good news to those without Christ in a manner that they can comprehend.

The movement's ecclesiology influenced its practical theology and how its contextualization process worked itself out in the local German parish. The nature of the church is essential in understanding the organization's goals and its very reason for existence. The ecclesiological basis will further reveal why the Association had difficulties contextualizing church growth strategies and why it was often the target of criticism. It will also explain why the founders of the organization saw fit to establish a new organization among so many well-established church renewal organizations and traditions. Is there always room for one more? The GCGA's understanding of the church holds the answer.

Knowing the history of the GCGA, with a view to grasping its ecclesiology, will allow practical applications to be drawn for missions in Germany. It serves as a case study for the contextualization of the gospel in any culture. Discovering the ecclesiology, or how the GCGA defined the church, will form the basis for an analysis of the GCGA from a biblical, historical, and cultural perspective. The German Church Growth Association made many logistical as well as missiological errors, but this does not diminish the fact that it attempted to interpret a worldwide movement for the particular German situation. Exploring these facts answers the question of how a modern American evangelical movement was contextualized within the traditional German *Volkskirche*. Hopefully this analysis will outline the pitfalls and opportunities of doing missions in Germany through the portal of the German Protestant Church, as well as any country boasting a strong national church.

A historical examination will reveal the GCGA's view of the church, and show how this view developed and evolved over the years. Further, an account of the Association's history will reveal how well it succeeded in contextualizing the Church Growth Movement in Germany. However, recording the history of the GCGA has its pitfalls. Norman F. Cantor stated it well: "We tend to discover the past we set out to find. This is not because the past is a willfully imagined fiction but because it is such a complicated and multifaceted reality."[72]

---

72. Lindberg, *The European Reformations*, 8.

Discussion Questions

1. What role does history play in contextualizing the gospel for a nation, people group, or tribe?

2. What watershed event(s) in your own culture have most affected the current spiritual climate in relationship to acceptance or rejection of the gospel?

3. Why is it important to know the history, influence, and practices of indigenous Christian churches and parachurch ministries already at work in a country, before a mission or missionary begins ministry in that country?

4. Why did the GCGA decide to work through the GPC? Discuss Hans Wilhelm's thesis that American missionaries failed in Europe because they refused to work with the GPC.

5. Many European countries have traditional national churches, the Church of England, for example. Poland is staunchly Catholic and Greece is historically Orthodox. Should foreign missionaries consider working in conjunction with these national churches for the sake of contextualization?

6. "And I tell you that you are Peter, and on this rock I will build my church, and the gates of Hades will not overcome it" (Matt 16:18). Given the success of East Germany's campaign against the church, how does one understand Jesus' statement?

2

The Formative Years of German Church Growth 1967–1979

In the historical thriller, *Valkyrie*, Tom Cruise played the role of one of Germany's most beloved historical figures, Colonel Claus Graf Schenk von Stauffenberg. Cruise is a member of the Church of Scientology, which is viewed with skepticism by many Germans. Scientology is under Germany's surveillance of organizations "that threaten Germany's peaceful democratic order."[1] So, the choice of Cruise to play the Colonel, one of the few true German war heroes, was not without controversy. However, because of the historical importance of the film, the Germans agreed to allow production. Colonel Stauffenberg, together with many other German officers, tried unsuccessfully to assassinate Adolf Hitler in July of 1944. The film was important for Americans, because it gave a glimpse into the shadowy world of the German resistance against Hitler.

It is a fact largely unknown in America that there was a resilient movement to do away with Hitler from the very beginning of WWII. Not all Germans were goose-stepping Nazis, bent on world domination. Many high-ranking German officers, as well as influential segments of the German society, sought repeatedly either by coup or assassination to rid Germany of the brutal dictator. Those planning the demise of Hitler were even found among the elite SS, Hitler's personal bodyguard troop. The common thread that bound the resistance together was abhorrence of Hitler's mad determination to rule the world. The goal of the resistance was to liquidate fascism and thus save Germany from total destruction.

---

1. "Hubbard's Church Unconstitutional."

The men who founded the German Church Growth Association also were bound together by a common goal to save Germany. They wanted to save the decaying German Protestant Church where 25 million Protestants—30 percent of Germans—held membership. Without the presence, support, and planning of Bernd Schlottoff, Jörg Knoblauch, Roger Bosch, and Fritz Schwarz, the GCGA never would have existed.

The Founding Fathers of the Future GCGA

Schlottoff and Schwarz were pastors in the GPC. Knoblauch was a German businessman, and Bosch was an American missionary with strong ties to the American church growth movement and Campus Crusade for Christ. It is essential to know what influenced these men, in order to understand their reasons for establishing the GCGA. In addition, the formative years of 1967 to 1979 will shed light on how each of the men developed certain evangelistic ideas that would impact the German church growth movement and how the gospel was contextualized.

The year 1967 marks the earliest point that postwar evangelism began to have a direct and practical influence on the future GCGA. By 1979, an informal organizational framework already existed, and in the same year, the first German church growth magazine, *Dynamic Church* (*Dynamische Gemeinde*) was published. The events of these early years shaped the ideas of the founders and, subsequently, the presentation of the gospel to the German people. This chapter will shed light on the people and events that led to the founding of the GCGA.

Bernd Schlottoff

Bernd Schlottoff was born in Gevelsberg, Germany in 1938. He completed his theological studies at the University of Münster. As a student, Schlottoff was interested by Karl Barth (1886–1968) and his *Dogmatics*, but historical Pietism influenced him the most.[2] Pietism was a reaction against the Lutheran emphasis on belief in doctrine alone. In the seventeenth and eighteenth centuries, Pietism sought to complete the Protestant Reformation by emphasizing individual conversion and personal piety. It gave birth to the Protestant missionary movement. Schlottoff

---

2. Schlottoff, interview by author, 10 October 2007.

was also influenced by postwar crusade evangelism, especially the evangelistic techniques of Billy Graham and the Janz Team. He found their practice of requiring respondents to come forward and make a public profession of faith astounding. The practice served to influence his future evangelistic efforts.

In 1965, Schlottoff became pastor of the GPC church in Wanne-Eikel. He invited the Janz Team from Canada to hold a series of evangelistic meetings at his church in 1967. The Janz Team was composed of ethnic Germans, who combined music with evangelistic preaching. Schlottoff's interest in crusade-style evangelism continued into the 1970s. He encouraged his parishioners to attend a Billy Graham crusade held in Dortmund in 1970. According to newspaper reports, an estimated 1,000 people from his parish attended the crusades.[3]

While on a preaching tour in Canada among German speaking churches in 1971, Schlottoff became interested in visiting some growing American churches. He was encouraged to visit Coral Ridge Presbyterian Church in Fort Lauderdale, Florida, and to investigate the Evangelism Explosion program instituted by James Kennedy, the pastor. In 1973, Schlottoff visited the Florida church and became interested in the possibility of implementing the Evangelism Explosion (EE) concept in Germany. Two years later, he was invited to attend the first European EE seminar held at the Anglican Church in Northwood, Middlesex, England. Archie Parish, the International Director for EE, came to Germany in 1976 and held the first German EE seminar.[4] Evangelism Explosion became an important part of the GCGA, especially in the beginning phases of the organization. Schlottoff became the German Director for EE and founded the Protestant Prep Course for Church Growth, a training program for GPC pastors and laity using the EE program. A full explanation of how EE functioned in Germany is found in the next chapter.

The impact of postwar crusade evangelism on Schlottoff was significant. He saw the "call to come forward and make a decision for Christ" during evangelistic crusades as revolutionary for Germany, and for him personally. Schlottoff's commitment to this methodology would lead him to impact other pastors, most notably Fritz Schwarz.

---

3. *Bekehrung bedeutet Freiheit.*
4. Ibid.

Fritz Schwarz

Fritz Schwarz, born in Germany in 1930, studied theology at the universities in Bonn, Göttingen, and Marburg. In 1967, he became the church superintendent for the GPC churches in the Herne church district in the Ruhr area located in the state of North Rhine-Westphalia.[5] His duties as superintendent brought him into direct contact with Bernd Schlottoff and a close friendship developed. Schwarz observed the evangelistic efforts of Schlottoff in Wanne-Eikel and desired to see a similar program in the entire church district of Herne. He developed his own evangelistic methodology for the local church, however, and did not copy Schlottoff's evangelistic model of EE. In fact, as the program unfolded Schwarz became critical of EE, finding its methodology unfit for the GPC. Although both EE and Schwarz's model began in the 1970s and continued into the 1980s, both programs ran independently of one another.[6]

Schwarz's program gained momentum and popularity to such an extent that other pastors came to Herne to observe Schwarz's model of local church evangelism. Because of the need for an explanation of how his evangelistic program functioned, Schwarz published a series of books between 1979 and 1981 called *The Manageable Church* (*Überschaubare Gemeinde*). This three-volume series revealed the philosophy behind the evangelistic program in Herne. The publishing of *The Manageable Church* was the beginning of Schwarz expressing his views on a church growth model having its roots in Germany. The full expression of his thought came in 1984 when Schwarz and his son published the first German theology of church growth, *Theology of Church Growth: An Introduction* (*Theologie des Gemeindeaufbaus: Ein Versuch*).

In order to understand Schwarz and his theology, examining the watershed for his church growth experience is required. Schwarz describes his eighteen-year tenure as superintendent of GPC churches as theologically unchallenging. He spent time not in theological reflection, but in endless hours of meetings, paperwork, and administrative boredom.[7] During this time Schwarz was convinced of "the sole efficacy of the sermon (*Alleinwirksamkeit der Predigt*)." This means, whenever a sermon is preached, whatever the topic may be, it is considered "preaching

---

5. C. Schwarz, interview by author, 18 September 2007.
6. Schlottoff, interview by author, 14 September 2005.
7. F. Schwarz, *Unter allen Stühlen*, 63–64.

the gospel." But, when asked by Bernd Schlottoff if he could name one person who had come to faith because of one of his sermons, Schwarz could not name anyone. This was the turning point. Schwarz later wrote that that was the "hour of birth for church growth" for him.[8]

There were other influences in Schwarz's life that affected his theological philosophy and ultimately his church growth thought. The question by Schlottoff and Schwarz's admission was a culmination of several factors that had been in process for many years. Schlottoff's provocative question was not the primary reason for his full conversion to church growth thinking; it was, however, the key element that brought several factors to a head.[9]

As a young man, Schwarz was a popular preacher in the GPC. During his years as a student, he was considered a very liberal theologian, and when he became superintendent in the GPC he also had the reputation of being non-controversial. However, his life changed when he began to have health problems. He realized he needed to think seriously about how he should invest his time, because he may soon have to stand before God and give an account. This led him to gather many of the things he had learned and experienced over the years in order to organize them in an effective manner for evangelism. His shift in priorities was controversial, because it meant that he spent the majority of his energies encouraging pastors to evangelize church members. His duties as superintendent were no longer Schwarz's priority. The entirety of these different factors, brought to a head by Schlottoff's question, led to the development of the program, The Manageable Church, which is discussed in chapter three.

Jörg Knoblauch

At the time of the founding of the GCGA, Jörg Knoblauch was the only man on the board with no theological education, yet he would become the main impetus in bringing the different elements and personalities of the GCGA together. He was a businessman who owned Drilbox, a company that produced toolboxes for drill bits located in Giengen, Germany. He was primarily interested in understanding how businesses grew. Why did some businesses prosper, while others failed? This entrepreneurial curiosity carried over to the church. While earning a master's degree

8. Ibid.
9. C. Schwarz, interview by author, 18 September 2007.

in Atlanta, at the Georgia Institute of Technology in 1974, Knoblauch observed churches in the Atlanta area that were growing. This was especially remarkable to him given the declining church in Germany.

He asked the same question that Donald McGavran had asked, while a missionary in India, "Why do some churches grow and others do not?" He was interested in the reason why churches in the United States were growing and churches in Germany were dying. The pastor of a local Atlanta church told him, "If you want to know why this church is growing, go to the bookstore and buy books by Win Arn, Peter Wagner, or Jerry Fallwell." Knoblauch followed the pastor's advice and read these books.[10] They revealed that American churches were growing because of an underlying philosophy called "church growth."

Another incident that had a great affect on Knoblauch was his visit to the First Baptist Church in Hammond, Indiana. The church, under the leadership of Jack Hyles, boasted the largest Sunday school in the world. When visiting the church in 1974, he noticed a street cleaner sweeping the church parking lot. He told the woman he was from Germany and was visiting the church for the first time. She asked him if she could ask him a question. She asked, "If you were to die tonight and you stood before Peter and he asked you why he should let you into heaven, what would you tell him?" Knoblauch replied, "Because I am a Christian." He then went into the church where he saw a group of men standing in the foyer. He asked them where the church office was and they gave him directions. Before he left the group, one of them asked if he could ask him a question. The man asked, "If you were to die tonight and you stood before Peter and he asked you why he should let you into heaven, what would you tell him?" Knoblauch gave the same reply as before. He made his way to the office and asked the secretary if it would be possible to bring a group of German pastors to visit the church. She responded that it would be an honor for the church to host the pastors. Before Knoblauch left the office, the secretary asked if she could ask him a question. She asked him the same question he had twice previously been asked. Knoblauch realized that in the course of less than ten minutes, he was confronted three times with the central question of Christianity. He realized a person could live their entire life in the GPC in Germany and never hear it asked once. This experience had a lasting impression on Knoblauch and impacted

---

10. J. Knoblauch, interview by author, 24 September 2003.

his desire to do something about the situation in Germany. More importantly, it would form the basis for his understanding of how the church grows.[11]

Knoblauch initiated the publication of the first German church growth magazine, which debuted in 1979 at the Church Days congress in Nuremberg. This magazine was originally published as *Dynamic Church* and later became known as *Church Growth (Gemeindewachstum)*.[12] That same year, while Schlottoff was on vacation in Florida, he became acquainted with Knoblauch. It was during this first meeting that the idea for an official organization to promote church growth and evangelism in Germany began to take shape. Schlottoff called this meeting "the birthday of the German Church Growth Association."[13]

Reading church growth literature and meeting American church growth leaders proved to be crucial for Knoblauch, and for the future contextualization strategy of the GCGA. Knoblauch was an entrepreneur who studied business models and practices. He wanted to know what made businesses fail and what made them succeed. This involved making very practical decisions for the success of a company. In American church growth leaders, he found like-minded men. Their interest was not what made an enterprise grow, but what made the churches grow. Their conclusions, however, were the same as Knoblauch's. Pragmatic decisions, based on certain universal growth models, could be implemented that would greatly influence the growth of the church. This mixture of American and German pragmatism would prove to be a volatile combination when confronted with the traditional practices of the GPC. This volatility was most often expressed in vastly different views on the role of the Spirit and the role of human planning. Those opposed to precise goal setting (pragmatism) would argue that it is not possible for man to control or dictate the movement of the Spirit of God.

Roger Bosch

The fourth key person involved in the founding of the GCGA was an American, and according to Jörg Knoblauch, he was the main component behind forming a church growth association for Germany. He was

---

11. Ibid.
12. GCGA Archives.
13. Schlottoff, interview by author, 14 September 2005.

the first person to present church growth principles in a systematic way in Germany.[14] Roger Bosch joined Campus Crusade for Christ in 1965. He first went to Germany in 1968 with the University Ambassador Team, and from 1968 to 1975 he focused on the initial stages of establishing a student ministry in Germany. After starting student ministries in West Berlin, Erlangen, and Freiburg, he felt that his work in the area of student ministry was complete.[15] From 1976 to 1979 Bosch attended Fuller Theological Seminary in California. While at the School of World Mission at Fuller, Bosch came under the tutelage of Donald McGavran and Peter Wagner. McGavran's book, *Understanding Church Growth*, was pivotal in convincing Bosch to invest his time and energies in implementing church growth principles.

From 1977 to 1979 Bosch was Peter Wagner's assistant. Wagner was Professor of Church Growth at McGavran's School of World Mission at Fuller. It was during this time that Bosch began to understand and appreciate Wagner's church growth philosophy. Wagner took McGavran's cross-cultural principles, applied them to the American church context, and later published his book *Your Church Can Grow*. When Bosch learned these principles, he knew they were applicable to the German church.

Wagner then challenged Bosch to undertake a research project and study the churches in Germany, which he did in the summer of 1977. The findings of the research project are discussed later in this chapter. Upon completion of the project, Wagner encouraged Bosch to return to Germany and no longer work in student ministry, but instead to build an institution for the advancement of church growth in Germany. Using his research project as a foundation, Bosch and his colleague, Dennis Griggs, formulated a church growth seminar that relied heavily on Wagner's own seminar material. Armed with the new seminar, Bosch returned to Germany in July of 1978 and presented the first German church growth seminar in Giessen the following September.[16] The pastors from the fifteen churches he had studied the previous summer attended the five-day seminar and their response was positive.

This meeting in Giessen was pivotal because Jörg Knoblauch also attended the seminar and met Bosch for the first time. The seminar impressed Knoblauch and he encouraged Bosch to continue his work

14. J. Knoblauch, interview by author, 24 September 2003.
15. Bosch, "Research Project," 2.
16. GCGA Archives.

exposing Germans to church growth principles. Since Knoblauch was a well-known Christian businessman, Bosch realized that he was the one person who could open doors for the seminar to the various regional churches. If Knoblauch could vouch for him and the seminar, it would be easier to gain access to churches. Upon completion of his studies at Fuller in 1979, Bosch returned to Germany and founded the Institute for Church Growth in Giessen. This new institute would serve as the source for German church growth research and church growth materials, specifically oriented toward the local GPC church.[17]

In summary, these four men provided essential elements for German church growth. Bernd Schlottoff and his EE emphasis brought an American evangelistic model to Germany. Fritz Schwarz with his Manageable Church program introduced a purely home-grown German evangelistic outreach. He also deserves the title of the father of German church growth theology since he published the first theology of church growth. Jörg Knoblauch with his managerial expertise was able to organize these men into a functioning organization. Roger Bosch was able to establish a permanent institute in Germany for the CGM.

The First Initiatives Promoting Church Growth

Bosch's first church growth seminar in Giessen was a major step in introducing German church leaders to the CGM. Other initiatives employed key tools and strategies at this early development of the GCGA to promote the church growth agenda among German church leaders.

One of the best tools for introducing Germans to church growth was the airplane. While Roger Bosch was ending his student ministry in Berlin, and Schlottoff and Schwarz were beginning their evangelistic strategies, Knoblauch was planning a study trip to the States. Taking groups of pastors and church workers who see only low church attendance to experience American churches with thousands attending a single service, was a sort of "shock treatment." These trips are discussed in detail in the next section.

But the most important tool for promoting church growth was a magazine. This quarterly publication gave advice for the pastor interested in growing the local church. The first issue of the magazine explained

17. Bosch, interview by author, 18 April 2007; Bosch, personal communication with author, 10 August 2003.

church growth and showed statistics that reflected the dire situation of the GPC. This first issue of the magazine is discussed later in this chapter.

Study Trips

After having been in the United States the previous year and experiencing growing and dynamic churches, Jörg Knoblauch organized a study trip to the United States for GPC pastors and church leaders. It was during this first study trip in 1975 that Knoblauch met three American church growth leaders who would strongly influence the formation of the GCGA: Win Arn, Peter Wagner, and Donald McGavran. McGavran's book, *The Bridges of God*, interested Knoblauch because it asked and answered the same questions Knoblauch was contemplating: "What are the roots of church growth, and why do some churches grow and others do not?"[18]

The 1975 study trip marks the beginning of the German church growth movement. It is the first time that an organized jaunt, specifically aimed at exposing German pastors to the American church growth movement, was undertaken. Study trips to America were essential for the development of German church growth. These tours were very popular in the initial stages of the church growth movement in Germany and continued to be a strategic tool for the GCGA up until the formal closure of the association. On one of these study tours as many as thirty pastors and lay workers traveled to the United States to experience American churches.[19]

German church leaders visited churches in California, Washington, Virginia, Georgia, and Florida. According to the organizers, the study trips were to allow German pastors to observe some of the most active churches in the world, and to get a vision for what God was currently doing. German pastors, most of whom were used to having forty to fifty worshippers on any given Sunday, needed to experience large, active, and attractive churches. When they were in a worship service in the United States with several thousand in attendance, perhaps they would lose their attitude of accepting and maintaining the status quo. German pastors needed new ideas on how to promote specific programs, ministries and events. Challenging their ways of thinking, organizing and leading in

18. Ibid.; McGavran, *The Bridges of God*, 6–7.
19. Schwesig, "Wo Gemeinden wachsen," 2–3.

order to bring change was a key ingredient. Another purpose was the cementing of relationships between both German and American church leaders, and increasing the visibility of the church growth in German-speaking Europe.[20]

There would be many study trips over the years. Most of these were to the United States; trips also went to England, South Korea, Hong Kong, China, and East Germany. The study trips followed a similar format. Participants visited specific churches to learn from experienced church planters and church growth specialists. A pastor or church leader explained how the church started, described the difficulties and problems confronted, and how they were overcome. Participants usually numbered between fifteen and twenty and visited church services, prayer services, home meetings, and church staff meetings to get an understanding of exactly how the church functioned.[21]

Trips were organized so that the Germans would have personal interaction with such American church leaders as Robert Schuller, John MacArthur, James Kennedy, and Jack Hyles. It was hoped that tour participants' exposure to church growth experts at Fuller Theological Seminary such as Donald McGavran, Peter Wagner, Arthur Glasser, and Eddie Gibbs would broaden their understanding of church growth. Tour organizers hoped this exposure would encourage German leaders to think practically, and to consider how to contextualize these principles within the German church. Not all of their experiences were positive. Many of the German theologians and pastors were favorably impressed with their personal interactions with the American pastors and their teams, although they were skeptical of a "salesman" approach to the gospel that they observed in one of the churches. Also, Fritz Schwarz was angry after interaction with one pastor because of his sermon on Rom 13:1–8, which seemed to stress unconditional obedience to governmental authority. Because of Germany's history, Germans are very sensitive to and skeptical of governmental authority. As a result, that particular treatment of the text was not well received by Schwarz and other German pastors.[22]

---

20. J. Knoblauch, interview by author, 24 September 2003; Yinger, personal communication with author, 18 March 2005.

21. Yinger, personal communication with author, 18 March 2005.

22. Ibid.

Gerhard Maier, a pastor in the GPC, analyzed the reactions of study trip participants.[23] The purpose of Maier's survey was to determine, from the participants' point of view, how well American church growth practices transferred to Germany. Maier surveyed 44 participants that included pastors, lay workers, church employees, and church members. Most of the participants gained a new perspective on what could happen in Germany if certain barriers no longer existed. For example, considering that many church leaders and the majority of pastors in the German Protestant Church have not trusted Christ as their personal Savior, it would be extremely difficult to implement church growth in Germany.

While the majority were encouraged about the future of the church after their trip to the States, most were very critical of the intense preoccupation with numbers by church leaders. Also, the majority criticized—what seemed to them—a staged spirituality and a naïve trust in the inerrancy of the Bible. Most thought American church growth principles would be difficult to transfer to the German GPC, but not impossible. The key to this contextualization was the German pastor. The pastor must discover how to evangelize and how to renew the local congregation; things that he was not trained to do at the university. Another factor concerned structures. American-style church growth is transferable to the *Volkskirche* if the church's structures become flexible and tolerant to new ideas.[24]

Twenty-eight of those surveyed indicated that their fellow church members could not comprehend what they had experienced in the United States. In spite of this, there were initiatives put into practice as a direct result of the study trips. Pastors indicated they began to preach more enthusiastically and practically, and encouraged their congregations to concentrate more on their personal spiritual growth. Cell groups for Bible study and prayer formed. Lay people were encouraged to minister in the church and training classes were started to prepare them for service. The majority further indicated they had communicated to their churches that not only was church growth possible, but that they should expect great things from God. Maier concluded from the survey that the study trips were an excellent method to experience church growth at its source. Participants could actually see church growth taking place, not

---

23. Maier, *Gemeindeaufbau*, 234–40.
24. Ibid.

just read about it in books. Furthermore, they could learn the great variety of church growth principles.[25]

Study trips became an indispensable tool for the GCGA. These church growth tours were a type of shock treatment for German pastors lulled into lethargy by an ever-shrinking church and habitually low Sunday morning worship attendance. These trips also revealed another issue that would began to surface slowly over the years, and eventually lead to a re-thinking of German church growth. At issue was the very foundation of church growth philosophy. This problem can be summarized by comments made by Chuck Smith, at that time pastor of Calvary Chapel in Costa Mesa, California and Robert Schuller, of the Crystal Cathedral. Smith told a group of visiting German pastors, "If your church isn't growing, then it's your fault!" Schuller told the same tour group, "The gospel is a necessary and good product. Success is determined by the packaging and sales techniques."[26] These comments, reflecting an American pragmatic approach to the church, would prove to be a serious issue for German church growth. As German church growth developed, proponents would have to answer critics of this pragmatic approach.

Study tours visited churches that had grown astronomically from their inception. Smith's church had grown from twenty-five to 25,000 in fourteen years. Schuller's started with forty-eight attendees, and twenty-five years later over 10,000 attend services each Sunday.[27] The question of cultural comparison arises. Is the American church situation comparable to the German Protestant Church? Is it intellectually honest and theologically sound to promote, or at least imply, that such growth is possible in Germany? These questions begged answering as church growth gained a foothold in Germany in the 1980s.

The Publishing of Dynamic Church

In 1979—six years before the founding of the GCGA—the first issue of the German church growth magazine *Dynamic Church* was published. The magazine came about primarily through the efforts of Jörg Knoblauch, supported by a small, informal committee. This committee, called Association for Church Growth (*Arbeitskreis Gemeindebau*), had been

25. Ibid., 237–38.
26. Schwesig, "Wo Gemeinden wachsen," 2–3.
27. Ibid.

organized after the first study trip in 1975. In order to gauge how well the magazine would be accepted, it was first distributed free of charge at the Church Day (*Kirchentag*) in June 1979. Approximately 6,000 copies were distributed and conference attendees ordered 4,000 more. The magazine became the primary means of disseminating church growth information throughout Germany. It offered a forum for German pastors, German laity, and American pastors, to strengthen, as well as criticize, church growth in Germany.

The introductory issue defined the purpose of the magazine. It was to be an avenue for the dissemination of the gospel via church growth: "Our wish is that every person in this country discovers Jesus Christ and grows to maturity in the faith. We want the church to grow!"[28] The *Evangelical Dictionary of World Mission* defines church growth as that discipline that investigates the nature, expansion, planting, multiplication, function, and health of Christian churches as they relate to the effective implementation of God's commission to "make disciples of all peoples" (Matt 28:19–20).[29] Church growth was also clearly defined for the particular German context in this first issue of *Dynamic Church*. As in the first installment, subsequent issues always contained practical advice for contextualizing church growth for the parish church. For example, the following section reviews how a survey was used to motivate pastors to consider church growth as a viable option for their church.

Church growth literature was scarce at the beginning of the German movement. Every book listed in the magazine was a translation of an American work. The magazine made the readers aware that there was more literature available, but only in English. This was not a great problem, since most German pastors could read English. As the church growth movement gained influence, more literature in German became available.

Contextualizing Church Growth

Roger Bosch explained the non-negotiable elements of church growth, using a 1977 research project that he and Peter Wagner had co-authored. They had analyzed fifteen growing churches in Germany during a ten-year period from 1965 to 1975. The purpose of the project was to

28. J. Knoblauch, interview by author, 24 September 2003.
29. Wagner, "Church Growth Movement," 199.

determine the factors causing these particular churches to grow. Bosch and Wagner wanted to discover if certain shared characteristics among these churches facilitated growth. For example, the survey revealed that these churches all had strong leadership and a vibrant worship service.

Along with the statistical graphs for Jehovah's Witnesses, Mormons, and the New Apostolic Church (a German-born cult), graphs for the GPC and Free Churches were also used. The research showed that only 4 percent of Protestants attended church, while 9 to 11 percent of Catholics attended Mass. The findings of this project revealed that the major cults in Germany were growing faster than the mainline denominations. The Mormons, Jehovah's Witnesses, and the New Apostolic Church, were growing much faster than the GPC, the Baptists, the Evangelical Free Church, the Methodists, and the Brethren Church. The Evangelical Free Church had modest gains, but the rest of the denominations were in serious decline. The only exception was the Church of the Nazarene, a Free Church, which was at that time the fastest growing church in Germany.[30]

Bosch's research project was important because it formed the basis for future analysis of local churches that would become involved in the church growth movement. The project aimed to discover the reasons why certain churches were growing. The study only included those churches that Bosch considered "growing churches." Since there were no comprehensive research statistics to indicate the growth of certain churches, Bosch relied on the observances of pastors, evangelists, and church leaders to point out churches that were experiencing conversion growth. Based on these observations, fifteen churches across the denominational spectrum were chosen.[31]

In conjunction with the project report and under the rubric, "What is church growth?" Bosch gave four reasons why church growth was a part of traditional evangelicalism. These proved to be too general.

1. Church growth theologically belongs in the evangelical camp.
2. Church growth emphasizes practical Christian living.
3. Church growth emphasizes the necessity of the personal decision for Jesus.
4. Church growth emphasizes the working of the Holy Spirit.[32]

---

30. Bosch, "Gemeindewachstum was ist das?," 2.
31. Bosch, "Research Project," 10–11.
32. Bosch, "Gemeindewachstum was ist das?," 2.

Bosch's presentation of this research project was Germany's first formal introduction to the fundamentals of church growth. However, there were some issues that Bosch did not address. Bosch failed to differentiate between evangelicals and charismatics. In America, charismatics are referred to as evangelicals, but in Germany they are distinguished from evangelicals. There was another issue Bosch failed to address. He gave no theological basis for the necessity of a personal decision for Jesus, which was crucial for the GPC. It would have been prudent for Bosch to take one reason at a time and explain it from a biblical basis. This would have gone a long way in making church growth more acceptable to the leadership of the National Church.

Bosch's article continued to outline the non-negotiable elements of church growth:

1. Jesus Christ is the Lord. Being obedient servants requires that the church grow in quality, as well as quantity (Luke 5:4–11; Matt 13:3–9; 18:12–14).

2. Men and women must be convinced to become disciples of Jesus, and become responsible members of a local church.

3. Clear evangelistic goals are a necessity. This is God's will in the New Testament. As a result, our efforts are measurable.

4. An effective and healthy evangelistic strategy will bring fruit. This will please God.

5. Social and behavioral sciences can positively add to a mission's strategy. Sociologists and psychologists can be of great assistance in enabling the church to do its work more effectively.

6. Effective evangelism depends on good research. Healthy evangelistic strategies require facts, not vague hopes, wishes, or promises.[33]

These six points were in fact an apologetic for the CGM. Each point is a statement defending specific aspects of the CGM that were already under scrutiny, or being challenged outright. Point one addresses the controversy of quality versus quantity. Detractors believed that the CGM emphasized quantitative growth at the expense of qualitative growth.[34] Point two speaks to the criticism that CGM only concerns itself with evangelism and not Christian ethics. Points three through six actually are

---

33. Bosch, "Gemeindewachstum was ist das?," 2.
34. McGavran, *Understanding Church Growth*, 86.

concerned with only one issue; it is God's will that a competent strategy be forged for the growth of the church. This is one of the crucial elements of the CGM. It serves as the bedrock of the movement and trumps all criticisms. Since it is God's will that the lost be found, then strategies must be developed to fulfill God's will. Thus, these four points addressed the criticism that church growth was too pragmatic and only concerned with methods.[35]

The publishers of the magazine wanted readers to gain practical tips, as well as church growth theory. Thus, a plan was laid for the renewal of the church and readers were encouraged to start working toward this end by getting involved in church growth. The logic was simple. If cults were growing in Germany, it meant that people were not closed to spiritual matters, but actually were spiritually hungry. It was the Christian church's responsibility to reach these seekers. If the church did not efficiently plan evangelistic strategies to reach these people, the cults would. The church must respond to this need, or she would continue to lose members to the sects.[36]

Roger Bosch took the lead as a church growth consultant for the GCGA. He was to be available to help local churches analyze their situation and come up with an effective plan of outreach. Practical help, tips, and interviews of successful pastors would be the earmark of the publication. In 1980 the name of the magazine was changed to *Church Growth (Gemeinde Wachstum)*, and according to Knoblauch, it grew to be one of the most read church growth publications in the world.[37]

EVANGELISM EXPLOSION

Evangelism Explosion was one of the earliest forms of church growth that would become a major part of the larger German church growth movement. The first issue of *Dynamic Church* introduced the German translation of James Kennedy's book *Evangelism Explosion*, under the title *Dynamic Evangelism (Dynamische Evangelisation)*. This was the first translation of the book in 1978. A second translation was undertaken in 1981, with the title *Handbook for Church Growth (Handbuch*

---

35. Ibid., 25–30.
36. Bosch, "Sekten wachsen schneller," 3.
37. J. Knoblauch, interview by author, 24 September 2003.

für Gemeindewachstum).[38] These two translations were too oriented toward the GPC, thus the Free Churches were not able to implement the program. For this reason both translations were later removed from EE circulation.

The second issue of the magazine highlighted EE's German director, Bernd Schlottoff, and his church in Herne as a model of a growing church. Schlottoff's articles about EE were standard in every issue of the magazine until 1984. Schlottoff's Protestant Prep Course for Church Growth, a study course that combined theory with practice of EE, was very popular among evangelistically minded pastors and lay leaders. It already had proven to be a successful method of witnessing in America, as well as in other countries. Many German pastors who first heard about the program were skeptical because of its American ties. However, upon going through the coursework and actually putting theory into practice, even the skeptics became true believers in the program.[39] This enthusiasm exhibited at the beginning of the program would only be temporary. The difficulties of implementing the much-regimented EE program in the GPC would prove to be insurmountable. The problems underlying the EE program are discussed in chapter three.

Grow or Wilt

In order to promote church growth in Germany it was necessary to provide appropriate literature. Using the avenue of *Dynamic Church*, later called *Church Growth*, a variety of church growth literature was offered to the readers. The first church growth book advertised in the magazine was by Win Arn and Donald McGavran. Originally published in 1973, *How to Grow a Church* appeared as *Grow or Wilt* (*Wachsen oder Welken*) in German in 1978. The book, a primer defending and explaining basic church growth principles, presented ideas using a dialog between Arn and McGavran.[40] In this question and answer format McGavran explained the motivation and goal of church growth. He explained that the church alone has the duty to fulfill the Great Commission.

According to McGavran, fulfilling the Great Commission is more than simply disseminating the gospel. People must have a chance to hear

---

38. Goseberg, personal communication with author, 7 August 2004.
39. Scharnowski, "3 aktuelle Berichte," 5.
40. McGavran and Arn, *Wachsen oder Welchen*, 5.

and experience Christianity from someone within their own culture.[41] McGavran also spoke to an issue that became a major criticism as the church growth movement took root in Germany; the importance of counting church members. McGavran countered this criticism by using the example of the emphasis on counting the conversions in Jerusalem in Acts.[42]

Grow or Wilt Contextualized: 10 Signs of a Growing Church

There was no attempt to contextualize *Grow or Wilt* for the GPC. A booklet by Horst Knöller published in 1979, *10 Signs of a Growing Church* (*10 Kennzeichen der wachsenden Gemeinde*) took excerpts from the Arn/McGavran book and applied them to the German Methodist Church. This booklet was introduced in the second issue of *Dynamic Church*. Its purpose was to serve as a point of dialogue for Germans interested in church growth. The ten signs listed were gleaned from the entire book and not simply copied from *Grow or Wilt*:

1. According to the will of God, the church can and should grow.
2. The present condition of the church must be analyzed.
3. Specific goals for growth must be set.
4. The church must be freed from many of its activities and concentrate on evangelism.
5. The "sleeping giant," the lay worker, must be trained for the work.
6. Personal evangelism must be a high priority.
7. New believers must be brought into the leadership structure of the church.
8. Small groups must be a major part of the church.
9. Follow-up of new converts is a necessity.
10. Prayer must play a central role if a church is to grow.[43]

---

41. Ibid., 41.
42. Ibid., 66–67.
43. Knöller, *10 Kennzeichen*, 4–18.

This booklet is important because it was the first attempt to interact contextually with American church growth. Horst Knöller, a Methodist pastor in Pliezhausen, did not simply list these ten signs, but also interacted with them from a German point of view by raising questions concerning their propriety for Germany. He admits what many Germans think concerning American church growth principles: "Here we go again—another sure-fire recipe for success from the Americans!"[44] He took issue with the idea that the spiritual health of a church was directly proportional to numerical growth. In his opinion, there may be other factors determining a healthy church. Although Knöller saw the necessity of lay involvement, he also took issue with the evangelistic training methods for personal evangelism. In his opinion, the type of regimented training presented by McGavran and Arn was too mechanical. He feared that evangelism would become too automatic and void of real feelings for the lost.[45]

The author also expressed sincere doubts that new believers should be integrated into church leadership, since they lacked maturity to lead the congregation. He feared that new Christians would eventually become frustrated and leave the church if they were thrust too soon into church leadership. Regarding prayer, Knöller raised the perennial problem with the CGM concerning the over-reliance on methodology rather than on the Holy Spirit. Although he offered no complete answer to alleviate his concern, he admitted that churches he had contacted within the CGM all exhibited active prayer lives.[46] Thus, Knöller presented an effective beginning model for a balanced church growth ethic. Pragmatic principles must be balanced with fervent prayer to help insure reliance on the Holy Spirit. This principle is essential to the future development of the GCGA and proved to be the most significant challenge for the organization.

---

44. Ibid., 3.
45. Ibid., 7–11.
46. Ibid., 15–18.

The Early Influences of American Church Growth Leaders

Donald A. McGavran

Donald A. McGavran coined the term "church growth," which came to mean all that is involved in bringing non-Christians to faith and fellowship with Christ and into responsible church membership.[47] McGavran's ascension to leader of the CGM began in 1955 with the publishing of *The Bridges of God*. The book challenged the prevalent missiological thinking of the day, which was that any vigorous mission work carried on for many years will result in great growth. McGavran also challenged the prevalent notion that the converted should be removed from their own culture so they could be trained. He founded the Institute for Church Growth in Eugene, Oregon in 1960, which five years later moved to the campus of Fuller Theological Seminary in Pasadena, California, where it remains today. This move pushed the CGM and Donald McGavran into the global arena of world missions. McGavran became the founding dean of the School of World Mission and the Institute of Church Growth.[48]

The Bridges of God had a profound effect on German church growth. As previously stated, the book raised the question most on the mind of Jörg Knoblauch: Why do some churches grow and others do not? However, there were other issues that McGavran espoused that influenced the early development of German church growth thought and practice. These fundamentals of church growth detailed by McGavran in a second book, *Understanding Church Growth*, guided the movement. The following fundamentals are not meant to be a summary of McGavran's church growth precepts, but list only those principles which had an immediate and profound effect on the early formation of German church growth.

The first foundational principle was that it is God's will that the Church grows. This is the core element, with all other principles branching out from it. This tenet forces the axiom that Christians then are compelled to be faithful to God and be involved in growing the Church. McGavran states, "Where there is no faithfulness in proclaiming Christ, there is no growth."[49] The spiritual health of a local church can then be analyzed, measured, and diagnosed by its involvement in this divine mandate. The

---

47. McGavran, *Understanding Church Growth*, xv–xvi.
48. Burkhalter, "A Comparative Analysis," 139–45.
49. McGavran, *Understanding Church Growth*, 5.

GCGA incorporated this principle as means to promote church growth on the local church level. After an initial analysis, appropriate seminars were offered to bring the local body to a healthy condition.

The second principle was "Church growth is basically a theological stance. God requires it. It looks to the Bible for direction as to what God wants done. It believes that Acts 4:12, John 14:6 and scores of other passages are true."[50] According to McGavran, this "theological stance" takes precedence over the theological differences of denominations. Denominational differences should be secondary for the sake of accomplishing church growth, especially when such theologies thwart the growth of the church. He admits that denominational theologians will criticize his view as a weak theology of the church. Herein lies a serious problem with the CGM that passed on to the GCGA. For some denominations, there are little or no "secondary theological issues." Many theological principles separating Christians in Germany were established long ago and are still in force today. McGavran's stance of setting secondary theological issues aside for the sake of the gospel guided the GCGA to make alliances with the Charismatic Church Renewal Movement, and promote church growth from various denominations all over the world. This denominational openness would have a profound effect on the ability of the GCGA to communicate its message to the GPC.

The third foundational principle that effected the early formation of the GCGA was the "harvest principle." This principle states simply that God seeks the lost. It is God's will that they be found. Matthew 9:37 records Jesus instructing the disciples to pray that God would send laborers into his harvest. McGavran emphasizes, "Seeing the responsiveness of a particular population, our Lord recognized the need for reapers. The whitened fields were God's."[51] McGavran also emphasized the fact that Jesus told his disciples not to spend a lot of time with those who were unresponsive, but to go to those who were responding (Matt 10:14). This means that those entrusted with spreading the gospel should go to those areas where the Holy Spirit is bringing in a harvest.[52] According to McGavran's harvest principle, the most fundamental question to ask before starting a church growth association should have been: Where is the German harvest?

50. Ibid., 7.
51. McGavran, *Understanding Church Growth*, 33.
52. Ibid., 32–39.

There was certainly openness for church growth ideas in Germany; however, that is not the essence of the harvest concept. Harvest means that large numbers of individuals are coming into the church to such an extent that new churches are forming. In the formative years of the GCGA this element was taken into consideration, but in regards to Germany, the founders believed the harvest lay in the future. McGavran did not rule out sending missionaries and money to unresponsive fields; however his emphasis was on reaching those in responsive areas. This is especially significant when during the formative years the German Free Churches were responsive to church growth ideas. Why was the decision made to work primarily within the GPC, when the Free Churches were so responsive in the formative years of the church growth movement? The fourth McGavran principle gives insight.

The fourth principle was the "homogenous unit." McGavran had introduced the specialized terms "people movement" and "homogenous unit" to describe how certain ethnic groups or tribes come to faith en masse. This was McGavran's most important contribution to the German church growth movement. Usually meant for people groups of like social and economic strata, the concept, in the German context, formed a huge basin holding most German Protestants. This basic concept urged propagating church growth within the *Volkskirche* rather than the Free Churches, since most German Protestants had ties to the church through tradition, infant baptism and the subsequent church taxation. During the early stages of the development of church growth in Germany, the Free Churches readily adopted the church growth, trained their own leaders, and promoted church growth in their churches. However, the fact that the GPC had a hold on most German Protestants was conclusive.

In order to contextualize church growth among the majority of Germans, the emphasis must be on the GPC and not the German Free Churches. This was a strategic decision that was made early in the German church growth movement.[53] The GCGA did not completely ignore the Free Churches, but the *Volkskirche* was the primary beneficiary. McGavran continued to emphasize that German church growth should concentrate on the German Protestant Church based on its strong ties to the majority of the population. As late as 1987 McGavran urged the GCGA to stay on good terms with the Protestant Church: "Do not intentionally

---

53. Bosch, interview by author, 18 April 2007.

provoke the GPC, because it is part of the German culture. You should strive to work as closely as possible with the *Volkskirche*."[54]

C. Peter Wagner

Donald McGavran retired from the School of World Mission at Fuller in 1981. His pupil, C. Peter Wagner, became the main spokesperson for church growth. Although McGavran's principles helped in the formulation of church growth ideas for the GCGA, Wagner had the greatest influence. His contribution to the movement continued well after the GCGA was founded, shown by his influence on Christian Schwarz, Fritz Schwarz's son and future editor of *Church Growth*.[55] He also had an early and profound impact on the missiological thinking of Roger Bosch, who was the primary person behind the church growth movement in Germany. It was Wagner who prodded Bosch to establish a German church growth institute. Wagner's contribution during the foundational years of the GCGA is formulated in his book *Your Church Can Grow*, in which he listed seven vital signs for a healthy, growing church. He developed these signs after observing the mutual characteristics of growing churches. The seven signs were:

1. A pastor who is a possibility thinker and whose dynamic leadership has been used to catalyze the entire church into action for growth.
2. A well-mobilized laity, which has discovered, has developed and is using all the spiritual gifts for growth.
3. A church big enough to provide the range of services that meet the needs and expectations of its members.
4. The proper balance of the dynamic relationship between celebration, congregation and cell.
5. A membership drawn primarily from one homogenous unit.
6. Evangelistic methods that have been proved to make disciples.
7. Priorities arranged in biblical order.[56]

---

54. McGavran, "Prof. Donald McGavran im Gespräch," 14.
55. C. Schwarz, interview by author, 18 September 2007.
56. Wagner, *Your Church Can Grow*, 41.

Wagner's seven signs reveal the ultra-pragmatic side of church growth thought. The signs also could easily be re-phrased to become the "seven signs of a growing company." This does not mean they are unbiblical, but does reveal the emphasis on pragmatism rather than biblical precision. It also reveals the tendency of church growth to use sociology rather than theology to support its claims. Wagner takes a sociological concept such as "goal setting" and elevates it to a biblical concept, such as "having faith." Within this context he urges churches to set high growth goals as an act of faith. Wagner's biblical interpretation was based on certain observations of successful churches. For example, he found that large, growing churches set high goals. Wagner then interprets goal setting as an indication of biblical faith.[57]

The weakness of Wagner's approach is especially apparent in attempting to link the first sign of a healthy, growing church to a biblical precept. In *Your Church Can Grow*, the chapter outlining the role of the pastor is titled, "Pastor, don't be afraid of power!" However, there are no scriptural passages cited to support this sign. In the accompanying Bible study guide, Wagner points to 1 Pet 5:2–5 as the supporting passage upon which this sign is based.[58] However, the passage seems to emphasize the opposite of power: "Be shepherds of God's flock that is under your care, watching over them—not because you must, but because you are willing, as God wants you to be; not pursuing dishonest gain, but eager to serve; not lording it over those entrusted to you, but being examples to the flock . . ." A legitimate interpretation of Scripture seeks to understand a passage's cultural, linguistic and historical context. Based on this, applications can be drawn. Wagner's pragmatism forces him to read into the text (eisegesis) to support his suppositions. Wagner's seven signs not only formed the matrix for Bosch's first research project in 1977, but also remained standard for his subsequent German church growth seminar and church analyses. The 1978 seminar was one of the most important tools for the GCGA and attempted to contextualize American church growth ideas for Germany. The seminar is analyzed in the following chapter.

Wagner wrote, "Lack of church growth is a serious disease, but in most cases a curable one. The cure, however, is not simple. Most often it requires as careful a diagnosis and therapy as a tumor on the ovary

---

57. Ibid., 45–54; Rainer, "An Assessment," 155–58.
58. Wagner, *Bible Study Guide*, 1.

or a coronary thrombosis."⁵⁹ The idea of the sick church had its roots in McGavran's work, where he states that it is God's will that the church grows. If a church is not growing it is out of the will of God. Wagner's diagnosis of the non-growing church was adopted by the GCGA. Wagner continues, "One of the central tasks of the church growth school is (1) to develop scientific techniques of diagnostic research for ailing churches and (2) to design instruments to be used in the kind of therapy which will restore normal church health."⁶⁰ This formed the basis for the GCGA's work: sick churches could be diagnosed using statistical analysis and a cure found. This appealed to many GPC pastors who had long suffered with declining congregations.

Wagner also defined church growth and his definition became the key element for developing and defining German church growth. Using 2 Pet 3:9 as his basic text, Wagner poses this question, "Is the church growth approach really spiritual or might it be carnal?" He continues, "The Bible tells us that one of God's desires is that all men should know him. Does God desire churches to grow? Sure He does! The Bible says that our Lord wants all people to come to repentance. Commitment to Christ implies commitment to the body of Christ. This means church growth!"⁶¹ This explanation had the greatest impact on church growth in Germany. As German church growth gained in recognition, many definitions and derivatives of church growth emerged. As a result, the GCGA continued over the years to return to Wagner's definition. In the first issue of *Dynamic Church*, Roger Bosch explained that church growth emphasizes the need for each person to make a personal decision for Christ.⁶² Conversion of the individual was the "growth" in church growth.

C. Peter Wagner's influence will go beyond the formative years; his ties to the charismatic movement would wield much influence in the development of the GCGA during the end of the 1980s as German church growth's influence began to peak. During this period, the GCGA became identified with the German charismatic movement. Wagner fully adopted the charismatic paradigm in 1982 when he taught a course with John Wimber at Fuller Seminary. The course was at first called "Signs, Wonders and Church Growth"; later it was renamed "The Miraculous

---

59. Wagner, *Your Church Can Grow*, 41.
60. Ibid.
61. Wagner, *Bible Study Guide*, 1.
62. Bosch, "Gemeindewachstum was ist das?," 2.

and Church Growth." Upon observing the "miraculous" during classes, Wagner became a full participant in the charismatic movement along with Wimber's Power Evangelism. Wagner referred to Wimber's emphasis on Power Evangelism as The Third Wave (of the Holy Spirit). The first wave had been ca. 1900 with the birth of the Pentecostal movement. The second wave came with the global charismatic movement of the 1960s. Wagner had a profound influence on the GCGA; his importance for the movement was illustrated through the influence of Fuller Seminary, the Third Wave, and his emphasis on the need for German church planting.[63]

Win Arn

Win Arn founded the Institute for American Church Growth in 1973, which three years later became a part of the School of World Mission at Fuller Seminary.[64] He became acquainted with German church growth in 1976 when Jörg Knoblauch brought a group of German pastors to visit Fuller's School of World Mission. Arn influenced the early formation of the GCGA philosophy and ecclesiology primarily through his seminars for German study trip participants at Fuller, his seminars held in Germany, and his personal interaction with Knoblauch. The unofficial Working Group for Church Growth promoted Arn's German church growth seminars in 1978 and 1979. As with Wagner, his influence continued well into the foundational years of the GCGA.

Arn emphasized the universality of McGavran's church growth principles; however, he underscored the fact that these were only principles, the implementations of which were in the hands of the German pastors. His key to contextualizing these values was to refocus the pastor's priorities, with "making disciples" as the main goal. Arn explained why pastors may need to re-organize their priorities: "Working harder at what we have been doing is not the secret to growth. Working smarter on the things that matter in order to reach new people for Christ and the church is what causes a church to grow."[65] This concept was not different from Wagner's emphasis on the pastoral role—Arn simply pushed the idea to its logical conclusion. Pastoral priorities must be re-aligned if church growth is to take place. Arn's emphasis on pastoral priorities was

---

63. Wagner, *The Third Wave*, 24.
64. Burkhalter, "A Comparative Analysis," 144–45.
65. Arn, personal communication with author, 8 September 2004.

incorporated into the future church growth seminars and important for contextualizing American church growth for the German situation.

Contemporaneous Efforts of Evangelism and Church Renewal

As the foundational elements of the German Church Growth Association forged together, there were other evangelistic and church renewal activities and efforts simultaneously occurring. It is crucial to understand that the GCGA was not created in a vacuum, and that other efforts to renew the German Protestant Church were widespread and not just the formulations of the new Church Growth Association.

Lausanne 1974

Billy Graham inaugurated The International Congress on World Evangelization to bring together persons from around the globe involved in evangelistic activity. It met July 16–25, 1974 in Lausanne, Switzerland.[66] The meeting in Lausanne was a watershed for German evangelicalism, according to Horst Marquardt, leader of the German delegation. For the first time, Germans from different denominations and theological persuasions who were engaged in evangelizing Germany became acquainted. Lausanne hosted 222 German delegates.[67] The delegates agreed, "The Americans had to invite us to a city in Switzerland, so Germans who are interested in building God's Kingdom could get better acquainted."[68] Lausanne resulted in a new commitment towards German evangelization, spawning evangelism conferences in Stuttgart, Hermannsburg, and Bielefeld where thousands attended.

Lausanne is but one example of an immense amount of evangelistic interest and activity during the formative years of the GCGA, but not arranged by it. This resulted in an initial openness to the church growth movement. The Office for Evangelism of the GPC, for example, showed initial enthusiasm for the GCGA. However, as the church growth movement matured, the early enthusiasm would be tempered by the German

---

66. Wirt, *Billy*, 222.
67. "Lausanne 1974."
68. Ibid.

Eberhard Winkler: The Church and Her Role

Winkler's work, *The Church and Her Role* (*Die Gemeinde und ihr Amt*), published in 1973 in East Germany, is important because it speaks to many of the same issues important to the Church Growth Movement in West Germany. As did its counterpart in West Germany, the East German Church suffered major declines. But unlike the GPC in the West, the East German Church had no church tax subsidies to shore up the institution, because it was not granted legal status. The decline of the East German Church under the communist state formed the background for Winkler's work.

Winkler first maintains that there is no theological basis for the separation of clerics and laity. They may be distinguished by the variety of spiritual gifts, but there is no scriptural basis for an institutional hierarchy. This became a major emphasis of the CGM in Germany. The pastoral role is a gifting of the Spirit and not an issue of institutional dogma. A pastor is on equal footing with the other gifts of the Spirit and this gift should be practiced in conjunction and in harmony with the others.

Second, Winkler urges analyzing current church structures to test whether they foster the practice of differing gifts. If not, change is advised. He urges allowing different forms of worship in the church, especially that of small groups. In allowing for structural flexibility, the church can promote the Scriptural principle of "the priesthood of all believers."[69] Winkler relies heavily on historical Pietism to bolster his ideas. In addition, he lays the blame for the current church crisis on an unwillingness to follow Pietism's flexibility of worship forms. He found the remedy, especially for the church under socialism, in allowing room within the church for the small church cell. Only in a small group can the "priesthood of all believers" rise from an unrealistic and uninteresting theory to something practical and meaningful.[70] The GCGA popularized the necessity of small groups. Winkler called for the resurrection of the small group more than a decade before the arrival of church growth in Germany. Thus, by promoting the small group, the German Church

---

69. Winkler, *Die Gemeinde und ihr Amt*, 9–10.
70. Ibid., 31.

Growth Association promoted what was already viewed as essential for the renewal of the GPC from the point of view of a respected East German theologian.

Hans Kasdorf: Church Growth as the Goal of Mission

Kasdorf's work is important because he urges both mission organizations and local churches to embrace the CGM. Published in 1976, *Church Growth as the Goal of Mission* (*Gemeindewachstum als missionarisches Ziel*) offered a critique of church growth from Kasdorf, a Mennonite-Brethren missiologist. The importance of his work is that he places the CGM in the context of missions and the local church, while explaining the movement from a Free Church perspective. At the heart of his concept is the importance of the local church and its health. Kasdorf agrees with the most basic premise of the CGM: "If a church is not growing, it is out of the will of God."[71]

Kasdorf also answers the two primary criticisms of the Church Growth Movement at that time. First, the CGM was often criticized for the apparent tension between quantitative growth at the expense, or negligence, of qualitative growth. Kasdorf explains that if a local body is healthy (qualitative growth), then it will grow numerically (quantitative growth).[72] Second, he finds the criticism that the CGM is too fascinated with statistics unfounded. He defends the use of analysis and statistics as the logical way to determine how the church grows and what steps to take to encourage more growth.

In his section on evangelism, Kasdorf speaks to the necessity of a theological foundation for evangelism. He admits that there are sometimes tensions between theologians and evangelists. However, without a theological foundation, evangelism loses its effectiveness and without evangelism, theology loses its relevance. The answer lies in an evangelistic message based on the Scriptures. This insures that the message is not minimized or corrupted by evangelists.[73] Unfortunately, the GCGA did not take Kasdorf's concern seriously. Kasdorf admitted that the CGM was still in the process of developing. It was a movement that was still evolving. Nevertheless, Kasdorf's endorsement of the CGM gave cre-

---

71. Kasdorf, *Gemeindewachstum*, 14.
72. Ibid., 82–83.
73. Ibid., 130–31.

dence to the fledgling German Church Growth Association during the formative years.

Theo Sorg: How Will the Church Become New?

How Will the Church Become New? (*Wie wird die Kirche neu?*) was published in 1977. At the time of its writing and publication, Sorg was *Oberkirchenrat* of the GPC in Stuttgart—the main administrative authority in the GPC.[74] Sorg's ideas are important because they are yet another attempt to offer solutions for the GPC during the formative years of the GCGA. Unlike Kasdorf, Sorg makes no mention of McGavran or the CGM.

Sorg wrote to offer specific guidelines for church renewal. He confirmed the common knowledge that the church was in serious trouble. The chief reason was not dislike of the institution, but indifference toward it. The majority of Germans simply no longer expected anything of the church. The church was not dead, however. Many young people were coming to faith and seeking a church where their faith could grow. The question Sorg asked was, could the GPC in its present form offer these young people and other moderns a church home where they could grow in the faith? This was the premise of Sorg's church growth perspective. He did not base his position directly on the Great Commission, or the need to save souls, but on the premise that people were coming to faith and they needed a church home. He also raises the possibility that if these people find no spiritual home in the GPC, they may be tempted to start their own fellowships or churches.[75]

Sorg's publication was important because it addressed crucial issues of church growth and renewal at the earliest stages of its development in Germany. He identified elements necessary for renewal, which were also key issues of church growth developed by the GCGA. Sorg dealt extensively with the role of the pastor, the necessity of small groups, the importance of the worship service, and the role of clear gospel preaching. These same elements also played a significant role in German church growth. Thus, the GCGA was not promoting anything new or exotic, but calling for change in areas that have long been considered obstacles for the regeneration of the GPC.

74. Sorg, *Wie wird die Kirche neu?*, 7–8.
75. Ibid., 9.

Summary: The Foundations of an Ecclesiological and Contextual Paradigm

The fledgling German Church Growth Movement was not promoting a novel initiative. The fundamental philosophy of church growth was already present, indicated through Lausanne and by the writings of Winkler, Kasdorf and Sorg. At the end of 1979, three streams of influence merged forming the foundation of the ecclesiology of the GCGA. These determined how the organization would contextualize the gospel in Germany.

The first stream was Evangelism Explosion. Bernd Schlottoff would take the lead in contextualizing this American and worldwide phenomenon for the GPC. The second stream was that of American church growth, represented by the influences of Donald McGavran, Win Arn, and especially C. Peter Wagner. Roger Bosch and the establishment of the Institute for Church Growth in Giessen, Germany represented this stream. Fritz Schwarz and his church growth concepts represented the third and final stream. Schwarz's church growth program, independent of any American church growth influence, played an important role in the development of an indigenous church growth theology and contextualizing the gospel within the framework of the GPC.

These three streams formed independently of one another, but would merge into a loose-knit organization as the 1970s ended. Jörg Knoblauch ultimately was responsible for uniting these different streams into one movement. Under Knoblauch's managerial expertise, they formed a common ecclesiological paradigm: it is God's will that the church grows, and the church is composed only of those who have a personal relationship with Christ. This means that baptized church members must at some point make a decision for Christ. When this occurs, the church experiences "growth." This common foundation would lead to the founding of the GCGA in 1985. Contextualizing this ecclesiological paradigm would conflict with the ingrained theology of the German Protestant Church, which held that infant baptism automatically assures salvation and entrance into the church.

Discussion Questions

1. According to Donald McGavran, God requires that the church grows. This is the most fundamental theological stance of the CGM. McGavran further states that denominations should work together and put aside "secondary" theological issues for the sake of reaching those without Christ. Discuss what "secondary" theological issues exist currently that hinder evangelism.

2. What was the question that hounded both Donald McGavran and Jörg Knoblauch? Discuss how this question could and should be asked today. What role does contextualization play in finding the answer to the question?

3. Discuss the comments made by Chuck Smith and Robert Schuller to a group of German pastors about church growth. What was at issue concerning the cultural differences between Americans and Germans? Why did Fritz Schwarz react negatively to a sermon on Rom 13?

4. What contextualizing error was apparent in the first German church growth magazine? Given the purpose of the magazine, was it even possible to address the concerns of theologians and pastors?

5. Which one of Donald McGavran's church growth principles was ignored by those in the German church growth movement? Why was it ignored? Discuss the benefits of this principle as well as the drawbacks.

6. Eberhard Winkler's contribution to church growth is extremely important. Why? He called upon the traditions of Pietism to revive the church in East Germany. What specifically was he referring to and is it still relevant today?

7. According to Theo Sorg why was the GPC losing members? He questions whether the GPC in its present form can meet the needs of those coming to faith. Why is church tradition so hard to change?

3

The Foundational Years of German Church Growth 1980–1985

The year 1980 was one of "firsts" for the German church growth movement. The first official German church growth organization registered with the government. The organization, called Church Growth: Association for Church Development in Germany (*Gemeindewachstum-Arbeitskreis für Gemeindeaufbau in Deutschland*), was the forerunner of the German Church Growth Association, founded in 1985. Subscribers received the first issue of the magazine *Church Growth*, and Bernd Schlottoff led the first training session for Evangelism Explosion at his church in Herne. Schlottoff called the training The Protestant Prep Course for Church Growth. Thus, the years 1980 to 1985 proved to be significant in understanding how the contextualization of German church growth developed. In addition to all this, the German Protestant Church declared 1980 as the Year of Evangelism.

Church Growth: Association for Church Development in Germany

Although Church Growth: Association for Church Development in Germany would not officially be recognized until the end of the year, the founders made key decisions in January of 1980 which would affect the future form and ministry of the church growth movement. One decision was to detach the association from Schlottoff's Prep Course for Church Growth. The reason for this separation was that Evangelism Explosion was just one method of church growth, and was not intended to be the face of church growth in Germany. Roger Bosch and the Institute for Church Growth, for example, dealt with many church growth principles, such as discovering your spiritual gifts, leading a cell group, evangelization, and publishing basic church growth materials.[1] As its goal, the German church growth organization would have not only the promotion of certain methods, but also the proliferation of ideas. Coordinating and promoting a variety of church growth activities and models should be the goal. Thus, the Prep Course would be only one aspect of German church growth. As a separate entity, it would become a member with other organizations, of an official German church growth association. The Prep Course will be fully explained later in the chapter.

There were two reasons for establishing a legally recognized non-profit association. First, the German church growth movement needed tax-deductible donations to carry out its purpose. Second, registering as an official German organization was essential for the contextualization process. Unlike in the United States where Christian organizations become non-profits in order to raise tax-deductible funds, in Germany registration serves two purposes. First, it allows contributors to receive tax deductions. Second, and most importantly, Germans take seriously and consider indigenous only those organizations registered with the government. Due to the presence of Americans, the foreign moniker was a constant concern. This became critical as more Americans came and established their own church growth organization under the auspices of the GCGA.

An official church growth organization was also necessary to ensure that church growth established an independent profile while working within the GPC structure. The founders believed that the *Volkskirche* had too many priorities, resulting in the most important mission of the GPC being lost. A recognized German church growth organization could continually remind the GPC of the necessity of evangelism. Further, it was impossible for the National Church's official evangelistic organization, the Office for Evangelism, to completely meet the evangelistic needs of the entire nation. The Office for Evangelism had many other duties outside its evangelistic mission, and as a result, evangelism often was not emphasized. Although the founders had no desire to compete with them, they wanted an organization that would concentrate only on church growth, which was something that the Office for Evangelism could not

1. GCGA Archives.

do. This also explains why the founders of the GCGA saw the need for a new and independent organization and chose not to work within an existing group, such as the Gnadau Society or the Confessional Movement. Other organizations may have included programs very similar to church growth, but it was not their main emphasis. The GCGA founders wanted good relationships with these groups, but chose not to join them.

The first step in contextualizing German church growth was instituting the American study trips, and the second step was the publishing of the magazine *Church Growth*. The founding of an official church growth organization was the third step in the contextualization process. Church Growth: Association for Church Development in Germany was founded on December 12, 1980. The organization's constitution defined its purpose:

> The goal of church growth is evangelistic church development. This means helping a church bring men and women, with no personal relationship with Jesus Christ, into fellowship with him and to actively serve him. This goal is to be reached through regional and local seminars, church growth consultants, magazines, practical literature, and study trips. The association is not confined to methods and programs. It desires to work with other groups in order to coordinate activities and to publicize events. In addition, it hopes that other organizations with church growth goals will join the association.[2]

The goal, part of Jörg Knoblauch's managerial philosophy, was always to work with other groups interested in propagating church growth ideas in Germany. The organization was not to be an entity in itself, but was to be a forum for other organizations with similar interests. According to Knoblauch, just one organization would be too weak to contextualize the church growth message. There is strength in numbers.[3] At the beginning, there were three organizations under the association's umbrella: Schlottoff's Prep Course for Church Growth in Herne, Bosch's Institute for Church Growth in Giessen, and Knoblauch's Association for Church Growth in Giengen.

At this point in the movement, the philosophy of encompassing a wide spectrum of church growth ideas was apparent and would continue to be a hallmark of the association. This fundamental premise of

2. Ibid.
3. J. Knoblauch, interview by author, 24 September 2003.

the movement explains why this first church growth organization, and the future GCGA, invited ideas from what many German church leaders considered controversial corners of the church growth movement: Robert Schuller, Paul Yonggi Cho, and John Wimber. Schuller was criticized for his emphasizing "positive thinking" at the expense of the gospel. Cho and Wimber were condemned for their charismatic theology.

The Magazine *Church Growth*

Church Growth appeared four times a year and was the single most important contextual tool for German church growth. While the study trips and conferences were important, nothing surpassed the importance of the magazine.[4] The mission of the magazine was clearly defined:

1. Church growth has a spiritual side and a structural side. The magazine will concentrate on the structure of church growth. We assume that the pastors who read the magazine are believers and that their theology is friendly to personal evangelism.
2. *Church Growth* will fill a specific need. Out of the fifteen German magazines appealing to Protestants, only *Church Growth* speaks to the needs of pastors, church boards, and lay workers in the GPC.
3. *Church Growth* will help the local church by offering the services of church consultants. These consultants will come to the church and help them develop a program for church growth.
4. *Church Growth* will promote both sides of the church growth movement: The spiritual side and the practical side.
5. *Church Growth* will not promote itself. It is a servant to the church.
6. *Church Growth* will serve as a platform for a variety of organizations. This family of groups will have an opportunity through the medium of the magazine to report on their activities.

The goal for 1981 was to have at least four hundred subscriptions to the magazine. By the end of the year over eight hundred people subscribed to the magazine. At the end of February 1982, it reached nearly one thousand subscribers. This was an amazing development and

---

4. Ibid.

surprised the members of the movement. In addition, there was a great demand for earlier issues of the magazine.[5]

Although the magazine evolved over the years, it maintained particular characteristics. Foremost, it propagated the praxis of church growth principles. Primary among these were promoting evangelism, encouraging pastors to implement church growth ideas, and, according to many, emphasizing the practical aspects of church growth at the expense of theological reflection. Many felt that *Church Growth* did not offer sufficient biblical principles to back up the praxis it promoted.

The role of the pastor for the success of church growth in the GPC was paramount. Without the enthusiastic support of the pastor, renewal within the local GPC parishes was impossible. As a result, *Church Growth's* goal was to aid the renewal of the spiritual life of the German pastor, as well as to give him or her practical helps. Although lay people could gain from the articles, it was clear that issues raised and discussed were oriented toward the GPC pastor.

During this foundational period, the organization decided to concentrate on the GPC and not the Free Churches. However, the founders of the association realized that church growth was oriented more for the Free Church than the *Volkskirche*. They had to contextualize an American concept for the parochial system. Thus, two levels of contextualization were necessary. First, church growth must be acceptable to the German culture. Second, the pastors in the GPC must be open to church growth. By working with the National Church, the first level of contextualization was successful. In order to breech the second level, the magazine came into play.

In order to aid the contextualizing process for the pastor, the third issue of the magazine began a series entitled "Pastors Ask–Pastors Answer" in 1981.[6] This encouraged pastors to ask questions, with the assurance that a pastor would answer the question. Issue seven began a column called "From Pastor to Pastor" offering practical advice for the parish *Pfarrer*.[7] The model churches used in each issue were also oriented toward pastors. The hope was to encourage pastors to consider church growth as viable for their congregations. Another indication of the pastor orientation was the "Management" column in each magazine.

5. Ibid.
6. "Pfarrer fragen Pfarrer antworten," 7.
7. "Von Pfarrer zu Pfarrer," 3.

Pastors who were able to manage their time and resources would be able to spend more time doing things that encouraged church growth. Given the fact that GPC pastors spent most of their time fulfilling their required roles as public officials and had little time for church growth, time management was a requirement.[8]

Satire became one of the most controversial and antagonistic literary tools used by the magazine. The fourth issue, published in March 1981, was the first to use satire to introduce an article. The title of the article, "How to Split Your Church," was an innocent attempt to gain attention. The article proceeded to tell the true story of a pastor who made too may errors in introducing a visitation ministry in his church. This article did not offend anyone, but it was a harbinger of things to come. A similar title in the ninth issue, "How to Get Rid of Your Worship Service," was not as well accepted. The article was a fictitious interview with a pastor who was deliberately closing down his church. Many readers found such satire sarcastic and not amusing.

As stated above, *Church Growth* editors favored pragmatism over theology. The magazine always gave helpful applications for the reader's church or small group. For example, the third issue contained an article that encouraged the discovery and practice of spiritual gifts. Under the "Church Research" section, the reader got practical pointers on how to grow the church through spiritual gifts.[9] This section addressed the important issue of the role of the pastor and the role of the lay worker. At this point, there was an effort to give theological basis to this concept. The article mentioned Rom 12:1, 1 Cor 12–14, and Eph 4 that emphasize the importance of the body of Christ. The hope was to encourage lay people to get more involved in the church by practicing their God-given spiritual gifts. Five "how to's" described how gifts could make a difference in the local church:

1. A clear theological basis is required. Through a thorough study of the Bible, the church should determine what gifts are still in use today, and determine where the church stands on the baptism of the Holy Spirit.

2. An atmosphere for practicing spiritual gifts must be available. It must be determined where in the church a person may practice his or her spiritual gift.

---

8. "Management," 7.
9. Bosch, "Geistesgaben," 2.

3. There must be a workable structure between spiritual gifts and church growth.
4. Discovering spiritual gifts is necessary.
5. Expect God to bless the church.

This concept is rooted in the Word of God so that the Body of Christ functions as a true body of believers.[10]

This short explanation of spiritual gifts is distinctive of the method used by the magazine. The point was not to develop a theology for a certain concept, but to promote the method as a way to regenerate the church. This practice drew the ire of many German theologians and pastors. The criticism was the lack of theological depth to these principles. Protagonists argued this was typical of American pragmatism. In spite of the criticism, the focus on practicality rather than theology continued to be the hallmark of the magazine.

The German Church Growth Contextualization Strategy Emerges

The structures for contextualization were complete. German church growth would identify itself with the traditional German religious institution—the *Volkskirche*—and the first German church growth association was recognized by the government. *Church Growth* and the study trips were successful in arousing hope that the GPC actually could be revived. Now, church growth had to be brought to the parish to prove if all the hype was true. Four elements crucial for contextualization emerged during the early 1980s: Evangelism Explosion, regional workshops, regional associations, and most importantly, a theology of church growth began to develop.

Evangelism Explosion

Bernd Schlottoff built his Prep Course for Church Growth based on the philosophy and methods of James Kennedy's book, *Evangelism Explosion*. In 1978 it was published in Germany under the title *Dynamic Evangelism (Dynamische Evangelisation)*. Schlottoff edited the book's

10. Ibid.

second publication titled *Handbook for Church Growth* (*Handbuch für Gemeindewachstum*) in 1981. He edited the book to contextualize concepts that were oriented solely for the American church. Although the methodology remained the same, he tried to make changes to comply with the German parochial and cultural structures.[11]

Fritz Schwarz wrote the book's foreword and explained the importance of training lay people in the art of personal evangelism: "The laity will never become evangelists, because most of the pastors have absolutely no idea how to lead someone to Jesus. How then can the laity be trained? There are pastors who not only do not know how to lead a person to Jesus, but with an ingenious theology actually prove it is something no one should be allowed to know."[12] This statement reflected accurately the spiritual climate in the *Volkskirche*, where any dogmatic definition of the gospel was soundly condemned as playing God. In addition, at this time in German history, relatively few of the GPC pastors could communicate the basics of the gospel.[13] The inability of pastors to explain the simple tenets of the Christian faith may have been due to a lack of training or it could indicate the absence of personal faith on the part of the pastor.

This provocative statement by Schwarz set the stage for problems between the GCGA and the *Volkskirche*. This would be the central issue dividing traditional church growth ecclesiology and the traditions of the *Volkskirche*. Who is a Christian and how does one become a Christian? This was rudimentary, but certainly the strategic issue shaping the contextualization process for the church growth movement. Schwarz's remark, at the very beginning of the German church growth movement, was predictive. It is around this basic Christian doctrine that the GCGA would face its most fierce detractors and would be forced to repeatedly re-emphasize its evangelistic mission and evaluate how church growth is contextualized.

Schlottoff was similarly candid in his introduction. He mentioned the positive signs of church growth all over the world and compared them with the dying German church. Like Schwarz, Schlottoff agreed there would be no church renewal without the engagement of lay people in local evangelism. Therefore, it necessitates having an institution whose mission is to train lay people for evangelism. If the church is to grow, it

11. Kennedy, *Handbuch*, 15.
12. Ibid., 7.
13. Schlottoff, "98 Prozent," 7–8.

must come through the work of the church members. He emphasized the traditional role of the pastor must change. The pastor is to fulfill the role of coach, who trains and leads his team of co-laborers.[14]

A review of the German EE program is necessary because of its close association with the GCGA. Further, there were serious flaws with the contextualization of this program. The greatest difference between the American and German brands of EE is how to choose the households to visit for a gospel presentation. In American churches, visitor cards with the name, address, phone number, and other pieces of information of those visiting a church service or event are collected. Without notification, these people receive a personal visit. This mode of operation would not be acceptable in Germany. Germans would feel uncomfortable filling out a visitor's card asking for so much personal information. Germans also do not like to have surprise visits at home. The *Handbook* laid out specific ways for German believers to carry out a visitation ministry. Schlottoff was not the only one teaching visitation. The Office for Evangelism also emphasized visitation evangelism, and this resulted in tension between the two organizations.

In addition to training of laity and visitation handling, the Prep Course also instructed participants on other important aspects of the healthy church. What are the ingredients of a healthy church and worship service? How do you integrate new people into the church? How does the pastor maintain his spiritual life, and how can he better manage his time? Schlottoff, Schwarz, Knoblauch, and Bosch formed the core group of instructors who answered these questions.[15] The participation of the founders of the GCGA indicated the confidence they had in the EE concept.

The EE program is very rigid and methodical. Choreographing each part of the witnessing process ensures the following of a predetermined map. For example, if the student is unable to follow the format for an evangelistic dialog then the trainer interrupts and finishes the witnessing process. In order to bring people to the point of making a decision, constructing each part of the witnessing process assures clarity. Controlling the conversation is not the goal, but it ensures a clear presentation of the gospel, and that there is a point of decision. The explanation of the gospel has three parts. First, the visitor introduces himself and gives

---

14. Ibid., 9–23.
15. Schlottoff, "Evangelisches Studienkolleg," 11.

some background information pertaining to him and the church. Second, the visitor then gives his personal testimony and this leads to asking the individual of his or her spiritual condition: "If you were to die tonight, do you have the assurance that you would go to heaven?" Depending on how the person answers, the conversation continues along prescribed lines learned from EE. If the person answers in the negative, the visitor leads the individual to make a decision for Christ. The person witnessing is given exact words to say to bring the person to pray a prayer of repentance and faith in Christ. Finally, after the person has prayed to receive Christ, the visitor is to give personal assurance of their salvation. The person should have no doubts concerning their newly found faith.[16]

The success of Schlottoff's church, the *St. Stephanus Kirche* in Herne, became well known. As a result, questions poured in to *Church Growth*: "How did the church grow from 250 to 900? We would like specific information on how this happened." Two entire pages in the June 1981 issue of *Church Growth* dealt with answering questions. Schlottoff emphasized the difficulties involved with the success of the church. He was candid and explained the cost of church growth for him and those working with him. First, success depended upon the work of those who ministered in the church before him. This fact kept the ego in check. Second, other pastors work just as hard, and do not have the success. On the other hand, it is a lie to maintain that all you have to do is preach the gospel and the church will grow. Third, the success in Herne was due to the cooperation of lay workers. Finally, Schlottoff admitted that American church growth only emphasizes the positive aspects of the growing church and this is unfortunate. Discussing the negatives is necessary.[17]

Schlottoff wrote of several problems relating to the church in Herne. First, the constant fluctuation of attendees was frustrating. Some Sundays the church was full. Other Sundays there would be a hundred fewer worshippers. The explanation was that some who came were not committed Christians and only came to church occasionally. Second, the laity became tired. As the church grew, so did the responsibility of a small group of loyal laity. According to Schlottoff, this was a serious concern facing his church, as well as any growing church, and he could offer no solution to the dilemma. Finally, the last problem dealt directly with the EE program. Many of those who came to faith because of EE, never grew in the

---

16. Kennedy, *Handbuch*, 46–73.
17. Schlottoff, "Eine Gemeinde wächst, aber . . . ," 6.

faith and eventually left the church. This was the most troubling aspect of the work. Schlottoff remarked that if the program failed to integrate new converts into the church, then the church's growth would be implausible.[18]

Evangelism Explosion influenced church growth in Germany from the very beginning. The fact that a German Protestant Church was actually growing at a healthy rate was extremely encouraging, especially for pastors and lay leaders wanting an evangelistic church. The program offered practical help for reaching those baptized as infants, but who had never received Christ. The program's prominent place for many years in *Church Growth* reflected its importance for church growth, as does the prominent place that Schlottoff held in the church growth association. However, the EE experiment failed in Germany. Although Schlottoff had success at his church, the EE program in Germany did not have the intended results. Evangelism Explosion was the first GCGA church growth methodology imported to Germany. However, EE was not a party to the CGM. It did not originate from Fuller Seminary or the sphere of the CGM influence. It was born from the ministerial experiences of James Kennedy at Fort Lauderdale. Kennedy's church was included in the writings of church growth enthusiasts and was on the itinerary of the German pastoral study trips. It would be a mistake, however, to include Kennedy's EE within the sphere of the CGM.

Kennedy explained the origin, development, and biblical basis for EE in his 1979 dissertation. EE began as the solution to two coinciding issues of the local church: "They are the laity and the task of evangelism or Christian witness, respectively. Concerning the laity, churches of all denominations have been asking such questions as: What is the place of the laity in the church? What authority or power should they have? What tasks are theirs to perform?"[19] The questions raised by Kennedy were similar to those asked by the GPC. As a result, EE in Germany was a true test case for the contextualization of an American-born evangelistic concept focused at the German parish level.

Kennedy's EE formula was based on the Great Commission, but propagated in the local church through the matrix of Eph 4:11–13. The laity was to carry out the Great Commission through the instrumentality of clerical oversight. This was the most fundamental concept of EE. This had direct influence on the German EE program. Pastors were not only

18. Ibid.
19. Kennedy, "The Genesis," 2.

to train the laity; they were to do this by "on the job training." Clerics were to practice evangelism themselves and then take volunteers with them when they made visits. In this way, the laity would gain practical experience on how to effectively evangelize. Kennedy viewed this as the biblical answer to evangelistic problems at the local church level. Clerical training coupled with pastoral example and "on the job training," formed the nucleus of the American EE movement that began in 1960.[20]

The success of EE at Fort Lauderdale gained attention in the United States and by 1981 EE programs had been established in many countries throughout the world. The program quickly evolved into a regimented training program. Austere regimentation ensured the success of the program.[21] This extreme adherence to a controlled training regimen led to the demise of EE in Germany. Modern Germans do not like extreme control. Dennis Griggs, a colleague of Roger Bosch, spoke to this problem of control, regimentation, and formality in his implementation of Campus Crusade for Christ's evangelistic techniques among German nationals. "One of the most clear observations of the old LIFE evangelism training seminars was that Germans perceived it as 'methodical' or 'mechanical,' like a Marxist five year plan which, of course, never succeeded."[22] This was only one area of the clash of concepts.

Michael Herbst, a prominent German conservative theologian, also expressed concern with the program. He found this form of home visitation not only out of context for Germany, but also annoying in its form of presentation.[23] Herbst found the *Handbook for Church Growth*, in spite of the editing from Schlottoff, unfit for the German situation and having the stigma of American mentality and culture. What disturbed Herbst was the rigidity of the questioning by the witnessing visitor. He sees the series of questions leading to the gospel presentation as selling the gospel message short. In his opinion, this method of witnessing lends itself more to the repertoire of a sales clerk than to an evangelist.[24] In addition to the reasons mentioned above, there was a systemic flaw in contextualizing the program: the requirement of clerical training of the laity. The job requirements of the GPC pastor do not allow for the time necessary for EE.

20. Ibid., 70–74, 86.
21. Cox, *The Secular City*, 54–60; Sproul, *Lifeviews*, 85–86.
22. Griggs, interview by author, 14 November 2007.
23. Herbst, *Missionarischer Gemeindeaufbau*, 264.
24. Ibid.

Pastors came to the weeklong program of EE training at Herne and were to bring at least one layperson with them for the training. Afterwards, they were to begin home visitation programs in their respective churches. This proved to be impossible. There is an extreme variance between GPC pastors and American pastors. American pastors have a tremendous amount of freedom to invoke various strategies to promote church attendance. GPC pastors do not. A single pastor may have the oversight of 6,000 church members, but less than one hundred attending services. In addition to traditional duties such as conducting Sunday worship, funerals and weddings, pastors visit the elderly on anniversaries and birthdays, attend civic ceremonies, and perform administrative tasks. There remains little time to faithfully adhere to the EE lay training regimen. Subsequently, many pastors attending the Prep Course simply dropped the program.[25] In 2000, Evangelism Explosion training ended. In 2001, Reinhard Goseberg, a Baptist lay worker, restarted the program in Germany, completely revising the material making it applicable for the Free Churches.[26]

Church Growth Conferences

Church growth conferences were another key element of contextualizing the church growth movement. The establishment of these workshops promoted church growth on a regional basis so that pastors and lay leaders could attend a church growth presentation in their own area. Germans do not like to travel long distances, so it was crucial to establish regional conferences in closer proximity to them. There was always a well-known church growth expert invited to speak. There were a variety of workshops and seminars on church growth available to participants:

1. Evangelistic Home Bible Studies: Embryo for Church Growth
2. The Holy Spirit: The Power for Church Growth
3. Courage Pays Off: First Steps for Church Growth

In 1989, there were twenty workshops with experts in their respective fields. Topics ranged from how to become involved politically and socially, specifics on establishing a tearoom, outreach for the youth, and

---

25. Schlottoff, "Erfolg Mißerfolg," 11; Schlottoff, interview by author, 14 September 2005.

26. Goseberg, personal communication with author, 7 August 2004.

arranging an evangelistic breakfast for women. Workshops on church growth basics, spiritual gifts, evangelism, and management were always available for participants. Regional church growth conferences were not just workshops. They provided pastors and laity, sometimes working in isolated German villages, avenues to learn about the latest evangelistic ideas and the most current technology and media for the church.

Regional Church Growth Associations

Regional associations were local church growth working groups for pastors ministering in close proximity to one another. These associations, comprised of four to six pastors, were necessary for contextualizing church growth. By the end of 1985 there were six regional associations. The goal of these associations was to provide spiritual and emotional support for pastors. Pastors who desired to implement church growth strategies in their respective parishes discovered this could be a lonely and stressful undertaking. The associations would serve as a forum for mutual support. As a rule, these regional associations met several times a year for encouragement, prayer, and exchanging of ideas.[27] There were seventeen regional associations by October of 1986.

A group of pastors could form an association by meeting certain requirements. Potential members must agree to the goals of the GCGA and work with the regional GPC officials. They had to elect a board composed of three persons. Those on the board must meet with Fritz Schwarz or Roger Bosch for training at least twice yearly and take part in the regional church growth conference. The official association saw these regional associations as a means to directly influence individual pastors by offering them personal contact with Fritz Schwarz and Roger Bosch, and providing them with information over the latest developments in church growth. This included making them aware of the latest literature and upcoming study trips.[28]

The Development of German Church Growth Theology

From 1979 to 1981 Fritz Schwarz published a series of three books that not only detailed the evangelistic program in the Herne church district,

27. T. Knoblauch, personal communication with author, 18 March 2008.
28. GCGA Archives.

but also laid the foundation for a church growth theology. Schwarz's writings began a process that many would have considered impossible: church growth became in a very short time the topic of discussion within the GPC. Schwarz became a well-known figure in the GPC after the publication of the three volume series, *The Manageable Church* (*Überschaubare Gemeinde*).

It is important to review the Herne program for two reasons. First, it was an evangelistic church growth program developed independently from any American church growth influences. Second, it ran parallel with the EE program within the same church district. This leads to an obvious comparison motif rarely available. One program was wholly American, the other purely German. A comparative analysis is necessary to learn how each one fared in the contextualization process.

The Manageable Church was not only the name of his book series, but also the name of the evangelistic program developed in the Herne church district by Fritz Schwarz. It spoke directly to the problems in the church and offered an outline for renewal. According to Schwarz, renewal was possible in the GPC, but only if serious evangelistic work took place within the parishes: "We can no longer allow the question whether we want to be evangelistic churches or not; the challenges are too obvious."[29] His comment reflected that of the German church growth movement. Schwarz's evangelistic idea was unique in that it was a regional program confined to one church district representing fifty churches, with over half of the churches participating. According to Schwarz, the church had betrayed the simple gospel by making it so complicated that no one could understand it. The gospel appeared only as a confusing theory, practically inaccessible and void of the joy that Schwarz emphasized. This assessment was based on two observations. First, he believed that most of the Germanic tribes had only been "Christianized," not "evangelized" in the sixth century. Second, his experience taught him that church members had difficulty answering the basic question, "Are you a Christian?" When asked, the person would reply that they "hoped they were" or that "they were trying to live a Christian life." There was no assurance of salvation and any sign of assurance was criticized as "self-confidence." The joy coming from knowing Christ had died for your sins was absent. Instead, individuals were taught that taking part in church activities and endeavoring to live a good life was all that was necessary.[30]

29. F. Schwarz, *Überschaubare Gemeinde*, vol. 1, 7.
30. Ibid., 18.

At issue was the difficult climate in the GPC concerning evangelizing church members. For example, those encountering the church had different needs and attitudes regarding the Christian faith. Schwarz believed that it was important for the Christian to hear the gospel message repeatedly. It firmed up the faith of the believer and changed wrong attitudes and behaviors. There were also those who were active in the church but had not yet personally received Christ. They believed themselves Christian because they had been baptized as infants. They appeared to be "insiders" but in reality, they were "outsiders." In order to reach this group, Schwarz suggested it may be better to speak of "renewing their baptism or confirmation," rather than of "conversion." He admitted that this would cause problems for those demanding an undiluted gospel presentation. There was yet another group who had rejected anything having to do with the church. The only thing they would respond to was a radical call to conversion. Finally, there were those in the GPC who did not attend church, but have had contact with the gospel message. It was also possible that there were individuals attempting to live out Christian principles without church contact. The importance of the Herne program was the effort to develop a program having the potential to navigate through this religious maze.

The pastors involved in The Manageable Church program viewed evangelism as an integral part of the church, not an event that took place occasionally. In order to meet this requirement, Schwarz developed "Open Discussion Evenings." Rather than a pastor, an established cell group was responsible for arranging these regular events. Not only did the program fit in with the rhythm of church life, but it provided an atmosphere where guests felt comfortable enough to discuss faith-related topics. Lay workers had the responsibility to build relationships with those who seldom, or never, attended worship services. For the sake of clarification, these folks carried the label of either "distant" or "anonymous" church members. Through informal contacts, lay workers invited people of both groups to attend an Open Discussion Evening. These informal meetings took place in a home or at the church. The participants met in a room tastefully decorated where the guests felt comfortable. The speaker gave a short presentation that always contained a gospel presentation. Afterwards, there was time to sit and discuss the topic of the evening. This program proved successful in bringing people to faith. However, Schwarz stressed that even if the program resulted in no conversions, the church was still responsible to proclaim the gospel. If a church does not proclaim the gospel then it is no longer the church. A church that seeks to maintain its status in the community at the expense of the good news has betrayed its true calling.[31] Because of the Herne program, a new perspective on contextualizing the gospel evolved.

Fritz Schwarz lamented the fact that many pastors in the GPC were laboring under the illusion that the church continued to hold an important place in German society. The goal for these pastors was to maintain the church through infant baptism and church taxation. Pastors did everything they could to maintain a respectable number of Sunday worshippers, but soon resigned themselves to the fact that little, if anything, would change. They hoped that if the GPC maintained its present status long enough, perhaps things would change for the better. Schwarz specifically addressed these pastors, who felt duty-bound to maintain or stabilize the church institution. These pastors rejected the evangelism of church members because they taught that everyone became a Christian through infant baptism. Fritz Schwarz rejected the teaching of baptismal regeneration, as practiced in the church. The only way it should continue is when the church follows up the baptism with evangelism. The children at some point must trust Jesus and have a personal relationship with him.

This drab picture of the GPC did not prevent Schwarz from praising many aspects of the church. He was thankful for the freedom the church gave him to minister, and for the church tax contributors, without whom he would have no salary. He praised the different structures in the church that allowed for outreach into the community.[32] Regardless of his praise, Schwarz's view of the GPC became a point of contention with the publication of his next book, *Theology of Church Growth: An Introduction* (*Theologie des Gemeindeaufbaus: Ein Versuch*).

The theology Schwarz refers to in *The Manageable Church* is what was taught in the universities. He said nothing positive about it in relationship to his evangelistic program. People come to faith in spite of theology, not because of it. Schwarz complained that theologians have made the gospel message so complicated that it became impossible to understand. This theology finds its way into the parish, and results in the pastor viewing any verbal confession of faith with doubt and skepticism. Schwarz felt that it is not the duty of theology to make the gospel too

---

31. Ibid., 22–29.
32. Ibid., 85–96.

complicated, to offer nothing concrete for lay workers, to make it difficult to grow in the faith, or not heed the modest concerns of a cell group. Emil Brunner (1889–1966), a prominent Swiss Protestant theologian, had the same conclusion relating to theology and evangelism: "Evangelistic theology removes the barriers between the hearer and the gospel." It is the duty of faculties at the universities to insure that future pastors are educated in the art of church growth. Schwarz observed that many pastors visited churches in England and the United States, and profited from it. He suggests transferring principles learned in other countries to Germany, and that German faculties should consider offering courses on church growth. However, he quickly points out that his program is German, and has only a small touch of Americanism. Sarcastically, he concludes that this should be acceptable in an age of ecumenicalism.[33]

To reach the point where a lay worker could explain the gospel to another person, Schwarz was careful not to expound a particular method. On the other hand, he made it clear that "the Holy Spirit would rather work with our sweat than with our sloth." Trusting the Holy Spirit is no excuse for lack of good preparation. Like the CGM, Schwarz emphasized God's will in relation to outreach. As a result, reaching non-Christians is not an option for the church. Likewise, Schwarz reached the same conclusion as the CGM: if the church is not responding to this principle, it is no longer the church.

The goal of the Herne program was to renew the GPC. What would this renewed church look like? Schwarz envisioned church members experiencing the power of the living Christ in their lives. This required discarding centuries-old, encrusted traditions, and silencing theologians decrying evangelism. Those proclaiming the gospel and those wanting social reform would unify to fight the ills of unjust economic and political policies. Christians in neighborhoods would open their doors to one another, start new cell groups, and share with one another. Pastors and lay workers would no longer complain about lack of funds, but discover that living with less has its own riches. Most importantly, the church would become attractive and authoritative, bringing hope to people in darkness.[34]

The Herne program was a good model for the GPC. First, it simplified church growth for the German pastor-oriented parochial system.

33. F. Schwarz, *Überschaubare Gemeinde*, vol. 1, 130–38.
34. Schwarz and Sudbrack, *Überschaubare Gemeinde*, vol. 2, 20–21.

Second, Schwarz reduced the complicated theological and institutional structure of the GPC to a manageable (*überschaubar*) entity. Mobilizing the laity to first build personal relationships with parishioners, before introducing them to the gospel, was crucial. This enabled the laity to form a natural bond with people, so that when they came to faith, they already would have formed relationships in the church. Most importantly, Schwarz explained the gospel in simple terms, so that the laity easily understood it and could communicate it. The criticism of GPC theology was also legitimate. Schwarz was correct to condemn a theology bent on destroying any effort to legitimatize personal conversion. However, he offered no real alternative. Instead of developing an alternative theological paradigm, he only criticized the predominant one. Schwarz recognized this and began to formulate the theology underlying the Herne program. The result was *Theology of Church Growth: An Introduction*, which is discussed later in the chapter.

Evangelism Explosion vs. The Manageable Church: A Comparative Analysis

Although Fritz Schwarz wrote in the foreword of the *Handbook for Church Growth* that there was a lot to learn from the EE program, he never adopted it. He recognized the fact that it was not culturally suited for the German parochial system.[35] Although the program in Herne was not the antithesis of EE, the differences in the programs illustrate the complexities and the dangers of contextualizing foreign programs into complex post-Christian cultures.

First, there were similarities. Both programs were based on the necessity for individuals to have a personal conversion. Thus, both programs operated under the same ecclesiology. Both Schwarz and Schlottoff believed in the full involvement of the laity, with the guidance of the pastor. Similarly, the two programs implemented home visitations as a way for the laity to make contact with other church members. There were individuals in the parish that had experienced conversion. However, the majority had not. It was the duty of the converted to reach those who were not. There was then a clear line of spiritual demarcation between Christians and non-Christians.

---

35. Kennedy, *Handbuch*, 7; Schlottoff, interview by author, 14 September 2005.

Second, there were vast differences in the two Herne programs. Because of the amount of in-depth coaching required by the pastor for EE, the program became impossible to maintain. This exposed one of the contextual weaknesses of the program. As already stated, pastoral requirements and expectations are poles apart from those of American pastors. The most important programming element of EE is "on the job training." The German pastor was not able to fulfill this requirement of the program over a long period of time, because of the number of traditional duties required. As a result, EE never produced the movement for which it hoped. The Manageable Church also required the full participation of the pastor. However, the training was informal and less regimental, and required less supervision.

This leads to another complex issue of cultural adaptability and sensitivity. The EE gospel presentation is not transferable to the German social or religious experience of those in the *Volkskirche*. How can an individual who has never heard the gospel respond in the manner desired by EE? This would be an appropriate program for those having been exposed to the gospel numerous times and who had some understanding of the consequences. However, for German society and the GPC, the approach is not culturally compatible. The EE program lacked a full appreciation of German cultural idiosyncrasies, because it was an American program based on American cultural themes. Germans do not like discussing private matters, especially religion, with strangers. The intimate discussion of one's spiritual situation is reserved only for a small circle of friends or acquaintances. It is within that closed circle that an informal discussion of religious perceptions would be a culturally acceptable venue for expression.

Schwarz also saw the need for personal contact over a period of time between individuals, so that both gospel and conversion would be more natural and more conducive to the German need for conversation, discussion, and fellowship. This model took into account that it may take a long period of time for someone to understand the gospel. They were able to hear it from different individuals on a one-on-one basis, from the pulpit, as well as from other venues specifically formulated for their needs. This would allow for a smooth transition into the life of the church after conversion. By contrast, this may explain why many EE converts later left the church, because they had not been slowly integrated into the fellowship.

Theology of Church Growth: An Introduction

There is a natural bridge between the publishing of *The Manageable Church*, and *Theology of Church Growth: An Introduction*. Schwarz saw the need for the Herne evangelistic program to be explained from a theological standpoint. This is noteworthy in light of the differences in American church culture and German church culture. In America, results are important. If a certain evangelistic approach results in increased numbers on Sunday morning, then it is deemed successful. The program is viewed, after the fact, as theologically sound because it worked. In Germany, this pragmatic approach is extremely questionable. Traditional German theology dictates that any church program must first stem from theological study. The methodology springs from theology. As far as German theologians were concerned, the Americans had the cart before the horse. Thus, Schwarz naturally saw the importance of a theological basis for his outreach program. However, he did not consider that he was following the American pragmatic course of discovering a successful method, then finding a proof text to back it up. He believed he was following the philosophy of historical German theology.

His purpose would be not only to give church growth theological foundations, but also give practical guidance to the church. This thought did not originate with Schwarz, but from Helmut Gollwitzer, a German theologian. Christian Schwarz explained the importance of Gollwitzer's contribution to his father's thought: "He (Gollwitzer) defined theology as, theory between praxis and praxis '. . . he meant that theology has its source in praxis, theological questions come from praxis, and theology must work out a system that then serves praxis."[36] Thus, the Schwarz theology was more than a church growth apologetic. It would be a redefining of German theological practice in relation to church growth. The Americans were not so far off, after all.

As stated above, Schwarz and his son wrote the first German church growth theology. It developed on German soil, in the traditional GPC. In addition, his church district was located in the most densely populated and un-churched area of Germany, the Ruhr area. Neither Donald A. McGavran, Peter Wagner, nor any other American church growth specialist influenced Fritz Schwarz. It is also important to recognize that *Theology* resulted in church growth becoming a topic of discussion in Germany,

---

36. C. Schwarz, interview by author, 18 September 2007.

as well as causing great consternation in some circles. The outline of the book revealed that it was a scathing polemic against the established German Protestant Church. The authors understood their book as a manifest of thorough church reform. The book divides into ninety-five points or theses, a direct reference to the Ninety-Five Theses of Martin Luther. This work is not simply another treatise defending church growth; it is a broadside against the *Volkskirche*.[37]

The fundamental premise of *Theology* is a clear, absolute, and continual divide between the institutional church and *ekklesia*. The institutional church is composed of church members who have never trusted Christ. The *ekklesia* is the true church, comprised of those who have accepted Christ as Savior. *Ekklesia* is the Greek word for "church." Matthew (16:18) uses it to translate Jesus' promise to Peter: "And I tell you that you are Peter, and upon this rock I will build my church (*ekklesia*). Unquestionably, this divide is the chief characteristic of the Schwarzs' theology and all church growth practice. Although it may not always be clear where this line is, drawing it is necessary. It may not be evident who needs to be converted, but close contact with individuals will reveal those who need Christ.

This clear demarcation between institution and *ekklesia* has consequences. Inevitably, it leads to a differentiation between those believing and those not believing. The GPC refuses to recognize this, and as a result it no longer encourages conversion. In addition, proponents of the status quo in the GPC condemn such division between believing and unbelieving as playing God. They defend this position by claiming that no one can judge who is and who is not a Christian. The purpose of such statements and criticism, according to *Theology*, is to create an atmosphere where questioning faith is limited, if not outright forbidden. This results in annulling any call to faith and fellowship. That being the case, *Theology* defined *ekklesia* as personal fellowship with Jesus, and with sisters and brothers working their faith out in love. Schwarz maintained that the purpose of any theology is to promote the growth of the true church. If theology fails this test, *it is not theology*.[38]

Fritz and Christian Schwarz were careful to explain that this in no way dooms theology to failure. When it serves to establish the continuation of *ekklesia*, theology establishes its true relevance, and secures its

---

37. Schwarz and Schwarz, *Theologie des Gemeindeaufbaus*, 5–10.
38. Ibid., 41–59.

continuation as a vital part of setting the compass for church growth. As a result, theology will no longer be in danger of only being a tool of the institutional church, whose sole purpose is to secure the church's continued domination over the true church. Theology, as it exists now, finds itself in a difficult position. While not denying the difference between institution and *ekklesia*, in order to maintain its present position, theology must support the notion that the institution *is ekklesia*. This resulted in a theology of paradox to explain the plausibility of impossibility, explains Schwarz. In the end, a hyper-logic has developed in the National Church to prove the fusion of institution and *ekklesia*.[39] The church is a fellowship of those who have a personal relationship with Christ, and who exercise their faith in love and service. Logically, defining the church is fundamental because it is the object of growth. Since this is not the case within the GPC sphere, categories have developed over time seeking to clarify or define what the church is (ecclesiology). Although understanding these categories may prove daunting, it is necessary to tackle them before attempting a definition of church growth in the GPC.

According to *Theology*, there are four categories or definitions of the church in the GPC. First is the concentric church, where degree of devotion to the church is decisive. The stronger the devotion, the closer one is to the center of the circle. The amount of time given to attending worship services and serving the church in some capacity determines the amount of devotion; the more time, the more devotion. The duty of the pastor is to strengthen and increase those in the center, while working to bring those on the periphery of the circle closer to the center. The most critical concern for the GPC is preventing members from cutting all ties to the church. "Cutting all ties," means the church member quits paying church taxes and is subsequently stricken from the church roles.

The second category or type of church is the "visible-invisible" church. The overriding theological premise is that spiritual growth is the sole work of the Holy Spirit, and occurs without human interference or influence. Lack of true spirituality has no influence on the work of the church, since spiritual growth occurs only in the "invisible" church. The "invisible" church takes form by maintaining the "visible" church, the institution. Third are the *ecclesiolae in ecclesia* (Latin: little churches in the church). Those in the Fellowship Movement fall into this definition. Those who consider themselves true Christians gather in fellowships

---

39. Ibid., 70–72.

(*ecclesiolae*) striving to live out their faith within the institutional church (*ecclesia*). They strive to bring those in the institution into their fellowships. These efforts usually fail and the fellowship takes the form of a protest movement against the church, exemplified by the Confessional Movement "No Other Gospel." Last is the latent church. Its task is to discover the church rather than build it, because it exists everywhere, even in areas denying the gospel. The duty of the believer is not to grow the church, since the church already exists and grows without human intervention.[40]

Schwarz explained these categories evolved because there is no lucid definition of the church in the GPC. It is within this milieu that his theology sought to define church growth: church growth consists of all activities having as their goal the establishing and building up of the *ekklesia*. Clear and simple definition of the church results in a plain definition of church growth. This excludes anything claiming to be church growth not having as its center the forming and proliferation of the *ekklesia*.[41]

The existence of the *ekklesia* is a prerequisite for evangelism to take place. Evangelism is something that happens within the context of the life of those in the true church. The Schwarzes viewed evangelistic events, crusades, or outreaches as anomalies rather than biblical evangelism. They preferred the "genesis of faith" developed by Emil Brunner, where the unbeliever is attracted to the fellowship because of the power emanating from it. The power and life in the fellowship is contagious, and the unbeliever wants to be part of it. Before he knows it the power of the Spirit overtakes him. This power resembles a magnet or the outbreak of an infectious disease, and before he is aware of it, he is carrying the infection.

Schwarz rejected the traditional GPC form of evangelism, which is the sermon. Most German pastors consider preaching, regardless of the topic, to be proclaiming the gospel. Before Schwarz's confrontation with Schlottoff, he too held this belief. A similar philosophy is that everything the church does is evangelistic. These misconceptions of what biblical evangelism entails required an unambiguous definition. However, engrained GPC tradition does not change easily, and any other definition of evangelism is suspicious. Schwarz hoped that evangelism would revert to its biblical roots where the *ekklesia* was the expression of the gospel.

40. Ibid., 52–53.
41. Ibid., 61–62.

"Preaching the gospel" was so clear and enticing that it drew people in. *Theology* concluded that without the *ekklesia*, there is no evangelism, and without evangelism, there is no *ekklesia*. Thus, evangelistic preaching emphasizes conversion, and simultaneously points to Christian fellowship.[42]

Fritz and Christian Schwarz admitted that the GPC continues to wield influence in Germany. The question is what vestiges of Christianity remain. As church growth became more widely discussed in Germany, two distinct paradigms emerged revealing what vestiges were indeed present. First, church growth was strengthening and growing the true church. Second, church growth was a way to return the church to its former glory days or at least stabilize the church to prevent further loss of its prestige.

In order to dispute this second paradigm, *Theology of Church Growth* described how church growth should operate in a post-Christian Germany. Church growth meant men and women were experiencing a personal conversion. The GPC rejected this paradigm and fought to repel it. The Schwarzes compared this stance to that of atheistic states bent on destroying the true church: "This church, that has never given up calling itself the church of Christ, has over the centuries, systematically and horribly exterminated the *ekklesia*, just as many atheistic countries today have done with their specific policies."[43] However, the reason the early church grew at an astounding rate was not that the conditions were conducive for the spreading of the gospel, but rather because they were compelled to spread the gospel. They were compelled because they had been commissioned by the risen Lord to make disciples of all nations and took seriously the Lord's promise to soon return (Acts 1:8–11). They perhaps firmly believed that upon completion of their mandate the Lord would return and set up his kingdom. The sooner the task was completed; the sooner he would return. The rejection of the institutional church by thousands of Germans does not mean people are not interested in the gospel. It meant that the church as an institution no longer had any meaning in their lives. Those leaving the church saw this as one of the only opportunities available to opt out of a government tax-driven program that proved to be irrelevant in their daily lives.

According to the Schwarzes, there has never been a time more conducive for evangelism than the present. The decline of Christendom

---

42. Ibid., 79–81.
43. Ibid., 281–89.

in Germany should challenge the church to return to her calling, the building up of the true church already in her midst. However, the GPC has never developed a strategy for church growth. In addition, they have previously labeled those defining the church as a body of true believers as separatists or fanatics.[44]

Theology served to provide a theological basis for German church growth. Precisely, it gave focus for the contextualization of church growth within the GPC. The role of church growth was to focus on the growth of the *ekklesia*, not the stabilization of the *Volkskirche*. Thus, the GCGA concentrated its efforts on the remaining vestige of the church—those truly converted—and providing them with the appropriate tools to accomplish their purpose. All of this was to transpire while maintaining a presence within the GPC institution, because contextualizing the gospel required it.

The Year of Evangelism: 1980

The first GPC church membership survey in 1974 was entitled *How Stable is the Church?* and revealed that the days of a constant and stable membership were over. Between 1969 and 1980, 1.2 million Germans left the church. Of those that remained, 17 percent were contemplating leaving. A continual decline of the German birthrate, the influence of foreigners on the culture, and the trend to break with tradition among those twenty to thirty years of age, pointed to a future of rapid decline for German Protestantism. This bleak outlook was the impetus behind the Year of Evangelism.

In 1918, immediately after the First World War, Gerhard Hilbert, a leader in the Office for Evangelism, proclaimed: "Germany has become a mission field."[45] Sixty years later, the statement still held true. Employing Hilbert's quotation as its motto, the GPC called all the district churches, Free Churches, and indigenous mission organizations to take part in a national evangelistic outreach in 1980. The goal of the Year of Evangelism was for committed church members to determine ways to reach out to the uncommitted and skeptical church members.

---

44. Ibid., 293.
45. "Missionarisches Jahr 1980," 1.

In preparation for 1980, the GPC leaders (synod) in Baden took up the subject of mission and evangelism.[46] Some fascinating observations were made which had a direct link to church growth principles. One observation was that the church should grow, in contrast to much of the thinking of that time, which believed that there was such a thing as "healthy decline." The synod leaders used the American church growth movement as exemplary of the attitude that the church should grow. Pointing to the rapid growth of the church in Acts, they emphasized that a growing church was biblical. In addition, the American "church survey" offered a means to discover a church's strength and weaknesses. The synod also encouraged pastors to consider the idea that not everyone in their church was a Christian. This addressed the problem of pastors taking for granted that all of the worshippers were Christians. As a result, sermons tended to be more on ethics than on the gospel. Practically, this required personal evangelism in conjunction with a well-organized visitation program.

Although no great revival resulted, the evangelistic year was deemed a success because it brought together the GPC, the Gnadau Society, and the Free Churches to work concurrently on a nationwide evangelistic endeavor.[47] It revealed the fact that although the Free Churches were relatively small, they had much to offer in evangelism. The reason for this was that they realized their very existence depended on evangelism, since they received no funds from the government.

The Year of Evangelism also made evident that there remained structures in the church that inhibited evangelism. There was a lack of follow-up for those who made personal decisions, and certain church traditions made the church worship services unattractive for visitors. For example, pastors wore clerical garb, seating was uncomfortable, sermons were predictable and boring, and the stoic atmosphere uninviting. In addition, it was obvious that the large and complicated GPC administrative machine left little room for personal initiative and creativity. The so-called evangelistic preaching lacked precision and clarity. A survey revealed that the majority of the pastors believed they had always promoted evangelistic outreaches in their churches. One third of the pastors, however, did not

---

46. "1980 Missionarisches Jahr und was nun?," 15.
47. "Bilanz," 1–3.

fully understand the term "evangelism." They had a negative understanding of the word and suggested finding another term.[48]

Although the program resulted in much discussion and debate concerning the meaning and motivations for evangelism, the desired evangelistic renewal did not take place. The primary cause was that the traditional structures of the GPC remained immovable. Parishioners view the pastor as a public employee, because their salaries come from German income taxes. The idea that the majority of church members need to be converted is abhorrent and goes against the culturally engrained tradition that everyone in the church is a Christian. Categorizing someone who faithfully pays the church tax as non-Christian is unacceptable. As a result, an evangelistic renewal movement had little chance of success.

The significance of this evangelistic outreach was the fact that many of the methods either employed or suggested came directly from American church growth. While the GPC discussed the realities of evangelism in their church, so did the founders of the future GCGA. It encouraged them that leaders in the *Volkskirche* were contemplating employing church growth principles. As the church growth movement gained momentum in the late 1980s, it would be attacked for its reliance on American church growth. This is ironic given the fact that those who promoted the Year of Evangelism enthusiastically endorsed key elements of American church growth methodology.

The Americans Arrive: Campaign for Church Growth

In 1981, three American families came to Germany wanting to work toward the renewal of the German Protestant Church under the leadership of Hans-Martin Wilhelm, an ethnic German. Overseas Crusades, an American missions organization, sent out the missionaries. Wilhelm was convinced that the best way to evangelize Germans was through the *Volkskirche*. Subsequently, he founded a new church growth group, Campaign for Church Growth (*Aktion Gemeindeaufbau*), and joined the GCGA as another member organization. Wilhelm initially met with Peter Schneider, the General Secretary of the German Evangelical Alliance. Schneider was at first skeptical given the history of his dealings with American missionaries. Experience had taught him that American missionaries arrived with a preconceived misperception of the German situation. They

48. Seitz, "Missionarische Existenz," 151.

came to Germany with a pre-packaged American style methodology and strategy already in place, well before they understood the country's very complicated religious landscape. However, when Wilhelm assured him that he had no agenda, and stated that it would be inept for an American mission to tell German Christians what they should do to renew their church, Schneider invited the OC team to come to Germany. Wilhelm's action was crucial for the contextualization of the gospel. It assured the Germans that these Americans had no intention of telling them what to do or trying to transplant an American church model on German soil. Wilhelm displayed humility and cultural sensitivity. Most importantly, it conveyed that the missionaries desired to learn from the Germans and serve them. Instead of propagating their own ideas, they wanted to help the Germans reach *their* goals.

The Campaign for Church Growth kept its promise. The German branch of Overseas Crusade did not promote its own material, but instead used that provided by the German Church Growth Association. Under the auspices of the GCGA, the Campaign offered seminars, church analysis, consultation, and study trips. The Campaign for Church Growth was a crucial addition to the association. First, it provided much needed manpower. The missionaries, all but one of whom had theological degrees, supplied the resources to expand the church growth mission. Three of these men were ethnic German, and requiring no language training, they began leading seminars immediately. Second, the Americans needed no financial assistance from the Germans. The missionaries raised their own funds from American churches and individuals to cover both living and ministry expenses. By 1985, seven additional American families had joined the Campaign.

Wilhelm was careful to convince GPC pastors that he was committed to working within the church structure and that the missionaries under his charge understood this.[49] The American families were discouraged from attending Free Churches, and urged to attend the *Volkskirche* located in their village. This was necessary to ensure the Germans that the Americans were indeed committed to the GPC, and not to following the typical American missionary pattern of shunning and condemning the *Volkskirche*. However, these efforts would not be completely successful. The American stigma would continue to be an issue with the GPC.

---

49. GCGA Archives.

The Second GPC Church Study 1982: What Will Become of the Church?

In 1984, one year prior to the founding of the GCGA, the second German National Church survey was published. *What Will Become of the Church?* (*Was wird aus der Kirche?*) portrayed the conditions inside the GPC and provided the immediate context of the formal founding of the GCGA.[50]

The survey revealed there were 10,662 churches, with 16,118 GPC pastors in West Germany. On any given Sunday, there were 840,000 worship services, along with 410,000 children's churches. Under its organizational umbrella, the GPC also had 12,980 institutes, homes, and hospitals for the care of the needy and sick. The church employed more than 1 percent of the 22.5 million workers in the country; these were engaged primarily in hospitals, convalescent centers, orphanages, and kindergartens.[51] Being such a huge organization with so many employees, it would be a mistake to view the GPC as simply involved with carrying on worship services each Sunday. This makes the loss of church members more complicated, because the loss of revenue affects much more than the pastoral salary. Church tax revenues support thousands of other initiatives of the church.

The 1984 survey concentrated on what church members thought about the church. What was important to them and how should the church respond? Of course, as in the 1974 survey, the issue of those considering leaving the church was of great interest. However, intensive discussions concerning the church's losses no longer occurred. The fact was that losses had become common and expected. Those still in the church were now accustomed to a declining church. From 1974 to 1984, 1.52 million Protestants had left the church. The church tax continued to be disliked, and was the favorite subject of church critics. Fifty percent indicated that the church income tax (8 to 9 percent) was too high.

The survey showed that there was some improvement concerning church attendance. Eleven percent of Protestants attended church almost every Sunday, while 35 percent never attended. In 1974, 8 percent were regular churchgoers, while 39 percent indicated they never attended church. However, a greater percentage indicated that they had

---

50. Lindner, "Programme," 210.
51. "Arbeitskreise," 12.

contemplated canceling their membership.[52] Indications were that leaving the church no longer carried the stigma that it once did. Instead of considering what the community might think, it is more important that a person decide for his or her own personal reasons. The results of the survey were not surprising to those in the German church growth movement. Most importantly for the movement, the statistics revealed that the GPC might be ready to try anything to increase worship participation. The sad truth was that the German National Church was facing a financial crisis and anyone offering a ray of hope would have at least a hearing.

The Founding of the German Church Growth Association

On May 19, 1985 the leadership of Church Growth: Association for Church Development in Germany decided to disband and establish a new church growth association. The association concluded that the theme "church growth" was becoming more popular in light of the increasing number of requests for church growth seminars and speakers. As a result, the Association, founded in 1980, needed a new concept and organization that would be conducive to reaching the entire country. This required the electing of a leadership board responsible for a nationwide church growth vision. This board would consist of elected members, as well as those invited from other like-minded associations. Contact with churches in Switzerland and Austria was increasing, so representatives from these countries should have a place on the board. This complete board would be responsible for public relations on a national scale by employing television, radio, and the print media. Board members would also be responsible for national church growth research projects. Increasing the number of board members would further enhance the possibility of increasing the number of regional church growth societies. The goal was to have associations in each of the ten West German states.

The primary function of this new organization would continue to be renewal within and through the German Protestant Church. This focus would serve to guide the new organization as it sought to contextualize and promote church growth in Germany. Although the GPC would be its primary interest, the GCGA would also endeavor to reach the Free Churches and the Catholic Church. This was something the former

52. "Arbeitskreise," 25–26.

organization had not done. The GCGA would continue the evangelistic emphasis of its predecessor: "to discover ways to bring men and women, who have no personal relationship with Jesus Christ, into fellowship with him and into active service for him."[53]

Summary: The Fundamentals of a Contextual Paradigm

The GCGA solidified its contextualization process by 1985. The GCGA defined the true church as a mission church bent on fulfilling the Great Commission. The *ekklesia*, fully distinct from the institutional church, was the true church. The foremost goal of the true church and the most essential characteristic was *growth*. This ecclesiology resulted in a distinct practical theology of conversion-oriented praxis. Subsequently, the GCGA would concentrate on persuading those in the *ekklesia* that growth was indeed possible, if it employed precise planning and correct methodologies. This fundamental ecclesiology and corresponding practical theology would motivate opposition in the coming years. An ecclesiological paradigm, characterized by a clear line of demarcation between Christians and nominal Christians, coupled with a pragmatic planning motif, would be the primary source of opposition to the movement. Thus, contextualizing the CGM in Germany would prove difficult.

Discussion Questions

1. Discuss the reasons why Evangelism Explosion failed in Germany.
2. Discuss why the Manageable Church program succeeded.
3. What was the thesis of *Theology of Church Growth: An Introduction*? How did the GPC respond to the thesis? According to the book, what is the role of theology?
4. The *Volkskirche* rejected the GCGA's definition of the church. Discuss the four categories of the church devised by the GPC.
5. Crusade, or mass evangelism, was once popular in the States. What cultural shift is responsible for the absence of this type of evangelism? How does this change effect contextualization of the gospel in America?

53. GCGA Archives.

A Case Study in Contextualization

6. What was one reason the founders of the GCGA chose to form their own organization instead of joining one of the other groups, such as the Office for Evangelism or the Fellowship Movement?

7. Regarding contextualization, is it ever wise for a missionary to work independent from an indigenous church or organization? Why or why not?

8. The GPC church survey in 1984 revealed much about why the church was declining. In relationship to the contextualization of the gospel, why is it necessary to know why people leave the church in a particular culture? Why did many of those won by EE leave Schlottoff's church?

9. One of the reasons the Campaign for Church Growth was a welcome addition to the GCGA was that the missionaries received funding from America. How could this situation be a hindrance to the work of missionaries on any mission field?

10. Why did the Free Churches have more to offer concerning evangelism than the GPC?

4

German Church Growth Takes Root 1986–1990

In 1531, Anabaptists, stark proponents of believer's baptism, had taken over the German city of Münster, and were threatening to spread their dissent throughout Germany. In June of 1535, a Catholic army led by Münster's former bishop besieged the city, killing thousands of its inhabitants. The killing went on for months after the city was taken. Their crime? Opposing infant baptism. In other German cities Anabaptists were burned at the stake. The blood lust took a rather macabre and ironic twist as hundreds of the dissenters were "baptized" in German rivers. In Holland Anabaptists were slaughtered, so they fled to England, where they were not welcomed. Fourteen Dutch Anabaptists were burned at the stake in various English towns in 1535.

Europe has never welcomed voices of religious dissent. If the history of European religious dissent reveals anything, it is that those opposing powerful churches should keep their mouths shut. As long as they remain quiet, nothing will happen. However, as soon as the dissent takes root, those invested in the status quo strike back.[1] This was the experience of the German Church Growth Association.

Contextualization Process Clarified

The organizations under the GCGA umbrella adhered to the principles that Fritz and Christian Schwarz solidified and publicized in their

---

1. Watts, *The Dissenters*, 9.

Theology of Church Growth: An Introduction.[2] The GCGA founders already understood that infant baptism did not equal Christianity, and that it resulted in the division of *ekklesia* and institution. This was especially decisive in clarifying the relationship between infant baptism and conversion. The authors of *Theology* rejected as unbiblical the prevailing belief that conversion was in a constant state of flux and indeterminable. They believed conversion occurred at that time when the individual made a clear decision for Jesus Christ, and this decision in no way elevated the human role in justification over the power and work of God: "However a person judges infant baptism, one thing is certain. A person can only rely on his baptism when he personally meets Christ through the power of grace. But then someone will surely mention the power of grace in baptism. Baptism has absolutely no power. That would be magic."[3] However, the authors never rejected infant baptism. If they had, they would have been excommunicated.

This explanation gave those in the GCGA an ecclesiological and contextual basis from which to work. Those member organizations understood this as the foundation from which to build a church growth philosophy within the GPC. Infant baptism was not to be outright rejected, but would be used to encourage personal conversion. Upon the onset of personal faith and conversion, one became a member of the true church, and validated the person's infant baptism. From 1986 to 1990, the organization solidified its ecclesiological stance and the subsequent praxis for contextualization. The practical implementation of church growth theory characterized this period, as well as increased opposition. There were three crucial issues concerning the new organization requiring clarification during this time.

Free Church or the Volkskirche?

The first issue was the GCGA's commitment to the GPC. Was the association true to the National Church or was it more oriented toward the Free Churches? Bernd Schlottoff, the chairman of the organization, explained that the GCGA was totally committed to working in the *Volkskirche*, however, they would not ignore the Free Churches. He discounted the idea of planting new churches. At this stage, the organization was enjoying a

---

2. J. Knoblauch, interview by author, 31 August 2005.
3. Schwarz and Schwarz, *Theologie des Gemeindeaufbaus*, 81–85.

relative openness to church growth within the GPC and as a result saw no reason to consider the establishment of new congregations, which would only be possible within the Free Churches.[4]

Compatriots or Competitors?

The second issue concerned the relationship to the Office for Evangelism, a division of the German Protestant Church. Why was there a need for a new organization whose mission was similar to that of an established GPC institution? Schlottoff explained that there was a need for a variety of activities leading to the renewal of the church. However, the GCGA endeavored to develop a close relationship with the office and coordinate with their efforts. Peter Mädel, director of the Office for Evangelism in the state of Hessen, was on the board. Further, the GCGA gained "guest status" with the office.[5] In order to encourage an atmosphere of cooperation, GCGA representatives met with church leaders in the state of Württemberg and associates of the Office for Evangelism for Württemberg in 1987.

The Office for Evangelism also specialized in advancing the GPC's perception of church growth and church consultation. The GPC viewed the GCGA as just another organization among many that were offering a series of prescriptions for the ills of the church. Further, it was evident they viewed church growth as something the church had always done. Church growth principles promoted by the GCGA were nothing new, and the representatives argued that church growth was continually being accomplished in all areas of the church. They saw church growth as accomplished through confirmation instruction, church music, worship services, evangelistic outreaches, and church visitation. This prompted a heated exchange between Schlottoff and representatives of the Office for Evangelism. Schlottoff countered that such generalizations of church growth amounted to a distortion of genuine church growth. He said that to minimize church growth as encompassing all activities of the church was one of the most refined satanic attacks against real renewal. If church growth were diluted to mean every church activity then nothing

---

4. "AGGA betont Zusammenarbeit," 14.
5. GCGA Archives.

substantial would ever occur.⁶ This argument was one that continued to follow the GCGA through the years.

Evangelicals or Charismatics?

Schlottoff said the atmosphere was so positive for church growth that there was room for several organizations working toward the same end. The goal must be to coordinate the efforts of those desiring to renew the *Volkskirche*: "The time of division between Christians is finally over. Now is the time to plan together, work together, and pray together."⁷ This statement leads to the third critical issue facing the new organization in the late 1980s. Schlottoff not only was referring to cooperation with those evangelical organizations with ties to the GPC, he also was signifying the future role of charismatics represented by the Charismatic Church Renewal Movement. There would be specific steps taken to involve the charismatic branch of the GPC in German church growth.

Wolfram Kopfermann, chairman of the Movement, was on the GCGA board. This was not without controversy and resulted in another reason to oppose German church growth. This move by the GCGA was based on a principle set down by Donald McGavran, the Father of the Church Growth Movement. As previously stated, he insisted that secondary theological issues should be set aside for the sake of evangelizing those without Christ. The problem was defining "secondary theological issues." One group's secondary issue may not be secondary for another.

Church Growth Gains Ground: How Was It Done? What Were the Signs?

Church growth was a recognized movement in Germany by the mid-1980s and gained in popularity and strength by end of the decade. In 1987, Theo Sorg, bishop in Württemberg from 1987 to 1994, observed: "At this time there is much written and spoken about the renewal of the church. The interest about this issue can be described as very enthusiastic. Basically, this is a joyful sign. It points to the fact that something is going on . . . Indeed, a lot of new things are going on." In regards to the

---

6. "Wie die AGGA," 6–15.
7. "AGGA betont Zusammenarbeit," 14.

GCGA he concluded: "Today everybody is talking about the catchword 'church growth.' This includes not only those organizations tied to the church whose goal is evangelism, service, and mission, but it is also a topic of discussion among church leaders and church councils." Sorg concluded that it was difficult to keep up with all the new books, magazines, and organizations that have sprung up as a direct result of the interest in church growth.[8]

Sorg reflected the observations of the GCGA regarding this particular period of time. The number of subscriptions to *Church Growth* had increased to four thousand by September 1988. There were three church growth conferences in 1988 that together drew approximately one thousand participants.[9] The organization postulated that this positive atmosphere was a direct result of church growth going through a series of steps or phases. These phases of development are instructive regarding the contextualization of German church growth:

1. Ignorance: Few people in Germany knew what church growth was. There was little interest.

2. Opposition: Skepticism greeted the proprietors of church growth as more information disseminated throughout the GPC. Many criticized the proposition that growth must be measured. Counting church members echoed "the sin of David" (2 Sam 24; 1 Chr 21). Opposition also arose because of the American roots of church growth: "After chewing gum and Coca Cola, now we have this nonsense. No Thanks!"[10]

3. Curiosity: After a time, curiosity replaced much of the opposition. However, church growth had the reputation of "disturbing" the GPC culture.

4. Reflection: Notice of church growth principles inaugurated the idea that they may be helpful. The accompanying concern was that implementing these principles might compromise traditional GPC theology.

5. Learning: Seminars, literature, and church growth functions facilitated the message that church growth was a positive development.

---

8. Ibid.; Sorg, *Christus vertrauen Gemeinde erneuern*, 14–15.
9. GCGA Archives.
10. Jacobsen, "Gemeindewachstum," 13.

6. Acceptance: For those willing to fully commit to the principles, church growth filled a needed void.[11]

These phases greatly generalize the evolution of German church growth, and are not an exact representation of the contextualization process. For example, phase six indicates that there was a relative acceptance of church growth. This does not mean that church growth had been embraced. It only shows that the number of pastors willing to accept aspects of church growth philosophy was increasing.[12]

The increase in the interest in church growth in the 1980s was noteworthy given the fact that ten years earlier church growth was seldom, if ever, mentioned. After 1975 church growth and its underlying principles became the subject of books, congresses, and theological discussions throughout Germany.

The Time Was Right for Acceptance

It is not an exaggeration to say that what began in the 1970s as a small faction of church growth supporters had blossomed into a full-fledged church growth movement by 1986.[13] Several contributing factors brought about this phenomenon:

1. According to the two church membership studies by the GPC, the church continued to decline. The church leadership sought answers to the problem.
2. Previous renewal strategies and reforming certain structures of the GPC had failed.
3. Evangelistic crusades alone did not guarantee church growth. Studies revealed that very few of the converted ever became active church members.
4. Many church leaders no longer viewed the Holy Spirit and church growth as contradictions. Spirit and method were viewed as one.
5. The fact that the church was growing worldwide was observed, and it gave hope that the church could also grow in Germany.

---

11. Ibid.
12. Ibid.
13. C. Schwarz, *Praxis des Gemeindeaufbaus*, 36.

6. The German culture was no longer bound to the traditional church. This opened new opportunities for the gospel, as well as new opportunities for those wanting to take advantage of it.
7. Church growth research was accepted as a scientific discipline. Examining churches to determine their growth patterns, and using the results to form a plan, was accepted as a legitimate practice.[14]

The initial acceptance of church growth was tempered by much skepticism and sometimes hostility. Outside observers felt threatened by the new movement because it accentuated the failures not only of the GPC, but also of the organizations, such as the Office for Evangelism, sanctioned by the GPC to reverse the negative trends. This revealed the fundamental problem of renewal movements; they were seen as threats. Regarding this, the GCGA avoided the term "renewal" (*Erneuerung*) in the foundational documents, because of the negative connotations that accompanied the word.[15]

The Case of idea-Spektrum

The most popular and respected Christian magazine in Germany was *idea-Spektrum*. At that time, the magazine had close ties to the German Evangelical Alliance and its relationship to the GCGA was at times strained. Initially the magazine refused to print any information about the new movement, going so far as to refuse any advertisement concerning congresses or meetings.[16] Over time this attitude changed, proving the influence of the GCGA in Germany.

One proof of the foothold that church growth had in Germany was an article in *idea-Spektrum* in June 1986. *Idea* published a series of articles dealing with the questions and issues surrounding church growth. The series recognized the growth of the church in much of the world and compared it to the dire situation in Germany. The prognosis for growth in the GPC was nil. If the current trends continued, the article lamented, current membership would be cut in half in forty-five years. They invited Jörg Knoblauch to discuss the qualities of a growing church.[17] Knoblauch named five crucial qualities of a growing church:

14. Ibid.
15. Wilhelm, interview by author, 8 February 2008.
16. T. Knoblauch, interview by author, 31 August 2005.
17. "Wie wachsen Gemeinden wieder?," 11.

1. The church has to know its condition before it can find the cure, i.e., the correct methodology to correct the problems. The local church must analyze its condition. Fear of the results of the analysis prevents churches from taking this first step.

2. The pastor's role must change from player to coach. The pastor's ministry must be one of coach and personal trainer. A trained laity is a necessity.

3. Worship must be encouraging, attractive, and inviting. Church leaders must understand that absence on Sunday was not the gospel's fault; it was their fault.

4. Cell groups are an integral part of the growing church. How does the church with only a small group of committed lay workers begin? They begin a cell group, a home Bible study, and invite people they know. The cell group is the door to the church.

5. Prayer is the foundation for the growing church. There are crafty people who can sell a refrigerator to an Eskimo, but craftiness has nothing to do with church growth. It is the work of the Holy Spirit. Without prayer, the church will never succeed.[18]

The willingness of *idea-Spektrum* to delve into this subject was yet another indication that church growth was becoming more widely known. The condition of the church had gotten so miserable, with no hope for the future, that many in the GPC were willing to listen to what was considered an American heresy. Knoblauch's point three was indicative of the CGM and resulted in intense criticism. Blaming church leaders for low worship attendance put too much of an emphasis on man's responsibility and not on the Holy Spirit. Knoblauch, however, was simply repeating what he had heard from pastors in the United States.[19]

The Radio: One Example of Promoting Church Growth

Gospel Radio (*Evangeliums-Rundfunk*), founded in 1959, was affiliated with Trans World Radio. The GCGA used it during the 1980s to promote, clarify, and contextualize church growth. These broadcasts were important because they came at a time when church growth was becoming well

---

18. Knoblauch, "Nicht Eskimos einen Kühlschrank verkaufen wollen," 2.
19. Schwesig, "Wo Gemeinden wachsen," 2.

known and provided another avenue to clarify precisely what church growth meant. From 1982 to 1988, Gospel Radio presented a series of thirty-minute broadcasts detailing the activities of the GCGA and its church growth program.[20] Schlottoff, Bosch, and Knoblauch, as well as pastors and laity, were interviewed for the purpose of explaining how church growth functioned in Germany. The format of the programs followed the rule of theory first, presented by the GCGA, then the practical aspects of implementation, explained by a GPC pastor or lay person.

The first broadcast explained the background of the CGM and how the movement changed the understanding of evangelism. Earlier evangelism was viewed as having primarily two forms, mass evangelistic campaigns and personal evangelism. Donald McGavran ushered in the new paradigm of church growth evangelism. That is, personal conversion was identified with the numerical growth of the local church. This basic premise formed the later fundamental issue of church growth, that a healthy church experiences growth in membership.[21]

Scriptural foundations were those used by the CGM for their methodologies. The spread of the gospel presented in Acts and the parables of the mustard seed and leaven were proof texts for the New Testament basis for church growth. These basic tenants were expanded to include the need for strong pastoral leadership and goal setting, training of the laity, and prayer. The programming was apologetic in nature, since there was already controversy brewing over the movement. At that time there was an ongoing debate over the role the Holy Spirit and the nature of human planning, as well as the relationship between quantitative and qualitative growth.

The tension between quality and quantity was explained as an important symbiotic relationship. When a church grows in its spiritual quality, it will correspondingly experience quantitative increase. If the church is not adding members this points to a lack of spiritual quality. The relationship between management and the leading of the Spirit was seen as a balance between prayer and human logic. Prayer is the basis for all church renewal and growth. However, the Holy Spirit works through us, using our logic and common sense. Logically, discounting planning would result in chaos in most social and commercial concerns. In

---

20. GCGA Archives.
21. Schlottoff et al., "Gemeindeaufbau was ist das eigentlich?"

relationship to the church, goal setting for church growth is an example of the Holy Spirit's leadership.[22]

Contextualization was also a concern. Although the church was growing in Africa, Asia, and the Americas, the German parochial situation was very different. Could methodologies used in the Asian church, for example, be used in Germany? According to Roger Bosch there were certain principles that were universal to church growth and would function within any church system: (1) goal oriented leadership, (2) laity training and involvement, (3) specific goals for growth, (4) personal evangelism, (5) cell groups, and (6) prayer.[23]

The radio transmissions were significant in that specific universal transferable concepts for church growth were aired indicating that church growth was no longer exotic to Germany. More importantly, GPC pastors and laity were interviewed explaining the actual implementation of church growth in their parishes. They revealed both the positives and the negatives of operating a church growth program in the GPC.

Positively, evangelism and the meaning of the gospel were issues that were being discussed. The nature and purpose of the church were also topics of interest in these local churches. The commonly held belief that every baptized church member is a Christian was openly being debated. This particular debate led to bitterness toward and rejection of church growth on the local level. According to one pastor, eventually there was an unofficial church split as a result of this issue. Another critical point was the discussion of the spiritual condition of the pastor. In order for a local church to be renewed, the pastor must also undergo a conversion. If the pastor has no relationship to Christ, then there is no hope for renewal.[24]

Church growth's center is not a certain theology, tradition, confession, or denomination. Church growth is not formulating plans, goals, and strategies. The church growth's center is the gospel of Jesus Christ. It is the conversion of individuals by the proclamation of this gospel. Schlottoff repeated the basic tenants of what this meant. First, people are sinners and cannot save themselves. Second, by God's grace salvation is offered. Third, salvation is accomplished through the atoning death of Jesus. Church growth occurred when the converted shared the joy of

22. Brüning and Brüning, "Gemeindeaufbau Methoden?"
23. Knoblauch and Bosch, "Gemeindeaufbau welche Erfahrungen gibt es?"
24. Schlottoff et al., "Gemeindeaufbau was ist das eigentlich?"

their salvation with others.[25] This rudimentary explanation was crucial at this time because misunderstandings grew with the popularity of the movement. Although this central theme of church growth was emphasized and repeated, criticism continued that church growth was only concerned with numbers.

The other importance of these transmissions was the GCGA was able to explain the biblical basis for its work. The Great Commission was the foundational scripture. As stated above, Acts also formed the impetus behind the idea of a growing and ever-expanding church. Acts 2:44–46 gave credence to their ecclesiological stance of personal faith, fellowship, and mission. Likewise, the body metaphor of 1 Cor 12 supported the emphasis on the discovery of spiritual gifts and the empowerment of the laity. This text was also employed to explain the danger of a church or body experiencing stagnation or decline. Since a healthy body grows, stagnation and decline were symptoms of a sick church that needed an examination to determine the root causes of the malady. Finally, Eph 4:11–16 was the basis for encouraging church leaders to form new priorities centered on developing the laity for the work of the ministry.[26]

There are no empirical studies from the 1980s indicating the number of individuals who actually heard the ERF broadcasts. It can be estimated, however, that approximately a million people listened to the church growth program.[27]

The Provocative Nature of *Church Growth*: Opposition Grows

Gemeindewachstum magazine subscriptions grew from 350 in 1981 to 3,953 by 1990. Estimations were that with five thousand subscriptions the quarterly magazine could be solvent. This was a dramatic increase from 1982 when two thousand subscriptions were required for solvency.

In 1986 Christian Schwarz became chief editor of *Church Growth*. The magazine would continue to have an editorial team composed of GCGA board members but Schwarz would have the final word as to the direction and content of the publication. Schwarz had studied theology in Bochum, Bethel, Wuppertal, and finally in Mainz. He also studied

---

25. Schlottoff, "Was steht im Mittelpunkt?"
26. Brüning and Brüning, "Gemeindeaufbau Methoden?"
27. "Umfrage des Emnid-Instituts."

church growth for nearly four months at Fuller Seminary in Pasadena in 1986. He inherited the wit, sarcasm, and edgy humor of his father and would change the tone of *Church Growth* by increasing the intensity of irreverence, satire, and humor for which the magazine was already known. Christian Schwarz's style was infamously called "Rambo IV Journalism."[28] He was criticized for allowing topics in the magazine that were deemed taboo, as well as for his satirical portrayal of the *Volkskirche*.

It is inaccurate, however, to label Schwarz as the only responsible party for the irreverent tone of the magazine. That fundamental problem began very early with the German church growth organization, and had continued until Schwarz took the editorial lead. Instead of responding from a theological foundation, too often the response was sarcasm or satire. From a philosophical standpoint, the organization could have appealed to the principle of providing a forum for various factions of the GPC to be expressed and debated.

Two illustrations of the provocative nature of the magazine stand out as exemplarily for the early period of Schwarz's tenure as editor. One example was Schlottoff's comments in issue thirty-two, regarding GPC pastors and evangelism. In the article he stated that his expensive and extensive theological training did nothing to prepare him for evangelism. In addition to this, he claimed that the GPC's baptism theology had become a "baptism ideology," which taught that faith was present at the moment of infant baptism. This belief muted any evangelistic endeavor for reaching the baptized church members, since they all were seen as converted at their baptism. There was no need for conversion, since faith was present. Individuals need only therapy to enable them to understand their faith. Schlottoff explained: "At my Protestant Prep Course I tell the pastors: Imagine that a person standing at your door says, 'Pastor, I really want to become a Christian, what should I do?' Now listen to the response I hear . . . absolutely nothing. They say nothing, because the question is too difficult for them."[29] In response to the question as to what percentage of GPC pastors could lead a person to Christ, Schlottoff commented: "I would say under 2 percent. When we have sixteen thousand Protestant pastors, then possibly three hundred could lead a person to Christ."[30]

28. C. Schwarz, "GW und der Rambo IV Journalismus," 3.
29. Schlottoff, "98 Prozent," 7–8.
30. Ibid.

The veracity of this comment was never seriously debated, but the propriety of publishing the quotation was. Ako Haarbeck, Superintendent of the Lippisch District Church, viewed the remark as a direct attack on the GPC. In a letter to all the pastors and vicars in his district, and subsequently published in *Church Growth*, Haarbeck wrote: "Surely he (Johannes Hansen, director of the Office for Evangelism in Westfalen and GCGA board member) will help the rest of his brothers in the GCGA not to be so unloving by kicking those in the shin whom they want to encourage and train in evangelism."[31] His criticism reflected that of a growing sentiment among GPC leaders. Johannes Hansen, himself, also questioned why the GCGA desired to alienate and anger the very pastors they were trying to reach: "'Ninety-eight percent of the pastors do not know how to lead a person to Christ.' Should you really use such a statement as a banner headline and publicize it to the world?" Hansen did not dispute the truth of the statement, but stated that such comments would only undermine the efforts of the GCGA. He further lamented that he was personally criticized at the national Church Day, because of his association with the GCGA. He indicated that if the GCGA desired to work with the Office for Evangelism, they must seriously consider changing their satirical journalistic practices. Matters were not helped when Schlottoff stated that he had no regrets for his allegation and would do it again, because he was only saying the painful truth. He admitted his assertion was provocative and he had meant it to be so. He explained his stance: "Allow me to be the mouthpiece for those in the church who have no voice. They are the millions of baptized people, who perhaps want to become committed Christians, but there is no one to lead them to Christ."[32]

The other most infamous example of the confrontational character of the magazine was issue thirty-four in 1988, the same issue reporting the backlash over Schlottoff's comments. Schlottoff's article in issue thirty-two had raised the question: "Pastor, I really would like to become a Christian. What must I do?" In response to the question stemming from Schlottoff, Schwarz interviewed evangelists and pastors asking how they would answer this question. Winrich Scheffbuch, the pastor of the Ludwig-Hofacker Church in Stuttgart, responded, "I do not want, I do not want, I do not want to appear in your magazine." Nevertheless,

31. "Ako Haarbeck," 14.
32. "Im Ton vergriffen?," 5–6.

Scheffbuch's picture, along with his response, appeared in the magazine. Paul Deitenbeck, a respected leader in the Confessional Movement, responded in like manner: "Please understand, I do not want to respond to you. God bless you." His picture and comment likewise were published. This was seen as highly offensive and disrespectful in the Christian community. This type of journalism breached the standard protocol of German Christian interaction. One could disagree and attack on any theological or ecclesiological front, but for many, deliberately embarrassing two very popular and prominent pastors from the Pietistic camp was viewed as an egregious affront. In order to repair the damage, Schlottoff published a letter of apology in the next issue.[33]

Regardless of the apology there were repercussions. Rudolf Weth was director of the Christian publishing house, *Schriftenmission Verlag*, which printed *Church Growth*, as well as other material on missions, evangelism, and church growth. In a letter to Schlottoff and Knoblauch, he stated that the publishing house was no longer prepared to print the magazine or support it, if the direction of the magazine did not change. He found it unbearable that such disrespect was shown to his brother-in-law, Winrich Scheffbuch. The prevailing attitude among the GPC leadership was that the GCGA only presented a negative view of the GPC and actually desired to harm the church. Weth appealed to the GCGA board to change the direction of the magazine and to take more responsibility in an editorial role. He further commented that his previous warnings had been ignored, as he had seen no change in *Church Growth*. He later broke ties with the GCGA, citing its close ties to the charismatic movement.

Schwarz defended his decision to print Scheffbuch's and Deitenbeck's responses on two grounds. First, it would betray fundamental journalism standards to only print facts or quotations deemed appropriate by certain individuals. Second, he only publicized issues that were pertinent to church growth. These facts were well known and assumed, but only talked about privately. When he published them, it made people angry that this truth was now part of public discussion. He believed it was an important contribution to speak about these things publicly. The real provocation was not the publication, but the facts that were made accessible by the publication. Second, specifically related to Scheffbuch and Deitenbeck, Schwarz decided to print their responses along with other quotes from other pastors, since he could not allow the person

---

33. Schlottoff, "Es tut uns leid," 11.

interviewed to determine what would be printed. That would have been unethical. In addition, he felt it was healthy for the church growth movement to have such provocative comments made public.[34]

Regardless of Schwarz's motives, the publication of Scheffbuch's and Deitenbeck's comments resulted in a rift between Schwarz and the GCGA board. In January of 1989, as a result of the Scheffbuch-Deitenbeck debacle, the decision was made to refrain from any further criticism of those in the Pietistic camp. In addition, an editorial board would be re-enacted to make the final decision on what articles would be printed. All articles criticizing or lampooning someone, or something, were to be submitted to the editorial committee before they were printed. These conflicts continued until the relationship between Schwarz and the GCGA became more contentious. This conflict ultimately resulted in Knoblauch dismissing Schwarz as chief-editor in 1997.[35]

Why would Christian Schwarz print an article that would alienate those in the Confessional Movement, as well as others in the GPC? Perhaps he should have used that same logic presented in the *Theology of Church Growth*, where infant baptism was not totally rejected so as not to fully alienate the GPC, thereby making further dialogue impossible. It would be prudent to maintain close ties and good relationships with those who have similar foundations such as the Pietists, and not deliberately publicize offensive articles making the enculturation of church growth more difficult. This was the reason the GCGA leadership was so incensed. Those in the Confessional Movement were, at least at that time, perceived as potential partners. As a result of the ensuing chaos, any cooperation between the two movements seemed improbable.

The Future of Renewal: Contextualizing the GCGA Ecclesiology

At the end of 1986 a two-day meeting was dedicated to future planning. The leadership planned for future seminars and training materials, and also set long-term goals for the GCGA. These goals laid out the fundamental prerequisites for determining to what extent church growth was being contextualized.

---

34. C. Schwarz, interview by author, 18 September 2007.
35. Ibid.

The Roadmap: Specific Goals

1. The GCGA ministry should result in hundreds of churches in German-speaking Europe being evangelistically active and characterized by powerful ministries, such as healing.
2. The GCGA should encourage the planting of new GPC churches where they do not yet exist. Ordained pastors would lead these churches and integrate them into the GPC.
3. The regional associations should be so numerous that pastors and lay leaders would not have to drive over fifty kilometers to attend a meeting.
4. No one should drive over twenty kilometers to attend a growing church.
5. A church growth school should be established, using the Fuller School of World Mission as a model.
6. Thousands of prayer cells should be started to pray for renewal.[36]

The Instrument: The Church Growth Seminar

Whereas *Church Growth* and ERF broadcasts spread the church growth message throughout the country, it was the church growth seminars that became the standard for contextualizing the principles being promoted. If church growth was to make a lasting impact, it had to do so at the local church level.

Two basic seminars were initiated to meet this need. The first seminar, a spiritual growth seminar, was strictly for personal spiritual renewal. The primary goal of this seminar was to ensure that each participant experienced spiritual renewal or personal conversion. This seminar provided the necessary spiritual foundation for the church growth seminar and was a prerequisite for it.

The second seminar on church growth was part of a five-step church consultation process:

1. Initial Contact: Contact was initiated with the GCGA by participating on a study trip, attending a regional church growth day, or subscribing to *Church Growth*.

---

36. GCGA Archives.

2. Presentation of Church Growth: The GCGA representative visited the pastor and would seek to build a trusting relationship. He might show a slide presentation to encourage the pastor that his church could grow and that the GCGA understood the special needs of the GPC pastor. The representative then suggested that the church host a church growth seminar. If the pastor opted for a seminar, step three was taken.

3. Church Growth Seminar: Preceding the seminar an analysis of the local church situation was initiated. The pastor, along with the lay leaders of the church, was interviewed to determine the strengths and weaknesses of the church. The seminar defined what the New Testament church is so church members could contrast their church with that found in the New Testament. After the seminar, the representative encouraged the lay leaders to establish a church growth committee to ensure implementation of church growth strategies.

4. Church and Seminar Analysis Presentation: Both the church analysis and seminar evaluations were discussed, and specific steps were outlined for the future. The newly formed church growth committee took steps to begin the church growth process.

5. Goal Development: Development of a specific plan and timetable for implementation was the final step. However, the church growth committee was encouraged to contact the GCGA representative every two months in order that the consultation process continued.[37]

The seminar appealed to the GPC audience because it claimed to answer the question that was continually being debated in the church: how do you increase church participation? The weekend seminar was important for two reasons. First, it was a tool to contextualize church growth for each particular parish. In conjunction with the consultation, the seminar could be customized for the peculiarities of the individual church. Second, after the presentation of church growth theory, practical applications were suggested.

The seminar also explained clearly the challenges facing the evangelistic-minded church in the GPC. This fundamental clarification laid the groundwork for the entire seminar and presented two conflicting

37. Ibid.

models of the church. The first was the preservation or maintenance model (*Versorgungskirche*). The church is understood as a public instrument and was there to provide a certain amount of public service. The pastor was to provide these services; in return, the church received public funds provided by taxation. The second model was the evangelizing church (*missionarische Gemeinde*). This church was supported by a group of committed Christians desiring to reach out to those not having a relationship with Christ or the church. Church growth occurred when those distant from the church experienced personal conversion. The goal was to reach non-Christian church members and integrate them into this group of committed Christians. The book of Acts provided the theological basis for this model.

Acts 2:40–47 clarified the distinction between the two models of the church. Participants were asked to compare the GPC situation with the church described in Acts. This led to five recognizable elements found in the verses that describe the New Testament church, as well as the true church of today:

1. The purpose of the church is not to keep the institution in order, but to win men and women to Jesus Christ (Acts 2:40–41).

2. The basis for membership in the GPC is infant baptism, not necessarily personal faith. The evangelizing church is dependent upon those who personalize the faith that was promised to them in their baptism. Their "yes" to Christ is the most important aspect of the New Testament church. Baptism, church membership, or regular church attendance does not guarantee a person has this personal faith (Acts 2:40–41).

3. The biblical church promotes a personal relationship with Christ and fellowship among believers. Where this type of fellowship is absent, then so is Christ's church (Acts 2:42–46).

4. People look to the preservation church structure to serve them. Those in the evangelizing church seek to serve others. Where service is absent, so is the true church (Acts 2:42–46).

5. Growth is the universal sign of life; otherwise, the organism is dead or sick. A healthy church should grow (Acts 2:47).[38]

---

38. Ibid; "Gemeinde wohin?," 9–10.

The German Christian had become conditioned to think that the church was at best stagnant, and at worse vanishing. The biblical basis for a growing church was essential for the German context, because there were reservations about numbers. The counting of worshippers on a given Sunday and using that to measure the success or failure of a church was a difficult cultural barrier to overcome. It was the goal of this weekend seminar to dispel the fear of numbers. In order to challenge these fears, the seminar enlisted the rapid increase in of the number of disciples in Acts:

Acts 1:15	120 believers gathered
Acts 2:41	3,000 were added to the church
Acts 4:4	The numbers (men) grew to 5,000
Acts 6:1,7	Number of disciples grew; many priests
Acts 8:1–4	Persecuted Christians spread the faith
Acts 9:31, 35	Many new churches were planted
Acts 11:21, 24	Great numbers believed
Acts 13:5; 14:1–21	Christianity spreads to Asia Minor
Acts 16:11; 17:4	Christianity spreads to Europe[39]

The point of these passages was that the primitive church grew in numbers and grew rapidly. Seminar participants were encouraged to compare what was normal for the early church and what should be the normal activity of today's church. Examples of the growth of the church in Africa, Asia, North America, and Latin America enhanced the biblical message of church growth in Acts. Growth was not just for the early church nor was it an anomaly, but the church was growing today at an astounding rate. The seminar leader compared Germany with the biblical and contemporary models of church growth. In Germany, the growth of cults such as Jehovah's Witness, the New Apostles Church, and the Mormons overshadowed the decline of the GPC. The true church is a growing organism, not a stagnant institution. The biblical pattern, as well as the historical, reveals a growing, thriving organism. The examples in Acts were meant to move the participants from an atmosphere of frustration and despair to one of optimism and hope.

39. Ibid., 11–12.

Two types of church structures used to reach people with the gospel were explained. There was the "come" structure and the "go" structure. Positive emphasis was given to the "go" structure, because "come" was interested only in inviting people to specific church events. The "go" structure, on the other hand, emphasized personal contact and building relationships. Most people come to faith through the witness of a friend or relative, not through an evangelistic event. This section ended with an exercise to write out the names of all their acquaintances that did not have a relationship with Christ. Participants received further instruction on how to start and maintain contact with people.[40]

This exercise was especially needed for the German culture. Germans have very few close friends because of the high level of commitment German friendship requires. Outside of this closed circle there are acquaintances. German Christians find it difficult to widen their friendship circle to include more people, especially those outside the church. Germans are not unfriendly or unloving. However, friendship is a serious matter for the German and great care is taken in allowing individuals into the inner circle of family and friends. This explains why Americans find Germans cold and aloof. Thus, this practical aspect of the seminar was the most important segment of the training. It forced the participants to consider overcoming a cultural barrier and allowing more individuals into their inner circle of acquaintances and friends.

The strength of the seminar was that it broke through several barriers barring church growth at the local level. The gospel and evangelism were explained in practical terms so that lay people not only could understand them, but also would gain confidence in communicating with others. Another strength of the seminar was its connection with the church survey. The pastor and lay leaders had an opportunity to gauge the strengths and weaknesses of the church. These sessions on analysis allowed discussion of issues that otherwise never would become known. Most importantly, seminar participants received specific tools required for evangelism. They understood what the gospel is in relationship to infant baptism. This was especially crucial for two reasons. First, it revealed that infant baptism did not equal salvation and that a specific response to the gospel is necessary. Second, church growth was defined in the context of personal conversion. Church growth only occurred when individuals responded to the gospel.

40. Ibid., 42–46.

The seminar also had several weaknesses. The emphasis on dramatic growth represented in Acts and the examples of mega-congregations in other countries served to give seminar participants an exaggerated expectation of local church growth. The seminar lacked a thorough explanation of the parameters influencing the early church that resulted in such rapid growth described in Acts. For example, the expectation of the eminent return of Christ and the miraculous signs on the Day of Pentecost certainly empowered the first Christians to action. There was also no explanation of the great dissimilarities between the GPC and denominations in other lands. This resulted in false expectations, both for the pastor and the local laity. The propagation of this false hope led to the second weakness.

There was no serious section on the various forms of subsequent opposition to the implementation of church growth. There would be opposition to the most important aspect of the praxis of the seminar: the evangelization of church members. It would have been practical to explain the sources of this conflict and explain that the implementation of church growth would take many years of struggle, given the structure of the GPC. For example, in the GPC church leadership, or even committed laity, may not be converted and thus might complicate the employment of a thorough evangelistic strategy. This was complicated by GCGA ecclesiology. The true church not only should grow, it *must* grow. If the local church did not grow, then it was sick, dead, or apostate. Glowing reports of worldwide church growth gave further foundation to this ecclesiology. What happens when the local church does not grow, or when someone only rarely comes to faith? Does this mean that the pastor and the laity have failed? Cultural and spiritual issues in Germany that gravely undermine efforts to grow the church were not discussed in depth, and the length of time it may take to initiate change was not emphasized. This failure to constantly illuminate the complexity of German religious and cultural barriers did not have immediate repercussions, but became evident years later as frustration and disappointment emerged among those involved in church growth.

East Germany Forms a Church Growth Association

In the spring of 1984, the first meeting between West German church growth representatives and East German pastors took place in East

Berlin. Fritz Schwarz and Klaus Eickhoff were the main speakers, with Schwarz introducing the Manageable Church program. In November the East Germans were introduced to Bernd Schlottoff and the EE program.

In 1986 Bernd-Ulrich Stock, an East German pastor, was allowed to travel to the West for the first time, where he took this opportunity to visit Schlottoff in Herne. During this visit the decision was made to form a closer working relationship with Schlottoff. After his return to East Germany, Stock, along with other GPC pastors Detlef Kauper, Friedhelm Müller, Bernd Vorwerk, and Jens Heil began to meet together regularly. These meetings led to the founding of the first church growth organization in East Germany, the Coordinating Committee for Evangelistic Church Growth (*Koordinierungsausschuß für missionarischer Gemeindeaufbau*). The first priority of the new organization was to implement the EE program in their local congregations. From April 21 to April 28, 1986 Schlottoff held the first EE seminar at the Lutherpark in Erfurt. Lutherpark is the cloister where the monk Martin Luther became a Christian. From November 1987 to August 1988, three church growth seminars and four EE training sessions were held over a fifty-two day period in East Germany, with 387 participants.[41]

According to Stock, the most important EE seminar was in November/December 1988 held at the Augustine Monastery in Erfurt. The seminar was crucial because the practical application of the seminar, home visitation, took place in Großrudestedt and Udestedt, two villages where Stock was the pastor. Unfortunately there are no records indicating the results of the visitation program.

After the end of the German Democratic Republic in 1989, the Coordinating Committee became an official branch of the GCGA. The GCGA continued not only to give guidance in setting up the new association, but also it provided financial assistance to set up an official office in Udestedt.

Ties to Charismatics Increase

German church growth was always open to the charismatic movement. Positive reports on the growth of the Central Church in South Korea under the leadership of Paul Yonggi Cho appeared in *Church Growth* in 1982 and 1985. News of Charismatic Church Renewal Movement

41. GCGA Archives.

seminars appeared regularly in the magazine. Wolfram Kopfermann, leader of this Movement, also wrote articles for the magazine and was one of the original signers of the GCGA foundational documents. He was invited to hold workshops on "Signs and Wonders" at regional church growth conferences. Fritz Schwarz made it clear that he supported the efforts of the Movement and its leader, Kopfermann. He pleaded with Pietists, especially those in the Confessional Movement and the Gnadau Society, not to cut themselves off from fellowship with charismatics simply because they had another doctrine of the Holy Spirit. Schwarz refused to chose sides between the Pietists and charismatics and this resulted in further opposition from anti-charismatics.[42]

The relationship between the GCGA and the Movement was again an issue during a joint meeting on May 2, 1988 in Hockenheim. Schlottoff suggested that a theological consulting committee be formed to discuss theological questions arising from this mutual cooperation. Further discussion centered on how to maintain the GCGA's identity in light of the increasing exposure with the charismatics. In order to do this, there should be separation between activities of the two associations. The GCGA should also exhibit less of a charismatic worship style. It was hoped that this would enable the organization to be accepted by those having difficulties with the charismatic movement. Finally, the organization must concentrate more strongly on promoting church growth.

These measures were not enough, however, to prevent the GCGA from being directly linked to the charismatic movement. The Billy Graham Association in Germany refused to print an article about church growth in the *Decision* (*Entscheidung*) magazine, because the GCGA was deemed "too charismatic." A prominent GCGA board member also resigned in 1989 because of the organizations continuing charismatic tendencies.[43]

The Reasons for Rejection of Charismatic Ecclesiology

Reactions against the charismatic movement in Germany were grounded in events beginning in the early 1900s. Understanding the history of a country is paramount in proposing a program for contextualization. Understanding the history of the Pentecostalism and Neo-Pentecostalism,

---

42. F. Schwarz, *Ich verweigere mich*, 1–13.
43. T. Knoblauch, interview by author, 31 August 2005.

i.e., the charismatic movement in Germany, is essential in knowing the reasons why many in the *Landeskirche* had reservations with anything remotely characterized as "charismatic." There are three reasons why many German Protestants view any movement with charismatic tendencies with great suspicion.

The Kassel Tongues Movement

As stated in chapter 1, the Fellowship Movement was greatly influenced by the Sanctification-Evangelization Movement. The initial influence of the movement centered only on the necessity of evangelism. However, the inner spiritual life and the sanctification of the Christian were made prerequisites for effective evangelism. This prerequisite called for a deepening knowledge of the faith and new "power from above" in order to reach non-Christians. Thus, on the heels of evangelism came the openness of the Fellowship Movement for a new spirituality. Both movements held views that would become, according to opponents, radicalized by Pentecostalism. This eventually led to a split in the Fellowship Movement.[44]

In 1901 the German evangelist, Johannes Paul, claimed that the actual goal of sanctification was the sinless life. Only those experiencing total sanctification could reach sinlessness, however. It was also during this time that the baptism of the Holy Spirit, accompanied by speaking in tongues, became irreversibly connected to the teaching of total sanctification, or perfectionism. Paul contributed greatly to the belief that true sanctification was accompanied by baptism of the Holy Spirit. In May of 1904, Paul was invited to the Gnadau Pentecost Conference, where he claimed that he had recently attained sinlessness. Although there was criticism of perfectionism, his teachings were widely accepted.[45]

In the fall of 1906 T. B. Barratt, a Methodist preacher and leader of the City Mission in Oslo, returned to Norway convinced of the Pentecostalism he had experienced in New York. Two women, Dagmar Gregersen and Agnes Telle, members of Barratt's church, also came under the influence of the Pentecostals and experienced the baptism of the Holy Spirit exhibited by speaking in tongues. Heinrich Dallmeyer, a leading evangelist of the Fellowship Movement, met the two women in Hamburg and invited them to a conference in Kassel in July 1907. The women spoke at

44. Holthaus, *Heil-Heilung-Heiligung*, 272.
45. Holthaus, "Einleitung," 5–6.

the conference and subsequently began to speak in tongues, which was a new phenomenon for those at the conference. As the meetings progressed, other "signs of the Spirit" emerged: "uncontrolled prophesying and revelations, gesticulations, dreams, visions, and singing in tongues." The conference continued for an additional four weeks, accompanied by an ever-increasing volume of manifestations. Authorities finally closed the meetings because of the unrest it caused in the community.[46] The Fellowship Movement had expected the conference to result in a spiritual revival; instead they were bitterly disappointed and embarrassed at the pandemonium that ensued. They subsequently distanced themselves from Pentecostalism and branded the movement as a work of the Devil.

Initially Dallmeyer defended the events in Kassel, but by the end of 1907 he concluded that Satan was the instigator of the excesses. Dallmeyer condemned the division between justification and sanctification, the low regard for infant baptism, the subjectivism, and emphasis on perfectionism and Spirit baptism. He excused his earlier support of the movement by claiming he too had been mesmerized by the Devil. Ernst Lohmann, Johannes Seitz, Bernhard Kühn, and Johannes Rubanowitsch, all leaders in the Fellowship Movement, likewise concluded the Devil was at work in Kassel.[47]

There were others in the movement who lauded the events in Kassel. Eugen Edel and Johannes Paul, as well as the majority of the Fellowships in Silesia, supported the furtherance of Pentecostalism. It was in Silesia in 1908 when the first split among those in the Fellowship Movement occurred over the tenants of Pentecostalism. The tensions in the movement continued and culminated in a formal division in Berlin in 1909. The meeting in Berlin culminated with the signing of the Berlin Declaration, which condemned Pentecostal teaching as satanic. The Berlin Declaration continues to foster division between evangelicals and charismatics.[48]

---

46. Böckel, *Gemeindeaufbau im Kontext*, 49–50; Holthaus, „Die Kassler Bewegung," 8–9.

47. Hollenweger, *Enthusiastisches Christentum*, 208.

48. Holthaus, "Die Kassler Bewegung," 8–10; Holthaus, "Die Berliner Erklärung," 11.

The Modus Operandi of the Charismatic Movement

In chapter one it was shown that Arnold Bittlinger was the primary promoter of the German charismatic movement. In 1962, influenced by charismatics in the United States, he instituted a series of conferences to promote the renewal of the GPC. Although the beginning was small, the movement soon gained momentum and resulted in the Charismatic Church Renewal Movement being founded in 1984 under the leadership of Wolfram Kopfermann.

The procedure for charismatic church renewal through the medium of conferences was initiated by Bittlinger and continued to be the modus operandi of future charismatics. That is, the German charismatic movement does not normally initiate new church plants, but purposely desires to influence established churches. This practice began in earnest in the 1950s and continues to the present time.[49] Charismatic conferences are planned with the hope that the laity from many denominations will attend and become convinced of the need of incorporating charismatic manifestations within their respective churches.

This strategy seems harmless. However, it is the source of much anger and criticism by many church leaders who have to deal with the aftermath of these conferences. It is common that church members returning from a charismatic conference began encouraging others to experience the gifts of the Spirit witnessed at a conference. This has not only resulted in fear, anger, resentment and confusion in the churches, but has also ended in many church splits. When the charismatic members' wishes are rejected, they leave to start a new church. This may not seem a crucial issue within the scope of a large church. However, this often happens in small, struggling congregations of less than one hundred practitioners. In such cases a church division is disastrous and leaves in its wake an emotionally, spiritually, and financially poor congregation. The conflict is further exacerbated when leaders of charismatic organizations fail to condemn such practices. To those outside the movement it appears that this is the normal venue of the charismatic movement to propagate its message. As a result, the charismatic movement has a questionable reputation among many evangelical leaders in Germany.[50]

---

49. Böckel, *Gemeindeaufbau im Kontext*, 103–8.
50. Stadelmann, "Ist zwischen Pietisten?," 24.

The Exit of Wolfram Kopfermann

On September 5, 1988 Wolfram Kopfermann met with his bishop, Peter Krusche, in Hamburg. At this meeting he announced his intention of leaving the GPC and founding his own Free Church, as well as a new denomination, The Protestant-Lutheran Anskar Church (*Die evangelisch-lutherische Anskar-Kirche*). Kopfermann explained that he could no longer tolerate the practices of the GPC. According to him, the practice of baptizing infants of non-Christians, the hiring of non-Christian church staff, and the calling of practicing homosexuals as pastors was intolerable. He lamented the fact that the *Landeskirche* was held together only by infant baptism and the church tax. In order to maintain an atmosphere insuring the continuation of tax revenues, the church was silent concerning false teaching, abortion, and homosexuality.[51]

Kopfermann's reasons for leaving the church centered primarily on "church polity." Under German law, anyone baptized and who faithfully paid the church tax had the right to run for church office. Any church member may run for church board membership whether or not they attend church regularly or regardless of their spiritual condition. This can lead to serious problems in a church, especially where there is a strong evangelistic-renewal presence. As long as likeminded people are elected to the church board, then the church can continue its journey toward church growth and revival. However, if new board members are elected having a different agenda, that spells doom for renewal efforts.

There are many cases where the church hierarchy refused to support the church growth efforts of pastors under their charge. This situation made it virtually impossible for pastors to carry out any form of serious local church renewal effort. In order for pastors to be effective, they had to have the backing of the church board, the committed laity, as well as the immediate hierarchy. Thus, Kopfermann's exit, although roundly condemned, was not without sound reasoning and personal risk. His leaving barred him from any future personal financial stability provided by the GPC. It also insured that the GPC establishment would closely scrutinize any of his future successes or failures.

This move not only ended Kopfermann's relationship with the GPC, it also broke his ties to the GCGA and the Charismatic Church Renewal Movement. His leaving the GPC sealed the fate of the GCGA in

---

51. "Der Bruch," 1; Kopfermann, *Abschied*, 14–23.

the minds of its opponents. Kopfermann embodied all those things held suspect by church growth antagonists: he was charismatic and no friend to the institutional church. His founding of a new church and denomination solidified the suspicions that the GCGA intended to plant new churches. This was an anathema for the GPC. Werner Hoerschelmann, senior pastor at the St. Petri Church in Hamburg, called the move by Kopfermann "diabolical." Rudolf Weth called the starting of a new confession "blasphemy."[52]

As a result of the affiliation with the Charismatic Church Renewal Movement and Kopfermann, the GCGA confirmed its reputation as a charismatic organization devoted to church planting, with a visible American pragmatic bent. This proved to be a volatile combination. Although American pragmatism endured and church planting among the Free Churches was tolerated, charismatic leanings were unacceptable.

The Issue of Secondary Issues

Donald A. McGavran, the Father of the Church Growth Movement, stated that church growth would not be possible unless denominations were willing to set aside secondary theological issues. In Germany's case, this meant that those needing to hear the gospel should take priority over any division promoted by the charismatic controversy. Although eighty years had passed since the Kassel incident, German evangelicals were continually reminded of the dangers of Neo-Pentecostalism and maintained strict lines of separation. There was the remaining legacy of the Berlin Declaration branding all charismatic expression as demonic. In addition, there was Kopfermann's much-publicized denunciation of and exit from the GPC, and the emotional scars left from split churches blamed, rightly or wrongly, on charismatics. The founders of the GCGA, although well aware of these problems, embraced charismatics from the beginning. These close ties came at a cost. It served to provide further proof for those in the Fellowship Movement and the Confessional Movement that the GCGA was charismatic, and as a result should be avoided, or outright condemned.

The Association based its insistence on close ties with the Charismatic Church Renewal Movement, in spite of the consequences, on church growth principles. In order for church growth to succeed, there

52. "Der Bruch," 3–7.

must be unity among Christians. This reasoning stems from a missiological, as well as practical perspective. If German Christians continued to harbor resentment originated by this theological disagreement, only harm would come to the church. There was also another important reason. From a global perspective, it was Pentecostal and charismatic churches that were experiencing dramatic increase in church membership. Thus, from the GCGA's point of view, it would be tantamount to ignoring the work of Holy Spirit to exclude or disregard the very group that God was currently using to reach the un-evangelized.

This idealistic stance resulted in the GCGA embracing one group, the Charismatic Church Renewal Movement, yet alienating the Confessional Movement and the Gnadau Society. Thus, the Association found itself in a dilemma. Acceptance by the two latter movements required repudiation of the former, which the GCGA would not do. As a result, it became impossible for the organization to form any close relationships with those in either the Confessional Movement or the Gnadau Society.

Opposition Solidifies and Intensifies

The tension between the *Volkskirche* and German church growth caused by the charismatic question was only one issue making the contextualization of church growth difficult. There were other church growth fundamentals that appeared to be at great odds with the GPC. In fact, there were those who felt that church growth was a tool used against the church and actually bent on destroying it. Besides the charismatic controversy there were three other problems facing the GCGA.

Ekklesia versus Institution

The publication of *Theology of Church Growth: An Introduction* in 1984 resulted in church growth being debated in wide theological circles for the first time in Germany. Not everyone was pleased with the basic tenant of the book, and it evoked widespread criticism. *Discussion on "Theology of Church Growth"* (*Diskussion zur Theologie des Gemeindeaufbaus*), published in 1986, was a forum for several theologians, pastors, and church growth proponents to express their opinion on the work of Christian and Fritz Schwarz. The opposition focused on the thesis of *Theology*; the separation of *ekklesia* and institution that led to a strict line of demarcation between believers and unbelievers. This was unacceptable for the majority of German theologians, pastors, and lay leaders. The idea that some tax paying, baptized church members could be labeled as non-Christians would never be tolerated in the *Volkskirche*.

The Office for Evangelism of the GPC

From the beginning of the vision of a church growth organization in Germany, it was clear that this entity would serve primarily the National Church. However, there was already an organization whose mission was to revitalize and evangelize GPC members, the Office for Evangelism. Thus, the stage was set for confrontation. The reason for this was simple; the GCGA offered local churches similar services as the Office for Evangelism. Another point of contention was monetary. Officials of the Office for Evangelism were salaried employees of the church and remunerated for their services. The missionaries and other GCGA representatives were not. This led to the belief that the GCGA desired to make the Office for Evangelism irrelevant. What made the situation more difficult was the success that the GCGA was enjoying at this time. For example, over four thousand people attended one of the first church growth conventions sponsored by the Association. The Office for Evangelism also sponsored a convention, but canceled it due to lack of interest.[53]

Three areas concerned the Office in forming a relationship with the GCGA. First, there was the ecclesiological problem. There was fear that the GCGA was more oriented toward the Free Church rather than the National Church. Second was the theological problem. According to the Office for Evangelism leadership, the charismatic movement had too great an influence on the GCGA. Third, there was a cultural barrier. The Office suspected that the Americans of the Campaign for Church Growth were guiding the direction of the GCGA. There was concern that these nine American missionaries had a different understanding of both baptism and the Scriptures and this could cause difficulties. In addition, American missionaries were criticized in general for their tendency to take credit for the success of others: "Americans are great at spraying their whipped cream over the success of others, and proclaiming, 'We did it!'" The office was willing to work with the associations comprising the bulk of the GCGA: the Prep Course in Herne, the Institute for Church Growth

---

53. J. Knoblauch, interview by author, 24 September 2003.

in Giessen, and the Working Group for Church Growth in Giengen. However, working with the American Campaign for Church Growth in Limburgerhof was out of the question.

Church Planting: This Means War!

Continuing the effort to maintain good ties with the Office for Evangelism, GCGA representatives met with the superintendent of the Church Council (*Oberkirchenrat*) for the state of Rhineland-Palatinate in Speyer in June of 1987. The meeting got off to a bad start. The superintendent expressed his consternation that a member of the Campaign for Church Growth started a home Bible study in a town under his jurisdiction, without informing the local pastor. The fact that the town was the headquarters of the campaign exacerbated the problem. The superintendant also had received a copy of an interview with Hans-Martin Wilhelm, director of the Campaign for Church Growth, in which Wilhelm discussed church planting.[54] The superintendant said it was outrageous that Wilhelm did not categorically reject church planting as a viable option for Germany. The superintendant stated, "If the Church Growth Association encourages church planting, that means war!"[55]

The superintendent was correct in his observations, and the threat of "war" accurately described the atmosphere facing the GCGA. In 1988, an entire issue of *Church Growth* was devoted to church planting and even broached the possibility of planting churches in the *Volkskirche*. In the eyes of opponents, this publication confirmed their accusations: the church growth movement was an enemy of the GPC and wanted to destroy it. Opposition to church planting centered on three observations:

1. Planting new churches results in splitting the church. Numerous denominations already divide the church. This has a negative impact on the church's witness. Starting new congregations, when there was already one present, splits the church up into even smaller groups.

2. Planting new churches is cultish. New churches only want their own church structure. Fundamentalist theologies, ideologies, and cult-like leaders often characterize new churches.

---

54. "Hans-Martin Wilhelm: Wir Europäer," 26–27.
55. C. Schwarz, "Wo steht die Gemeindeaufbau Bewegung?," 14.

3. Planting new churches damages the National Church. Leaving the local church to plant a new church inside or outside the GPC only further erodes the church.[56]

Regardless of this endemic opposition, church planting became a new element in the renewal arsenal of German church growth, resulting in an ever-widening divide between the GCGA and the National Church.

Summary of the Contextual Paradigm

From 1986 to 1990, the GCGA enjoyed success in many areas. There were significant gains in the number of regional church growth associations, subscriptions to *Church Growth* continued to grow, and the amount of German church growth literature vastly increased. The establishment of church growth organizations in Austria, Switzerland, and East Germany, pointed to the wide acceptance of church growth.

In January of 1986, European church growth representatives met for the first time in Limburgerhof, Germany. Church growth consultants from eight European countries attended the meeting to discuss the current atmosphere for church growth in Europe and plan for future contact with one another. Representatives from Switzerland, Norway, Sweden, Denmark, France, Holland, Germany, and Great Britain reported on church growth in their respective countries. According to the representatives, the decline of the church resulted in opportunity for renewal. Thus, the cultural rejection of the church had a positive side. They also determined that the best prospects for renewal were in England, and the only growing denominations in Europe were the Pentecostals.

The meeting in Limburgerhof was not the last. The representatives planned other meetings to continue the process of repeatedly gauging church growth in Europe, as well as exchanging ideas. Working in isolation from one another and in difficult circumstances would eventually spell the end of church growth in Europe. This belief led to the founding of the European Church Growth Association in Brussels in 1988. This was an important factor in contextualizing church growth for the European situation and indicated the far-reaching influence of the German organization. Without the leadership of the Germans, European church growth would have had little impact.

---

56. "Die vier grössten Hindernisse," 16–17; Seitz, "Wer die Kirche verläßt, hölt sie aus . . . ," 3–4.

As the 1980s ended, the GCGA refined its purpose and vision. Church planting would begin to play a larger role in the organization's strategy. The emphasis on working within the *Volkskirche* would shift to include the Free Churches. In the past, *Church Growth* had a deliberate orientation toward GPC pastors and laity. In the 1990s, the magazine would begin to include help for cell group leaders, Free Church pastors, and church planters. The leadership also would change. Schlottoff had been Director of the Board since its inception in 1985. Exempted from most of his pastoral duties in order to lead the organization, he would return full-time to his Herne church in 1990.

Discussion Questions

1. The GCGA did not outright reject infant baptism in order to work within the GPC. Was this an appropriate compromise, or did it result in a diluted gospel? Was it biblical not to require new converts in the GPC to undergo "believers' baptism? What theological beliefs may be compromised for the sake of contextualization?

2. Compare the differences in how the Office for Evangelism and the GCGA defined church growth.

3. The Church Growth Seminar used the rapid growth of the church in Acts to prove that God desires the church to grow. What important aspect did the seminar fail to mention that was responsible for the rapid increase of the church in Acts? Is it theologically honest to compare the church in Acts with the church today?

4. Was it a contextualization error to embrace the charismatic movement at the expense of losing the Confessional Movement and the Gnadau Society, as well as others in the GPC?

5. What contextualization issues arise when dealing with infant baptism, the charismatic issue, or other religions in other cultures?

6. The GCGA propagated the church growth principle that if a church was not growing then it was out of the will of God. Is this always true? Is there a situation where a church should not expect to win new converts on a consistent basis?

7. Is it valid to compare the rapid growth of the church on one continent with the decline of the church on another? What variables must be considered before such a comparison is made?

5

The Zenith of German Church Growth 1991–1995

Theological divisions of the church are commonplace. Martin Luther's Reformation is the most well known church split resulting in Protestantism. Luther's problem, among other things, was the Catholic Church's practice of promising early release from purgatory for deceased relatives in exchange for money; the more money, the earlier the release from the sufferings of purgatory. However, the most egregious split came centuries earlier, and remains a mystery to most Christians.

Before 1054 the Catholic Church was composed of two branches; the Greek Church in the East, and the Latin Church in the West. The center for the Greek Church was in Constantinople, modern day Istanbul, Turkey. The seat of the Latin Church was in Rome. The Eastern Church leader was called a patriarch, while the Western Church referred to its leader as pontiff or pope. Over the centuries, there was constant friction between these two wings of the church over certain traditions. For example, Eastern priests were required to marry and wear beards. Western priests were celibate and beardless. In 1054 the disagreement over the kind of bread used in the Lord's Supper was the straw that broke the camel's back. The Eastern Church refused to use unleavened bread as mandated by the Roman pontiff. The ensuing dispute led the patriarch to excommunicate the pope, and likewise, the pope excommunicated the patriarch.[1] The split that had been brewing for centuries was now complete. This division of Christendom is known as the Great Schism. To this day, the Orthodox and the Catholic Churches remain divided. The

---

1. Latourette, *A History of Christianity*, 571–75.

reason for the schism may seem as though it was caused by a secondary theological issue that should have been resolved for the sake of church unity. However, as the GCGA learned, one church's secondary theological issue is another church's primary theological issue.

Contextualization Climax: Four Nationwide Church Growth Conferences

In 1991 Roger Bosch returned to the United States, leaving the Institute for Church Growth in German hands, and Klaus Eickhoff began his first full year as chairman of the German Church Growth Association. Eickhoff was no novice to the German Protestant Church. He worked for six years at the GPC's City Mission in Berlin. Afterwards he served in the Office for Evangelism in Hannover until becoming pastor of a parish church in Uelzen for five years. In 1981, he was sent to Austria to revive the dying Austrian Protestant Church, and there became director of the Office for Evangelism and Church Growth, where he remained until 1991.[2]

The years 1991 to 1995 represent the zenith of the influence of German church growth. Jörg Knoblauch judged this time as the most important in the development of church growth in Germany.[3] During this period the contextual paradigm of the GCGA finalized its development. The coalition between the GCGA and the Charismatic Church Renewal Movement (CCRM) produced a series of four national congresses. These congresses emphasized the depth of the relationship between these two church renewal agencies, as well as the continued division between evangelicals and charismatics.

The Congress for Renewal and Church Growth—1991

The purpose of The Congress for Renewal and Church Growth in Nuremberg was to unify German Protestantism. Klaus Eickhoff believed that without Christian unity, renewal would remain elusive for the German church: "Real revivals have always crossed over denominational boundaries."[4] The primary barrier to this unity was the continued

2. "Klaus Eickhoff," 23.
3. J. Knoblauch, interview by author, 31 August 2005.
4. Eickhoff, "AGGA Vorsitzender," 13.

The Zenith of German Church Growth 1991–1995

animosity between charismatics and evangelicals. Eickhoff was convinced that church growth on the national scale was impossible without unity, because the task to evangelize Germany was too daunting. Instead of single denominations or groups carrying out their own home mission agenda, all sections of the church should form a mission-oriented cooperative and unify their efforts to reach Germany. Not only did this revolve around encouraging a renewal movement, but also the authenticity of both the GPC and the Free Churches was at stake. If there was no reversal of past trends and a new commitment made to the priority of evangelism, there would be reason to question their very existence.[5] Eickhoff was emphasizing two of the foundational principles of the Church Growth Movement already reviewed in previous chapters and embraced by German church growth. First, secondary theological issues should be set aside for the sake of the gospel. Second, when the church ceases to grow through evangelism, it is no longer the church.

Jörg Knoblauch described the Congress as an earthquake for the German Protestant Church.[6] Peter Wagner, the heir apparent of the worldwide church growth movement, was the keynote speaker. Wagner was an outspoken proponent of church planting and spiritual warfare, as well as a critic of the *Volkskirche*. He criticized the church for their stance against church planting and the charismatic movement. Wagner was known as one of the chief supporters of the worldwide charismatic movement, which immediately made him suspect. The German Evangelical Alliance would not allow the GCGA to hand out brochures for the congress at one of their meetings in Stuttgart due to their concerns about Wagner's involvement.

Pressure from the Lausanne Movement, a product of the Lausanne Congress in 1974, came when representatives tried to get the GCGA to retract Wagner's invitation because of his comments regarding evangelicals and charismatics. Wagner had predicted the day would come when charismatics and evangelicals would work hand in hand. *Idea-Spektrum*, the most respected Christian news magazine in Germany, refused to print advertisements for the congress. This resulted in an immediate response from the GCGA. Jörg Knoblauch informed the editors that perhaps Germany needed another magazine similar to theirs that would print *all* Christian advertisements. He insinuated that he might start

5. "C. Peter Wagner kommt," 10.
6. J. Knoblauch, interview by author, 31 August 2005.

another magazine to compete directly with *idea-Spektrum*. After this exchange, *idea-Spektrum* printed the advertisements. However, it took an additional four weeks for the information to be published and this hurt attendance at the congress.

The congress, which attracted over five thousand participants, was the fulfillment of several years of planning. The participants came from both sides of German Protestantism, with 63 percent coming from the GPC and the rest from Free Churches.[7] The GCGA and the CCRM viewed the congress as a historical milestone in the laying aside of theological differences that had separated evangelicals and charismatics for decades. Eickhoff went so far as to suggest that the writers of the Berlin Declaration had erred in labeling Pentecostalism and its stance on the charismatic gifts as satanic. There was also a united call for the church to accept all the charismatic gifts set forth in the Scriptures.[8]

This congress ended with the proclamation of the Nuremberg Manifest. The manifest stated that the reason national renewal had failed in the past was because of the disunity of the German church. This was the message of the congress. Without church unity, reaching Germany with the gospel would be impossible. The desired unity was not ecclesiastical, but rather a willingness from both charismatics and evangelicals to work together for the sake of the gospel.

As in previous years, many opposed the plea for building bridges between charismatics and evangelicals. The connection to Wagner was especially troubling, because Wagner was a colleague of John Wimber and praised the ministry of Paul Yonggi Cho, in South Korea. Cho was pastor of the largest church in the world. In the eyes of German evangelicals Wimber and Cho were synonymous with everything that was wrong with the charismatic movement. Wolfgang Bühne, a staunch anti-charismatic and prolific author, opposed the practices promoted by Wagner, Wimber, and Cho. According to him, their beliefs bordered on the bizarre and had all the markings of the occult. Bühne pointed to the fact that "visualization" and "resting in the spirit," are inherent to the occult.[9]

Although the GCGA had no formal ties to Wimber, the CCRM did. In 1987, 1988, and 1992 the CCRM sponsored congresses by Wimber

---

7. "Gemeindekongreß 1991," 26.
8. "Schulterschluß," 1–2.
9. Bühne, *Dritte Welle*, 102.

that altogether drew over fourteen thousand participants.[10] However, the GCGA in no way distanced itself from Wimber, but encouraged Wimber's "Power Evangelism" program. Wimber believed that miracles were necessary for effective evangelism. The German Church Growth Association saw signs and wonders as the primary characteristic of growing churches worldwide; these therefore should be embraced and encouraged.[11]

Bühne understood the Nuremberg congress as the uniting of three very dangerous factions, using the GPC as its podium. First was the Third Wave represented by C. Peter Wagner; second was neo-Pentecostalism, embodied by the CCRM; and third was the Church Growth Movement represented by the GCGA. The term "Third Wave" was coined by Peter Wagner to describe the phenomenon of the worldwide charismatic movement. According to Wagner, the first wave of the Holy Spirit was the Pentecostal movement in the 1900s and beyond. The second wave occurred in the 1960s ushering in the charismatic movement or Neo-Pentecostalism. The Third Wave began in the 1980s in connection with the power evangelism movement of John Wimber and C. Peter Wagner. It is not lost to critics that all three of these waves began in California, the mecca of drugs, illicit sex, strange cults, and just plain weirdness. Bühne criticized any coalition that included charismatics. He viewed the actions of Billy Graham and the German Evangelical Alliance to include charismatics for the nationwide evangelistic outreach ProChrist '93 as unbiblical.[12] ProChrist is a European wide evangelistic event that takes place every two to four years and transmits gospel messages via satellite throughout Europe.

Rolf Scheffbuch, chairman of the Pietistic Ludwig-Hofacker-Society in Württemberg, also expressed apprehension concerning cooperation with charismatics. Scheffbuch pointed out that the evangelicals had already united on many fronts for the sake of the gospel. Although there were differences in the understanding of the sacraments, church government, and church offices, there was unity concerning the unsaved. For example, evangelicals united under Billy Graham for ProChrist '93. Therefore, it was not appreciated that those at Nuremberg ignored this

---

10. "4.500 Teilnehmer," 14–15; Böckel, *Gemeindeaufbau im Kontext*, 147–48.
11. Schlottoff, "Keine Angst," 4.
12. Bühne, *Die "Propheten" kommen!*, 163–64.

fact and proceeded as though there was no unifying element ever present among German churches and denominations.[13]

The most revealing insight by Scheffbuch was his conclusion that the call for an evangelical-charismatic coalition required that evangelicals become charismatic. He was convinced that the tenor of the congress was a unity that came at the expense of non-charismatics. It was required, thought Scheffbuch, that Pietists become charismatic. He also pointed to the fact that at Nuremberg the charismatics claimed that after the Berlin Declaration, Pietists had rejected all gifts of the Spirit, which was blatantly false. Scheffbuch came to the conclusion that the renewal promoted by the charismatics concerned only the raising of hands in prayer, emotional singing, and speaking in tongues, or "outward forms of worship." Since charismatics found these worship forms helpful, they should continue them and no one had the right to contest them. In turn, charismatics had no right to force these practices on others or to maintain that these manifestations are universally necessary for faithful obedience. In spite of his clear polemic, Scheffbuch supported the basic tenant that evangelicals and charismatics should coalesce for the sake of evangelism.[14]

The congress in Nuremberg brought together the three most divisive elements in Germany regarding German church growth: the charismatic movement, church planting, and American pragmatism. The identification of the GCGA with the charismatic movement assured the positions of the Confessional Movement and the Gnadau Society that close ties with the GCGA were impossible. Identification with church planting resulted in the suspicions of the GPC being confirmed, that the GCGA was bent on destroying the church. American pragmatism with its triumphalism mindset was seen by the GPC as incompatible with the purely spiritual nature of the growth of the church.

The Congress for Church Planting in the Volkskirche–1992

In October 1992, the Congress for Church Planting in the *Volkskirche* was held on the grounds of the University of Erlangen. This congress was billed as a forum to discuss church planting within the parochial structures of the GPC. As with the Nuremberg Congress, the GCGA and the CCRM sponsored the event. Criticism of the event began early.

13. "Müssen die Pietisten 'charismatisch' werden?," 10–11.
14. Ibid., 12–16.

Manfred Seitz, professor of practical theology at the University of Erlangen, gave the introductory address, and was criticized for even attending the congress, thereby lending it a measure of academic and theological legitimacy. Seitz countered these criticisms by stating that, even when unconventional, the university allowed an atmosphere of freedom of thought. Seitz emphasized the fact that although church planting was a legitimate topic for church renewal, leaving the GPC to plant another congregation would only cause further damage to the church.[15]

Only 450 people attended this congress. This was a disappointment for Knoblauch, who had hoped for a much larger attendance to discuss such a crucial strategy. Nevertheless, Klaus Eickhoff made it clear that nothing short of reform would bring change to the *Volkskirche*, and that church planting offered the most efficient avenue to accomplish this. He criticized the religious rites practiced in the *Volkskirche* as "hypocrisy and theater" and that "a corrupted church operates on cheap ingratiation."[16] Eickhoff also addressed the preaching in the GPC that never mentioned eternal damnation or the need for Christ. He continued his polemic by claiming that only the church tax kept the church afloat.[17] According to Eickhoff, certain GPC structures stood in the way of real change, and considerable modifications would be required in order to address the issues:

1. The worship service, which stemmed from the Middle Ages, had to be changed to meet the needs of the modern Christian.

2. The parochial system that forced a Christian to attend a particular church must be changed. For example, if a person wanted to attend church in another parish where the pastor was a Christian, this was not allowed. People should have a choice of the church they want to attend. New churches could offer forms of worship targeting a certain group.

3. Theology must be changed to emphasize the need for evangelism.

4. The pastoral role must be changed to include lay pastors.

5. The hierarchal structure must be changed to allow local churches more independence and the right to finance their own ministries.[18]

15. "EKD: Missionarisch," 4.
16. "Gemeinde Kongreß Erlangen," 11.
17. "Eickhoff," 4.
18. Hempelmann, "Gemeinde gründen," 23–24.

These reforms meant a total change in the GPC. Nothing short of starting new churches would allow for such radical reforms. This fact was not lost on those attending the congress. However, it was emphasized that these new churches would not leave the framework of the GPC.

Opponents were quick to point out that there was little at the congress that would encourage church planters to remain within the confines of the GPC. The weight of the conference was on church planting, not on staying in the *Volkskirche*. When the *Volkskirche* was mentioned, it was criticized. Instead of using the available possibilities and structures of the GPC to forge new strategies, the congress only accentuated the negatives. In addition, the emphasis was on independent church plants, such as those encouraged by the DAWN (Discipling a Whole Nation) group, and most of the literature centered on starting independent churches, not planting them within the GPC.

Critics were quick to mention that there were already structures within the church to allow for various expressions of worship. These churches outside the normal church were called Trend Churches (*Richtungsgemeinden*). The GPC hoped that allowing these new groups to operate within the parochial structure would prevent independent churches from springing up and thus losing people to them. The GPC leadership also saw the Erlangen conference's call for church planting as more criticism of the entire GPC. Bishop Klaus Engelhardt felt that those presenting the need for new churches expressed little love for the GPC. Engelhardt did not reject church planting outright, but rejected it if new churches were started as protest against the GPC.[19]

The reactions were not all negative. The church leaders realized that Germany was changing and that the church had to learn to operate within a pluralistic society where many were open to new ideas and movements. If the church was going to stem the tide of those leaving the church, they were going to have to adjust to this ever-changing culture. Heinzpeter Hempelmann, from the Office for Evangelism in Württemberg, encouraged the GPC not to view church planting as an attack, but as a positive challenge to re-define the church to meet the needs of a pluralistic society. Hempelmann saw the possibility that the debate on church planting could be a "holy provocation."[20] That is, it might move the *Volkskirche* to reevaluate its long held traditions. The charismatic movement within

19. "Im Gespräch: Klaus Engelhardt," 11–12.
20. Hempelmann, "Wie kann heute evangelisiert werden?," 3.

the GPC served as a good example. Would the current church structure make room for this brand of religious experience, or would the movement be forced to start a new denomination? Charismatics discovered that the ever-present praise of pluralism within the GPC had its limits as far as they were concerned.

The detractors of church planting promoted the idea that this was another wedge to divide the church. Church planting cynics promoted the idea that the GPC was a unified whole. This was a false picture. Under the motto of "Protestant freedom," the GPC is a conglomerate of competing ideologies (religious pluralism). The GPC also divides itself into two large divisions. There is the *Volkskirche* that embodies all church members, and there is the "core church" consisting of church members taking an active role in parochial church life. These two groups are then sub-divided into those who are completely "alienated," "somewhat alienated," and "committed." These divisions are in addition to the main denominations of Reformed, Lutheran, and United. Nonetheless, the GPC proclaims, "We are one *Volkskirche!*"[21]

The Willow Creek Congress:
Vision for Post-Christian Germany–1993

The Willow Creek Congress in Nuremberg was billed as a new strategy to reach those alienated from the church as highlighted in the 1992 survey. Over four thousand people came to hear Bill Hybels, the pastor of Willow Creek Community Church (WCCC) near Chicago, the second largest church in the United States. The specialty of the church was "seeker services" to reach those who had never attended church, or who no longer attend. This was the group that not only the GPC desired to bring back to the church, but also whom the GCGA wanted to reach. In 1993 WCCC boasted fourteen thousand worshippers each Sunday. Although there was nothing resembling the GPC situation in the States, the idea of reaching those estranged from the church resembled the circumstances in Germany closely enough. Hybels' ideas were appreciated because the Willow Creek strategy was exactly what German mission-minded churches were facing. There were masses of people who knew of church, but had lost all

---

21. Ulrich, *Die Kirche*, 42.

interest in it, and the hope was that if the church would change certain practices then this group could be reached.[22]

Willow Creek's concept of conversion also corresponded well to the situation in Germany. WCCC understood conversion to be a process. They did not expect for someone to come to church on Sunday, hear an evangelistic sermon and immediately convert. Conversion for those distant from the church was viewed as a slow procedure involving a progressive integration into the life of the church. For the first time, the Methodists and the Baptists in Germany co-sponsored the Willow Creek Congress. This turned out to be a crucial occurrence in the development of the WCCC program. The Baptists adopted the program and began to implement it in many of their churches, as well as publish WCCC materials.[23]

The GPC, as a whole, remained skeptical of Hybels, and following the trend of previous congresses, the tone of the congress toward the GPC was negative. The lack of church attendance was not caused by secularization, as the GPC claimed, but by the church actually hindering people from coming. The remedy echoed the findings of the Erlangen Congress: Germany needs new churches. Klaus Eickhoff stated that at least fifty thousand new churches were needed to meet the needs of Germany.[24]

After the congress in Nuremberg, there were subsequent mini-congresses promoting WCCC methods for reaching children and youth. In 1996 over four thousand people took part in a congress in Hamburg. Most of the participants came out of the Free Churches, primarily the Baptists. In 1998, around seven thousand attended a congress in Oberhausen, but this congress brought in a majority of GPC members.[25] The difference in the two congresses reflects exactly what the GCGA experienced over the years. Free Churches were the first to accept new ideas and models. The GPC was skeptical at first, remaining distant, observing how the new methodology worked. Then a small minority of the GPC leadership and laity would adopt the new trend. In 2003 at a WCCC leadership congress in Oberhausen, eight thousand participants came to hear Bill Hybels and Gordon MacDonald, another prominent American evangelical.[26]

22. "Willow Creek," 4–5.
23. GCGA Archives.
24. Hempelmann, "Vision," 361.
25. "7.000 Willow Fans," 7.
26. "Der Willow Creek Leitungskongress," 5.

Willow Creek made immediate headway in Germany because it offered specific ways to reach postmoderns. It was also effective because Hybels emphasized the history of WCCC, explaining how long and difficult the struggle was to reach their present stage. WCCC was not a charismatic church, and it was a growing, successful church. There were those, however, who had problems with Willow Creek coming to Germany.

Wolfgang Simson, the leader of the DAWN movement in Germany, saw it as just more new wine for old GPC structures. Simson understood Hybels' model to be just another wave from America that will soon run out of steam. He likened WCCC to a vitamin given to the dying patient, the GPC. According to Simson, Germany does not need another wave from America, but needs new churches with moldable structures.[27] Simpson expounded one of the critical issues facing the GCGA during this time. The GCGA, in conjunction with the CCRM, had instigated two new concepts that put them in direct competition with the GPC. Church planting coupled with the charismatic dimension brought much criticism. Now, an additional American model was promoted in the midst of these other very controversial church growth paradigms. A pragmatic pattern was emerging that reflected not a fundamental German church growth model, but an American philosophy of promoting one idea after another without considering the theological and cultural repercussions. There were also objections from the Confessional Movement, rejecting the seeker service approach as being oriented toward psychology and marketing methods rather than the Scriptures. Further, they said the worship service is for true believers and should not be re-constituted for unbelievers.[28]

The euphoria over Willow Creek was tempered by the reality of smaller churches struggling to implement seeker services. Christian Schwarz pointed out the problem of small congregations, with limited resources and limited talent. It was impossible for small German churches to match the professionalism of the WCCC staff. There were also problems convincing church members that the worship service should be changed to accommodate post moderns instead of Christians. One of the positive aspects of WCCC in Germany was its insistence on evaluation of current programs to determine their achievement of intended goals. If

---

27. Simson, "Willow Creek?," 35.
28. Schwark, *Gottesdienste für Kirchendistanzierte*, 99–100.

the programs are not functioning as intended they should be changed or discarded.

The Church of the Future–The Future of the Church Congress–1995

The fourth congress, The Church of the Future–The Future of the Church was also held in Nuremberg. This 1995 congress echoed the theme of the Willow Creek Congress. This time, however, Walter Kallestad, a pastor from the Community Church of Joy (CCJ) in Phoenix, Arizona was invited to speak. This was a Lutheran church, and he was billed as "a second Bill Hybels."[29] It was primarily Lutheran pastors, in conjunction with the GCGA and CCRM, who took the initiative and invited Kallestad. This church, a small congregation compared to WCCC, had three thousand worshippers each Sunday. Founded in 1978, the church grew to a congregation of over ten thousand by 2001. The strong point of the church was the same as Willow Creek; the desire was to reach the unchurched. However, there were real differences between the two churches. The CCJ maintained its traditional Lutheran style of worship, but in contemporary form. It was not lost on worshippers that they were in a Lutheran church with corresponding liturgy. This naturally resonated with those in the GPC. Here was an example of a growing Lutheran church that had not lost its tradition or identity. In addition, it was a Lutheran church that had been recently planted but maintained its traditional Lutheran ties.

There was little reaction to the CCJ congress. In comparison to the controversies stemming from the other congresses in 1991 and 1992, there was none. Many saw the ability of CCJ to bridge the gap between the unchurched and the churched, and the seekers' subsequent integration into the liturgical life of the church, as a positive model for the *Volkskirche*.[30] This may be the reason for the tepid response to the congress. Since the church was Lutheran and maintained its liturgical and ecclesiological ties, there was little room to complain. In addition, the CCJ maintained no real presence in Germany. As a result, the CCJ remained in America and did not press its program on the traditional German GPC.

Although the CCJ was closer to the German tradition than Willow Creek, and a congregation of 3,000 was more imaginable than Willow Creek's 14,000, the Community Church of Joy never gained the

---

29. "Gemeinde Kongress 1995," 8.
30. Böckel, "Gemeinde für andere," 155.

popularity or had the nationwide impact that Willow Creek enjoyed. There were two reasons for this. First, the CCJ program never caught on with the Free Churches, as Willow Creek had done. GPC churches were slow in adopting anything new so the CCJ never got a foothold. Second, there were no follow-up congresses planned. Kallestad was invited back to Germany to speak at congresses, but there was no continual presence of the CCJ as was the case with Willow Creek. As a result, the CCJ never evolved into a full-fledged movement.[31]

The Third GPC Study on Church Membership–1992

The decade between the second and third church surveys had brought great change to Germany. In 1989, East Germany, along with the Berlin Wall and the Iron Curtain, collapsed. Within a few months the two German states united. After unification a new phrase entered German vocabulary; there was the time "after the change" (*nach der Wende*) and the time "before the change" (*vor der Wende*). Unification not only occurred on the governmental level, but also brought a formal ecclesiastical unity. On June 27, 1991, at the GPC church council in Coburg, the churches of East and West were united. For the first time, the members of the GPC in the East could be surveyed about their relationship to the church. Because of East Germans being included, the percentage of those calling themselves Christian in Germany fell from 84 percent to 72 percent. The East German regime had been very successful in throttling the East German *Volkskirche*.

The surveys in 1972 and 1982 sought to determine the subjective attitude of West Germans toward the church. The 1992 survey, however, paid special attention to those church members who had little or nothing to do with the church. Under the best circumstances, those in this category would seek contact with the pastor for baptisms, confirmations, marriages, or burials. Beyond these occasions, they felt no need to have contact with the parish church. Given the large number of Germans having no church affiliation, the survey in 1992 sought to determine the attitude of this group towards religion in general and the church in particular. The preliminary results of the survey were published in 1993.[32]

---

31. J. Knoblauch, personal communication with author, 5 March 2006.
32. Engelhardt and von Loewenich, *Fremde-Heimat-Kirche*, 11–13.

Analysis of the Survey

The radical downward trend of GPC membership that began in the 1960s continued into the 1990s. Between 1960 and 1993 the western part of Germany lost 13 percent of its church members. These were the ones who made a conscious decision to leave the church. The church also, not including baptized infants, added membership. For every five members lost, the church gained one.[33] Thus, the seriousness of the church's situation led again to analyzing the cultural and religious inclinations of the church members. In 1972, 12 percent felt very connected to the church. In 1992, 10 percent felt very connected. In 1972, 12 percent felt no connection all, and two decades later 8 percent felt no connection at all. The increase in the number who felt "considerably" or "somewhat" connected was attributed to the tendency of people to avoid extreme positions. People felt more comfortable somewhere in the middle where there was more flexibility. For example, 31 percent felt somewhat connected in 1972. Twenty years later 35 percent felt somewhat connected. The increase was not attributed to an actual change in attitudes toward the church, but a change in cultural attitudes toward extreme positions.[34]

The amazing thing about the results of the survey was the relatively large percentage of East German Protestants who believed in God, as compared to their West German counterparts. Thirty-five percent of East Germans believed in God, who revealed himself in Jesus Christ, while 42 percent of West Germans agreed with the statement. The percentage is remarkable considering the decades-long attack on the church by the Marxist regime. On the other hand, the percentage is discouraging since it represents the peoples' response to the most basic tenant of the Christian faith.

The study revealed what was already expected. There existed in the two German States two distinct church cultures. The forces that affected the church population in each state were very different. In the West, decades of religious pluralism had an eroding effect on the church, while East Germans dealt with a socialism that punished church membership. The conclusion was that the church had a serious communication problem in dealing with the East. Western Germans, who had distanced themselves from the church, still had some knowledge of Christianity;

---

33. Ibid., 310.
34. Ibid., 35–37.

those in the East had none. There was no point of contact. This meant the church had to rethink its communication models both in the East and the West.[35]

Communication was not the only problem for the GPC. The survey revealed what was already suspected, that the church had lost its hold on the culture and that the monopoly of the institutional church no longer existed. The analysis suggested that the trends uncovered in previous studies continued. Social programs, once the sole realm of the church, were increasingly coming under the control of the state. As a result, the church was slowly losing its profile in the German culture. In addition, there was more competition facing the church; many Germans were investigating new religions, cults, psychologies, new age, and the esoteric. Added to these things were the classic temptations that kept people away from church: sports, pursuit of money, and desire for success.

The solutions to these problems were a serious matter for discussion. Nomenclature absent from previous discussions began to appear. Words like "business-like," "promotion," and "initiative" were used under the rubric "marketing" to describe what the church must do to attract members. The church must not change its basic message, but it had to make the message understandable to the masses. To do this the church must change its methods, and the language of the business world communicated what the church must do. This echoed what the GCGA had been promoting for years. The GPC was living in the past and there was a need for specific strategies and attainable goals actively seeking members. Although there was no mention of any church growth organization or church growth literature, the nomenclature was the *lingua franca* of the church growth movement.

Why no GPC Renewal?

There was no need for a statistical study for the GCGA to understand that church renewal was not taking place as they had planned. However, as in the decades before, the GPC took a survey to determine the status of the church in relationship to its members. Previous studies had shown that church losses were growing and that no positive change could be predicted in the future. This survey only accentuated what German church growth leaders already knew—that there had been no renewal.

35. Ibid., 345–46.

Theological Differences Blamed

The first public acknowledgement by the GCGA that church renewal or revival had not yet taken place occurred at the Nuremberg Congress in 1991. The fourth and fifth points of the Nuremberg Manifest acknowledged that there was no revival, renewal, or awakening. The reasons for this were blamed on the ongoing fight between evangelicals and charismatics. The manifest acknowledged that theological differences, as well as an unwillingness to unite for the sake of the gospel, were the reasons why God had not sent a spiritual awakening within the German church. The manifest did not directly blame opponents of church growth. However, it was evident that those opposing the unity with charismatics were to blame.

This wholesale charge against charismatic opponents greatly weakened the purpose of the document and served to further underscore the above mentioned objections to the GCGA. The manifest failed to acknowledge that there were legitimate reasons for the critical distance of non-charismatics. It would have given the manifest more weight if the theological and historical problems relating to Neo-Pentecostalism had been seriously addressed. For example, the manifest could have contained a statement criticizing the excesses exhibited at Kassel in 1907. The manifest also wasted an opportunity to speak to issues concerning spiritual warfare and spirit baptism that were deemed by charismatic opponents as unbiblical. These omissions, as well as the lack of any charismatic criticism, only served to further divide the two opposing groups rather than bring them together.

The Secular Society Blamed

The GCGA labored under the impression that the church was growing worldwide, and many countries were experiencing renewal. Awakenings were happening in many corners of the world, but not in Germany. For Klaus Eickhoff the question remained, especially since the GCGA had committed so much to the hope of renewal and reform, where is the German revival? Why does renewal remain so elusive in German-speaking Europe?

The GCGA had been in existence for almost a decade, and although much had been accomplished, renewal remained elusive. Many churches

The Zenith of German Church Growth 1991–1995

were still empty and the number of people leaving the church each year continued to rise. According to Eickhoff, the problem was not the secular German culture. False reasoning blamed continued losses of the church on the evil world. Eickhoff blamed the continued erosion on the church itself. According to him, the secular man was an empty shell that continually sought fulfillment. The secular society was a seeking society, filled with people oriented toward religion. The church at large erred in thinking secularization brought with it an anti-religious bent. This secular populous was finding fulfillment in all kinds of pseudo-religious groups and cults. Why did these secular seekers not find the church? Was not the church open to the whole world? The church as a whole believed that the problem was the secular person. Eickhoff concluded that the opposite was true; the church was the problem of the secular person.[36]

The Church Tax Blamed

Jörg Knoblauch also had ideas as to why there was no real change in the GPC. According to him it was not the lack of models to choose from. There were plenty of strategies and proven methods that would help jumpstart the ailing church. The problem was that the GPC leadership saw no real need to start new churches, or to be concerned with failing membership, because there was still tax money to rely on. According to Knoblauch, it was taxation that kept the church from fulfilling its responsibilities and kept the church enslaved.

Knoblauch likened the situation in the GPC with the communist-controlled economy in the former East Germany. No matter what the production or quality of the merchandise, the workers got their wages. This was a planned economy. The quantity and quality were pre-planned by the central communist committee, and the plan would be fulfilled. It did not matter if reality proved otherwise. As a result, there was no incentive either to work harder or to improve the product. Efficiency was never rewarded; wages were always paid; there was no possibility of being fired. This was the problem with the GPC. There was no incentive to improve the church or to make changes to improve the atmosphere for worshippers. No matter how many came to church or how bad the church service was, the pastor got paid and had his retirement package

---

36. Eickhoff, "Heute?," 10.

intact. Knoblauch's remedy for church renewal was to do away with the church tax.³⁷

Church Growth Adapts to the Reality

In 1992 the magazine made major changes. Issue 49 had a new look and a new focus. It maintained the same title, but with some changes. The magazine was now called *Church Growth Plus*. It was no accident that this issue focused on home Bible studies, or cell groups. This change was not made because of falling subscriptions. From 1990 to 1992 subscriptions had increased from 4,309 to 5,398. There was, however, a clear indication that the readership had begun to change.

Since its inception, the GCGA had viewed *Church Growth* as a magazine for futuristic thinkers. According to the GCGA, these once loyal readers had moved on to other things and should now be tapped to provide new and vital information for the magazine. *Church Growth Plus* no longer offered them the challenges it once had. These radical thinkers could now be called on for advice and expertise for the new generation of church growth followers. The magazine would need to change its focus in light of the changing needs of the readers.³⁸

The magazine, formerly oriented primarily for pastors in the *Volkskirche*, now sought to reach pastors of Free Churches and the laity of all confessions. *Church Growth Plus* now oriented toward "multipliers" (pastors, deacons, deaconesses, and local as well as regional church leaders). It sought to help those who worked on the local church level (Bible study leaders, cell group leaders, and others who served the local church). *Church Growth Plus* now included a copy of *Church for Tomorrow* (*Kirche für Morgen*), a magazine fully committed to the practical aspects of church service.

In 1995 the magazine went through another change. This time a new magazine name accompanied the change in focus; *Church Growth Plus* became *Praxis*.³⁹ There would be little or no church growth theory. Everything printed in the forty-eight pages would be applicable for the local church pastor and lay leader, whether *Volkskirche* or Free Church. The format and layout made it clear for whom the magazine was intend-

---

37. Knoblauch, "Wovon reden wir?," 24.
38. GCGA Archives.
39. C. Schwarz, "Editorial," 2.

ed. It appealed to the younger, more moldable church leader, who had a tendency to try out new things. Contrary to the reason for changes made in 1992, this new focus was in fact the result of a recent dip in subscriptions. This loss of readership in 1995 was the first sign that the influence of the GCGA was beginning to wane.[40]

Two New Strategies for Church Growth

The 1990s brought intense opposition, but there were also two new strategies for reaching Germany that took form during this decade. The DAWN strategy focused on planting new churches in Germany and Natural Church Development concentrated on local church analysis using Christian Schwarz's newly developed program. Neither of the models was new in the sense of being something totally exotic. There always had been new efforts to evangelize through the medium of the church. However, these strategies came at a time when there was openness to new trends. As a result, they found acceptance that previously had not been present.

DAWN: Discipling a Whole Nation

DAWN (Discipling a Whole Nation) is a church planting strategy developed by Jim Montgomery.[41] Montgomery was a missionary with OC International, the same American agency that sponsored the Campaign for Church Growth. His missionary stations included Taiwan, the Philippines, and Guatemala. While on missionary furlough in 1963 he studied under Donald McGavran at Northwest Christian College in Eugene, Oregon. The focus of the DAWN strategy was the fulfillment of the Great Commission in each country through the medium of church planting. This was to be accomplished by "mobilizing the entire Body of Christ" in a country to plant new churches or cell groups in every area where there were no evangelistically oriented churches.[42]

In 1987 Wolfgang Simson, a former missionary and founder of Wolfgang Simson Publishing in Lörrach, Germany became involved with GCGA-Switzerland and subsequently became acquainted with Kopfermann and Knoblauch in 1989. They encouraged his further participation with

---

40. J. Knoblauch, interview by author, 31 August 2005.
41. Montgomery, *Eine ganze Nation gewinnen*, 7–8.
42. "Deutschland braucht 87.000," 26–27.

the GCGA.⁴³ Simson, however, viewed the GCGA as a great hindrance to church growth because of its reliance on reviving existing churches in the GPC rather than church planting. He met Jim Montgomery at the 1989 Lausanne Conference in Manila. Simson, like Montgomery, was influenced by the CGM. He had translated and published *Understanding Church Growth* in Germany in 1990. His work on the book was key to his understanding of church growth principles. He understood DAWN as the foundational strategy necessary for the evangelization of Europe.

Simson sought to establish a bridgehead in Germany by first determining the actual condition of Christianity in the country. *How Christian is Germany?* (*Wie christlich ist Deutschland?*) was a research project sponsored by DAWN to reveal the true nature of Christianity in the country.⁴⁴ The hope was that a tangible picture of the condition of the church would shock church and confessional leaders into joining forces and to begin strategizing how to plant churches in areas where there was no adequate Christian witness. The specific goal was to start a church or cell group for every one thousand people. For example, if a city had 100,000, the goal would be to plant at least one hundred churches in that city. According to the DAWN formula, Germany, with a population of eighty-seven million, needed 87,000 evangelizing churches. The main issue at hand was the problem of contextualization. According to Montgomery the strategy had proved successful in the Philippines, El Salvador, Ghana, and Indonesia. It was not successful in Japan and it had not yet been tried in a country with a *Volkskirche*.

As in Japan, DAWN never materialized as a viable church planting strategy in Germany. The blame was laid, as in Japan, at the feet of the indigenous church for not fully adopting the movement. The question was not one of the propriety of a movement for the particular ecclesiastical peculiarities of a given country or the problem of contextualization. Rather, if DAWN was not contextualized, then it was the fault of an uncommitted indigenous church, not a dysfunctional or inappropriate methodology.⁴⁵ This was the case in Germany. In order for the DAWN strategy to function, cross-denominational cooperation was required. Since this cooperative effort never materialized, DAWN never materialized. Frustrated with this lack of cooperation stemming from what he

43. Simson, personal communication with author, 22 September 2008.
44. "Wie Christlich ist Deutschland?"
45. "Deutschland braucht 87.000," 26–27.

considered an engrained traditional *Landeskirche* mindset, Simson left the GCGA and Germany in 2001.

Natural Church Development

Christian Schwarz introduced the basics of Natural Church Development (NCD) in *Church Growth* in 1991. Critical issues surrounding the German church growth movement fostered the initial stages of development of the new program. Schwarz observed that simply training local church laity in the praxis of church growth did not automatically result in church growth. According to Schwarz, this was the norm rather than the exception.[46] In 1989, he analyzed 176 churches of various denominations in Germany, Switzerland, and Austria. Schwarz adapted and modified Peter Wagner's seven signs of a healthy church and developed his own eight basic principles for churches exhibiting growth. He believed his eight basic principles were confirmed when over one thousand churches in thirty-two countries on five continents were surveyed from 1994–1996.[47] The churches that were growing exhibited these eight qualities:

1. Empowering leadership
2. Gift-oriented ministry
3. Functional structures
4. Holistic small groups
5. Inspiring worship service
6. Need-oriented evangelism
7. Loving relationships
8. Passionate spirituality

Thus, the basic intention was not to identify which church growth models were or were not being employed, but rather to recognize what distinctive principles had previously naturally developed and precipitated the growth of the church. This would allow churches to observe functioning qualities common to hundreds of churches instead of a church growth model practiced by only a few large churches. Schwarz concluded this would change the typical church growth "model oriented" concept to

46. C. Schwarz, "Der Praxis Report," 23.
47. C. Schwarz, *Natural Church Development*, 19.

a more natural "principle oriented" concept.[48] This new paradigm would change the traditional American pragmatic church growth model, oriented on quantity, to a new paradigm oriented on quality.[49]

Schwarz labeled the traditional church growth approach as technocratic, or mechanistic. As a result, church growth models have failed to be universally transferable. He believed the biggest flaw in technocratic thinking was the total neglect of growth automatism or spontaneity. Technocracy results in each part of the church being viewed as an entity, instead of an integral part of the whole. One ministry of the church may be succeeding while others are suffering decline. In order to grow "naturally" as God in nature intended, each ministry must be interrelated with each other. Instead of concentrating on increasing the number of those in the worship service, for example, the emphasis is on increasing the quality of each of the eight basic principles. These principles encompass a holistic understanding of the church as an organism, instead of an institution defined by the sum of its parts. The goal of Natural Church Development is to help churches discover which of the eight basic principles is the "minimum factor," or that principle exhibiting the weakest development. According to NCD, when the quality of this "minimum factor" is improved, it will have a positive qualitative effect on the remaining principles. This in turn results in "quantitative growth." Schwarz sought to distinguish his methodology from church growth tradition:

> A look at church growth literature can be confusing. An entire array of programs claim: 'Do what we do, and you will get the same results.' Unfortunately many of these concepts contradict one another. One group pushes for megachurches as the most effective way to reach a community with the gospel, while another suggests the optimal church size is a small group, almost like most home Bible studies. Some suggest that the key to success is a worship service targeted toward non-Christians, while others emphasize that the goal of a worship service is worshipping God and equipping the saints. One group is convinced that marketing strategies must be integrated into church planning, while another enjoys healthy church growth without even having heard of such methods.[50]

---

48. Ibid., 58–60.
49. C. Schwarz, *Die dritte Reformation*, 11.
50. Schwarz, *Natural Church Development*, 16–17.

This particular criticism of church growth may be true concerning the CGM as a whole. However, it is an overstatement in the case of German church growth. From the earliest stages of the movement, beginning with the study trips, the leadership constantly encouraged participants not to copy the American models, but to seek out transferable principles and concepts. This was particularly true regarding the study trips to the United States.

By 1998 Natural Church Development had become fully independent of the GCGA and had taken the name Institute for Natural Church Development. The new organization had trained 150 consultants and pastors in the United States and training conferences were scheduled for Australia and Denmark. Additional conferences were planned in over fifty countries.[51]

The Culmination of Contextualization: Analysis

This period brought to a close the zenith of the German church growth movement and culminated with the completion of the GCGA contextual program. As previously noted, GCGA contextualization was based on its definition of the church; the true church grows with the number of those converted. It is God's will that the church grows. However, under the influence of Peter Wagner and hyper-pragmatic church growth thinking, this foundational ecclesiology added a caveat. Not only does the true church increase, it must consider all elements related to promoting growth. This resulted in a conservative stance on the nature of the gospel, while following a progressive or liberal approach to methodology.

As a result, the theology of spiritual gifts, which was foundational to German church growth, became clouded. There were no precise theological definitions of this most important concept, because in the realm of pragmatic church growth thinking, there was no need for it. Since charismatic churches were growing, they must be conforming to the will of God. Thus, by the end of 1995, charismatic spiritual gifts became an integral part of the GCGA ecclesiology and subsequently became part of the contextualization process.

---

51. "Natürliche Gemeindeentwicklung," 6.

Discussion Questions

1. What church growth principle was the underlying reason for The Congress for Renewal and Church Growth in 1991? How valid is this principle today for the contextualization of the gospel?

2. Discuss Rolf Sheffbuch's concerns regarding the Pietists closing ranks with charismatics.

3. The Evangelical Alliance welcomed Billy Graham's evangelistic efforts, regardless of his inviting charismatics to take part. Why then were they opposed to the Congress in 1991?

4. Why was the Willow Creek strategy a relative success in Germany? Why was Willow Creek's concept of conversion easily contextualized? Why did some churches struggle implementing the Willow Creek philosophy?

5. Was the GPC church survey in 1992 able to indicate if the GCGA had made progress in its contextualization process? What statistics would indicate the success or failure of the contextualization of the gospel in a culture? What kind of statistics would you expect a missionary involved in church planting and evangelism to keep?

6. As a result of the 1992 church analysis, what conclusion did the GPC reach regarding the church's traditional role in the German culture?

7. How did the GCGA respond to the change in the German culture toward the GPC? How can the church in your culture become aware of cultural changes that affect its contextualization of the gospel?

6

The Decline of German Church Growth 1996–2003

On May 1, 2003, President George W. Bush climbed into a seat of a Navy S-3B Viking military jet. His destination was the USS Abraham Lincoln, which was returning to San Diego after ten months at sea supporting Operation Iraqi Freedom. Bush wanted to thank the sailors for their service as well as announce the end of major combat operations in Iraq. In preparation for the speech on board the ship, Bush's staff had prepared a large banner to be displayed behind President Bush as he was giving his speech. The banner read "Mission Accomplished." Bush later explained that the banner was intended as a tribute to those serving on the USS Lincoln. However, news outlets interpreted it as a "victory dance" by the President. As the Iraqi ground war dragged on and American casualties mounted, the "Mission Accomplished" slogan became canon fodder for opponents of the Iraqi war and was used to mock the President. Bush later lamented that the banner "was a big mistake."[1]

"Mission Accomplished" was also the reason given for the closure of the GCGA. The leadership believed they had accomplished their mission. Unlike President Bush, they had no regrets concerning their pronouncement of "Mission Accomplished." After careful evaluation they stood firmly behind their decision to officially close the GCGA. This chapter, and the next, will explore the reasoning behind this explanation and determine whether the GCGA indeed had fulfilled its mission. The underlying intention of the GCGA's original mission meant stopping the loss of church members. Realizing this could not be done, the GCGA

---

1. Bush, *Decision Points*, 378–80.

adjusted the mission goal to become one of introducing church growth concepts within the GPC.

There were many reasons that the GPC could not be revived. However, there were three overriding factors that led the GCGA to realize that the GPC was incapable of revival:

1. The traditional role of the pastor was ingrained in the German culture and would never change. In order for revival to take place the pastor's role had to change from public official to mentor.
2. The belief that infant baptism equaled salvation would never change. Revival required that those baptized must experience personal conversion.
3. The universities held a steadfast monopoly on pastoral training. True revival could only happen when liberal theology no longer served as the bedrock for biblical teaching in the universities.

Although there was no specific date when these three realities became evident, the GCGA understood that it was time for reevaluation of its ministry in 2001. This reevaluation laid the groundwork for the eventual closing of the GCGA in 2003.

Positive Trends for German Church Growth

The years 1996 to 2003 were characterized by two positive trends that, at least in the early stages, pointed to gains for the German church growth movement. One of the most encouraging trends was the interest in founding new churches both in and out of the *Volkskirche*.

Church Planting Conferences

Opposition to church planting by the GPC did not initially stop the church planting movement. In 1996 the first church planting conference specifically oriented around the GPC took place in Karlsbad-Spielberg and a second in Basel, Switzerland. In 1998, a third conference took place in Giengen.[2] The goal of each conference was to promote church planting on three levels. First, the conferences promoted church planting on a national level. Second, specific areas were targeted for church

---

2. "Mit Gemeindepflanzungen," 7.

plants on the state level, for example Württemberg and Westfalen. Third, church planting would be encouraged on the regional level by networking church planters.

These conferences helped participants understand how to plant a new church within the structure of the GPC. They emphasized the unique possibilities, as well as the challenges, of starting a new worship service in proximity to a *Volkskirche*. In addition, the conferences emphasized the basics of GPC church planting: (1) how to determine the target group; (2) how to find and train workers; and (3) how to get the necessary funds to start a new work.[3] The main church planting models came from the Anglican Church in England where the church hierarchy encouraged the founding of new churches in Anglican parishes. The German church planters, within the GPC, welcomed this because the church structure in England mirrored the parochial system in Germany. This helped the German church planters in that models were coming from Europe and not America. Church planting within the GPC was actually a continuation of the Willow Creek Community Church concept of developing strategies to reach the unchurched. As a result GPC church planting was a union of two foreign concepts, one English and one American.

Another advantage was the motive for church planting from the English. The purpose was not simply to save the institutional church, but to save the lost. The literature promoting English church planting made this evident. Church planting was united with evangelism. Bob Hopkins, an English church planter, made clear that incorporating new Christians into the life of the traditional church could be difficult. As a result, new churches need to be established that would make it more conducive for new Christians to grow in their faith, resulting in an atmosphere for these new Christians to share their faith.[4] This missionary motive was evident in both philosophy and methodology of the church planting programs sponsored by the GCGA. Thus, the GCGA continued on unabated within the church planting framework. The church continued to be defined as a fellowship of those having a personal relationship to Christ. This fellowship would then form the foundation for mission in the world exemplified by service, as well as the proclamation of the gospel. This proclamation was not only meant to increase the number of conversions for a specific

---

3. GCGA Archives.
4. Hopkins, *Church Planting*, 6–7.

local church, but it should also show evidence of a mission-oriented society by encouraging the multiplication of churches.

Leadership Congresses

There were two reasons for the development of leadership congresses. First, Jörg Knoblauch was a well known Christian leader in Germany. He had won awards for business leadership and was a coveted speaker at business conferences. His interest in leadership led to his organizing conferences to help Christian leaders develop more attractive worship services and encourage the development of leaders in their churches. Organizing the conferences also revealed an important change in attitudes. Horst Marquardt, who led Germany's Gospel Radio for thirty-three years and had been one of the GCGA's most vocal critics, worked closely with Knoblauch and became chairman of the Christian Leadership Congresses.

Second, these additional congresses were a result of those held from 1991 to 1995. Feedback from these congresses was positive and reflected a desire from both pastors and laity for additional conferences. In order to meet this need, the GCGA planned a National Laity Congress and a National Christian Leadership Congress.[5] In conjunction with the November, 1996 Willow Creek Congress in Hamburg, an official Willow Creek Community Church Germany Association was established. Wilfried Bohlen, a Baptist pastor, led the new organization. Promise Keepers was also in Germany and found a strong following among German men. Study trips were planned to introduce the American Promise Keepers movement to the German movement. These new initiatives were viewed as positive signs for church growth in Germany. However, they also accentuated one of the problematic characteristics of the movement at this time in its history; instead of seeking to determine the real strength of the organization or re-orienting toward its core church growth philosophy, the GCGA tended to adopt the next newest trend from the United States.

---

5. GCGA Archives.

Negative Trends for German Church Growth

The first sign that something was amiss was the realization that there was nothing new to say about church growth. Everything had already been explained numerous times and in a multitude of ways. There came a point where the GCGA leaders knew that the church growth message had run its course. There were four negative trends pointing to the decline of the German church growth movement.

Praxis Subscriptions Plummet

The magazine, *Praxis*, had reached a readership of 5,490 by the end of 1993. Fears had been expressed in 1995 that *Praxis* had reached its peak, and this became a reality in 1997. The magazine not only peaked, but its readership began to decline. The number of subscriptions sank to around five thousand and it continued to lose readers in the coming years. By 2002 the total financial loss for publishing the magazine had reached sixteen thousand Euros. If losses were not curbed, the magazine would lose around five thousand Euros per issue. The losses were of concern because the magazine was the voice of the GCGA. Subscriptions to *Praxis* were viewed as a gauge in determining the increase or decrease in the interest for church growth in Germany. This decline was especially disappointing because much effort had gone into increasing readership.

There was also a change in editorship with Christoph Schalk replacing Christian Schwarz. Schwarz's dismissal as editor was not overtly done, but was accomplished primarily through slowly delegating his editorial responsibilities to others. The process of fully terminating Schwarz from any editorial duties began in 1988, finally coming to completion in 1997.[6]

In 2002 Oliver Schippers replaced Knoblauch as business manager for the GCGA. His main duty was to concentrate on rebuilding *Praxis*. There was much hope that he could reverse the negative trend, but the reversal never materialized. This concentration on the magazine only postponed the inevitable closing of the organization. Since its inception in 1979, the magazine had always been the most important tool of the organization, not only serving to disseminate information, but also allowing feedback from the readership. The number of subscribers indicated how well the message was being communicated. Without the magazine

---

6. C. Schwarz, personal communication with author, 10 September 2008.

the GCGA would become mute and as the number of subscribers lessened, they realized that the days of the organization were numbered.[7]

Editorship changed hands again in 2003 when Christian Koslowski took over the reins of *Praxis*. Those once loyal to the magazine had moved on to other church growth issues and priorities. Where they had once profited from the magazine they now had other church growth sources. This was a victory of sorts for the German church growth movement, because these other Christian magazines were publishing articles on church growth principles. For example, *idea-Spektrum* began reporting on the largest churches in Germany and printing responses from church officials. Other magazines appeared, such as *Focusswisse/DAWN*, *New Wine*, and *Morning Star* that promoted church growth concepts. This was understood by the GCGA as a great advance for church growth in Germany because until the efforts of the organization, characterized chiefly by their publication, church growth was relatively unknown in Germany.[8]

It was also obvious in scanning *Church Growth*, *Church Growth Plus*, and *Praxis* that articles and topics tended to repeat themselves. In the ongoing search to find new subscribers, the pool became smaller as an increasing number of readers became familiar with the themes. In 2003, the decision was made to combine *Praxis* with *Relax* (*Ausatmen*), a popular Christian magazine. *Praxis* would maintain its appearance and message but it would now simply be an insert within *Relax*. The remaining twenty-five hundred subscribers to *Praxis* now became subscribers to *Relax*.[9]

Church Planting Efforts Stagnate

The GPC church planting emphasis was ten years old, and according to Jochen Hackstein, one of the leaders of the Paulus-Institute (Berlin), there was little to show for it. Church planting congresses, seminars, and literature had done little to spur on any kind of real progress. The GPC leadership as a whole had rejected the idea and it was no longer a topic of discussion.

Illustrative of this stagnation was the Anskar Church denomination, founded by Wolfram Kopfermann. In 1988, Kopfermann left the

---

7. T. Knoblauch, interview by author, 31 August 2005.
8. J. Knoblauch, interview by author, 31 August 2005.
9. Schippers, "Aufatmen und Praxis," 2.

GPC to start his own church. At that time he predicted that by the end of 1993, five thousand churches would be planted in Germany. This did not happen. Kopfermann underestimated the difficulty of church planting in Germany. He had hoped that other disgruntled pastors would follow his example, cut ties with the GPC and start new congregations. Many of the pastors that had rallied behind him and encouraged him refused to follow his example. According to Kopfermann, they were not willing to give up a guaranteed salary, benefits, and good retirement, in exchange for the insecurity of a Free Church pastor.[10]

The opinion existed among leaders of the GCGA that there were no examples of a GPC planting a daughter church or of even planting a GPC church in any area considered a mission field. There were also differences as to what constituted an authentic church plant.[11] Some leaders were of the opinion that a church within the traditional GPC had been planted. The Oasis Church in Giengen was, according to Jörg Knoblauch, an authentic new church. It was not an additional church service for a particular target group, but a church with its own leadership, spirituality, and financial basis. Others had a different opinion. Oliver Schippers of the Paulus-Insitute, a church growth consulting organization, indicated that Oasis was not a true church plant. He felt that a group of Christians from a local church beginning another worship service in the same area, as occurred with Oasis, was a church mutation, not a church plant. Authentic church planting only occurs when Christians from one area go to another region and establish a new congregation where there is no credible Christian witness, and this scenario simply was not happening in Germany.[12]

Regardless of the difference of opinion, the Oasis Church was touted as the first GPC church plant. The church began with thirty-nine members and had its own constitution. It was a part of the GPC in Giengen, but it took two years of discussion with the regional church authorities to gain permission to start this new church. This church also began a church planting movement resulting in the initiation of other GPC church plants in twelve cities, including one in Austria. The purpose of the Oasis Church initiative was to make the GPC aware of church planting possibilities within the parochial structure, and to present a positive

10. "War der Ausstieg ein Abstieg?," 15–16.
11. "Gemeindepflanzung in Deutschland ist tot!," 7–8.
12. Ibid.

model. There was much fear about church planting within the GPC, and it was hoped that the initiative would change the perception from being a threat to being an asset for the *Volkskirche*.

The reason that GPC church planting stalled was the result of an antagonistic church leadership. Whenever a new idea originating from the GCGA was presented to the GPC, the reaction was skepticism. This limited the possibility of church renewal within the GPC. Successful church planting required an aggressive local church leadership that would be willing to battle the regional and local church hierarchy for permission to start a new church. This fact was the crux of the church planting problem in the *Volkskirche*.

The willingness to tackle the GPC hierarchy was not enough, however. If church leadership did not want any new forms of church services or church plants, the fate of a new work was sealed. In England, the Anglicans had the encouragement of the hierarchy to start new congregations. In Germany, the hierarchy was the constraint to any momentum for starting new churches. The only way to overcome this was civil disobedience: start new churches in spite of the disapproval of church leaders. The reasoning was simple; these leaders were deliberately holding the Kingdom of God captive only because they did not like the concept of new churches and believed it a threat to their power. This attitude persisted even though the GPC continued to lose thousands of church members each year. In fact, in 2003 there were more Catholics in Germany than Protestants. An end to this trend was nowhere in sight. The resistance of GPC pastors was evident in the aftermath of the congresses held between 1991 and 1995. Although these congresses were the apex of the GCGA movement, the GCGA concluded that GPC pastors refused to allow their people to implement any of the strategies presented at the congresses.[13]

The lethargy of GPC church planting was in contrast to that of the Free Churches. Running almost parallel with church planting efforts in the GPC were church planting efforts within denominational and independent Free Churches. Within a ten-year span (1990 to 2000), over fifteen hundred new Free Churches were planted in Germany. These were small churches, fifty to a hundred members, and usually charismatic oriented, with names like Jesus-Center, or Missions Church. Some churches formed associations such as the Protestant-Lutheran Free Church with

---

13. T. Knoblauch, interview by author, 31 August 2005.

forty-two churches and 1,800 members.[14] The Union of German Baptists and Brethren planted seventy-five churches from 1992 to 1995. The number of Brethren churches grew 15 percent from 1997 to 1998, numbering 140 congregations in 2000. The Evangelical Free Church planted six to eight daughter churches per year, and now has plans to work with the Baptists to plant more churches in the former East Germany. Russian immigrants of German heritage have planted over four hundred twenty churches in Germany.[15] In addition, the Seventh Day Adventists, the Mennonites, the Pentecostals, the Vineyard, and the Church of the Nazarene all developed strategies to plant new churches.

In contrast to the GPC, Free Churches were experiencing a church planting boom. The reason these Free Churches were experiencing an authentic church planting movement is that the motivation and strategies originated from both regional and national leadership. There was a frustration at the local level because of the lack of growth. In response, church leaders encouraged the local churches to evangelize with the view of planting new churches in un-evangelized areas. In further contrast to the GPC, Free Church leaders understood the benefits of planting new congregations, especially in Germany.

No one denomination could reach all the different types of people that called Germany home. There was a need for different churches with diverse goals and styles to reach the various segments of society. Also it must be remembered that Free Churches survived financially from their church members freely giving their financial support. Free Churches received no funds from the government, derived from the church tax, like the GPC. Thus, the Free Church had real incentive to change church ministries to meet the needs of the people. A final important aspect of the positive trends among the Free Churches was that they prescribed to a much more conservative view of the Scriptures than the GPC.[16]

Regional Associations Decline

The regional church growth associations for GPC pastors also suffered decline, for several reasons, but the primary reason was lack of leadership. At one point there were sixteen functioning groups throughout

14. "1.500 'neue' evangelische Gemeinden," 6.
15. "Die Brüder sind im Kommen," 12.
16. Machel, "Brauchen wir neue Gemeinden?," 6.

Germany, three in Switzerland, and two in Austria. Maintaining this network with GPC pastors became a very difficult task requiring personal contact with the association leaders in order to encourage and motivate them. It was the responsibility of the director of the GCGA to keep the regional associations informed and motivated. Because of time constraints and different leadership styles, the GCGA leadership failed to provide this personal contact. While some regional associations did an excellent job of promoting church growth in their areas, many struggled, and other regional groups simply died off.[17] Over time this important link between GPC pastors and the GCGA was broken. As a result, the Association had no way of gauging how church growth was faring at the parish level.

The GPC's Reluctance to Change

The decline of the German Protestant Church was evident at the GPC Synod in Leipzig in 1999. The entire thrust of the Synod was the need for evangelism and mission within the church, the same issues that had plagued the church for decades. There remained an ecclesiological vacuum in the church that begged to be filled. This meant that church leadership lacked the desire for mission or evangelism. The self-evident nature of the biblical mandate for both mission (sending) and evangelism (proclaiming) was absent from the GPC. As a result, the church needed to reverse this trend and fill the ecclesiological vacuum.

Frustration on the part of the GCGA, and others committed to evangelism, was again caused by comparison. Comparing the spiritual landscape in Germany with church growth movements in other countries was one element accompanying the birth of the GCGA. Why were churches in other countries flourishing, while the church in Germany was dying? This question plagued those involved in church growth, and was the same one asked by Jörg Knoblauch back in 1974. From the beginning, the slackness of the German church was compared with growing congregations in the United States and other parts of the world. This practice of comparing continued as new ideas, strategies, and methods came to the forefront on the church growth scene. Why was the German church always slow in responding to new ideas? While in the United States, and in other parts of the globe, churches were responding to the Natural Church Development program from Christian Schwarz, barely

17. T. Knoblauch, interview by author, 31 August 2005.

a hundred churches showed any interest in Germany. Churches in other European countries had shown unity in working with the DAWN initiative. Germany, on the other hand, showed only reluctance.[18]

Between 170,000 and 190,000 Germans were leaving the GPC each year, and this caused many German Christians to be eager to try new methods of ministry. These new ministry methods usually originated in the United States and eventually found their way to Germany. Although many Germans were interested in the Willow Creek model, others saw it as just another fad from the States that would soon pass into oblivion—leaving thousands of disappointed German Christians in its wake. There was some truth in this critique. German Christianity had seen its share of so-called successful church growth strategies over the decades, each promising to deliver the long sought-after awakening. John Wimber came with the Vineyard movement and Power Evangelism. Peter Wagner came representing worldwide church growth, the church planting movement, as well as spiritual warfare. After the church growth movement ran its course, Bill Hybels arrived with the "church for the unchurched" agenda. Promise Keepers later arrived with help for German Christian men. Study trips were organized to visit Promise Keepers leaders in America. Rick Warren and his *Purpose Driven Life* book and Forty Days of Purpose program held the interest of many German Christians for a period of time. The frustration lay in the fact that these different models, with their negatives and positives, brought only minimal change compared to the great need. The GPC remained basically unchanged.

The Ingrained Church Structure

The institutional structures in the church had always been perplexing. Fritz Schwarz had pleaded for a scenario where the ecclesiastical institutions served church growth. This scenario appeared only sparingly within the GPC where the structures remained barricades instead of bridges to any church growth effort. There were several reasons for this. First, the institutions were equated with the church or the *ekklesia*; therefore, change or criticism was seen as an attack on the true church. Similar to this was the idea that the institution's integrity and unity were equated with the integrity and unity of the church. Second, church duties were reserved only for pastors. This strangled the concept of a gift-guided laity,

18. Simson, personal communication with author, 22 September 2008.

co-laboring with the pastor. Third, the institution wielded its hierarchical power to quell evangelistic efforts and to discourage discipleship. Finally, prescribed institutional by-laws, rather than the message and mission of the gospel, guided the direction of the church.

Peter Brierley, director of Christian Research in London, believed institutional churches were bound to decline. They had structures that developed over several decades and could not simply be exchanged without turmoil. They could not be expected to suddenly drop their ingrown traditions to respond to the postmodern culture. His best illustrations of the problem were the church buildings. These historically valuable structures could not simply be remodeled or sold when they became viewed by modern culture as antiquated. In the same way, institutional churches would continue to decline because of the inability to change their own culture.[19]

Brierley also listed theology as a major obstacle for the Anglican and GPC Churches. They viewed themselves as guardians of Christian religion and theology and were hard pressed to change course or allow the laity to play a major role.[20] This was especially true in Germany where the historical-critical method was the major premise underpinning the theological training of GPC pastors. The fundamental premise of the historical-critical method of interpreting Scripture is that the Bible is not inspired by God. The damage of this theology to the German church was obvious; since the veracity of the most common elements of Christianity are called into question by the historical-critical method, why then a need for mission and evangelism? As long as the church tax guaranteed salaries and retirement, and offered some financial stability, why seriously consider changing anything? After all, those crying for change actually believed that God would judge those without Christ, and their beliefs were based on the Bible that is filled with error.[21]

At this point the reader may be asking, "Why are these people pastors in the first place? If they do not believe the Bible and the truth of the gospel, why then are they pastors?" The answer is that they see their role as a social service. National Church pastors are mostly serious people who want to counsel and encourage the parishioners. They see themselves as offering a public service of being able to speak directly to people

---

19. Brierley, "Warum institutionelle Kirchen schrumpfen," 6.
20. Ibid.
21. Stadelmann, "Nehmt den Bibelfaktor ernster!," 9.

about the problems they are facing. These pastors understand problems to be focused on the disparity between the rich, the not so rich, and the poor. Caring for the environment and sharing Germany's wealth with the poor in the third world are also paramount. Because church buildings are very important, it is also the duty of the pastor to make sure steeples, bells, organs, and pews are maintained in good working order. This maintenance of the real estate is very important for the GPC church community, especially in small towns and villages. While working with seminary students in the former East Germany, I learned that the most important issue was the repair of steeples and organs, not preaching the gospel. The maintaining of both social and real estate structures are seen as the primary duties of the typical GPC pastor.

Regarding the immovable structures of the GPC, Jörg Knoblauch observed that personal demons were a demonstrable fact for Christianity in Africa and Asia. He concluded that in contrast to these places where demons infested individuals, demons in Germany had invaded church structures and had found a home in the entire church organization. Knoblauch emphasized this by pointing out that no matter how bad the statistics were, the GPC continued on its present course. It defied any logic that the GPC would not consider major changes. The only explanation was that something supernatural was in play:

> What does the church want? In which direction should it go? Could it be that in contrast to Africa where missionaries have to deal with people possessed by demons, that we have a satanic invasion of our church structures? That is, demons have not so much possessed individuals, but have they not much more demonized entire organizations . . . demonized structures?[22]

Knoblauch was a businessman and a pragmatist. He saw the church structures of the GPC, along with the shrinking statistics, and wondered why there was no attitude of alarm. No business would allow itself to get into such a situation when there were so many alternatives. In the same way, it defied any logic that the GPC would continue on the same course when there was possibility of positive change:

> Whoever analyzes the sick *Volkskirche* will quickly realize that a timely healing is not possible, because the sickness lies too deep within. One realizes that using medicine or putting the patient on a diet, etc., is no use. Here is a body that is deathly ill and on

22. J. Knoblauch, "Wie Stabil ist die Kirche wirklich?," 103–4.

top of that, has diabetes and asthma . . . in business management you would say, "We need crisis management, real turnaround management is needed." Spiritually you would say, "Here only Jesus can bring the transformation."[23]

The Immovable Traditional Role of the Pastor

The barriers to church growth in the GPC were many. One appeared to be uncompromisingly immovable, yet it was the key to any hope of church renewal. The role of the pastor had not changed and had stood its ground against any hint of alteration. It was necessary to revamp the pastor's role and readjust the congregation's perception of what the pastor was to do. From the early days of the fledgling church growth movement in Germany, this had been one of the essential components of any renewal effort within the GPC system. The office and role of the GPC pastor was not only a hindrance to renewal, but also was a destructive force that muted church growth. If renewal and growth were to happen, the role of the pastor had to change.

GPC congregations viewed the pastor as a public official who performed required rites and duties and the pastors also understood their role in this way. As a result, the exercise of spiritual gifts of the laity and a biblical functioning church were impossible. In 1999, Klaus Eickhoff suggested ways to do away with the "church-destroying pastoral office":

1. Literature must be published dealing with this issue. Articles could be written confronting local church boards with their lethargy so they would understand the nature of this crisis. In addition, a literary forum for a "church without hierarchy" could be established to promote dialogue and an exchange of ideas on ways to abolish the contemporary office of pastor.

2. Local church structures must change. The laity could and should take over all responsibilities of the pastor. (The Reformation paved the way for this, but the church never took advantage of it.) The role of the local church board must change. Boards should no longer be able to micro-manage church affairs. The local church must finance itself, independent of the church tax, which eventually

---

23. Krause, "Verheißungsorienterter Gemeindeaufbau."

should be abolished. The parish church must have complete control over its role and responsibility before God.

3. House churches must be promoted. House churches could change the local church from a parochial church to a personal church. Parish church services would continue, but not in the present form. Parochial house churches would meet regularly for Sunday worship, but not as GPC institutions. They would be independent of any GPC hierarchy. This would subsequently abolish the traditional pastoral office. [24]

These steps would be a major undertaking and require not renewal, but a continuance of the Reformation. Following in the steps of Pietism, the GCGA saw itself as the second part of the Reformation. Luther promoted the concept of the priesthood of all believers and the integration of the laity into the duties of the church. However, according to the GCGA, this part of the Reformation was never fulfilled.[25] The chief reason it never reached its goal was institutional structures. These structures were in place well before church growth came on the scene and they had to be dealt with in order to renew the church. However, the analysis of the GCGA leadership failed to take into account the most fundamental aspect of the Reformation. It was not the reforming of church structures that was necessary, but a re-discovery of the authority of the Bible (*sola Scriptura*-by Scripture alone). It was the emphasis on the veracity and final authority of the Scriptures scriptures that led to the Reformation, not the desire to replace archaic ecclesiastical structures. In essence this remained the vacuum in the GPC, the church of the Reformation.

As a direct result of the loss of *sola Scriptura* came the decline of *sola fide* (by faith alone), and subsequently the vanishing of *sola fide in Christum membra ecclesiae constituit* (only faith in Christ can establish the members of the church). The most important aspect of GCGA ecclesiology, which determined its contextualization philosophy, was its independence from the ingrained institution of the GPC. It was formulated on a clear and conservative (*sola Scriptura*) understanding of the gospel as found in the Bible.

---

24. GCGA Archives.
25. Eickhoff, *Gemeinde entwickeln*, 56–58.

Ignored Opportunities for Change

There were two reasons why this institutional structure remained steadfast. First, it was traditional. The role of the pastor and state entitlements were historical norms that had been in place for hundreds of years. Although the church was no longer a monarchial state church, the attitude of church privilege remained. Second, it was a matter of pride, defensiveness, and humiliation. Church decline was not sudden, but a slow and grueling process. When renewal was mentioned in the context of the church, it accentuated the fact that something was wrong; the current situation needed change and those in charge were on the wrong course. Immediately, church leaders were put on the defensive. As a result, those favoring renewal had to fight for every inch of church renewal ground.[26]

There were two opportunities in the history of the GPC to make major changes with potential for institutional and structural alterations. The first was when the German monarchy came to an end—and with it the oversight of local rulers. For the first time in hundreds of years, the church was free to chart its own course. However, anti-democratic forces took control and a church hierarchy took over the role of the monarchy. This resulted in the continued consciousness in the laity of reliance on a hierarchy. Subsequently, the German laity never developed into what Luther had envisioned.[27]

The second opportunity for renewal came with the change of government in East Germany. For the first time in German history, the German church had the chance to remain a church with ties to the people instead of a church tied to the government. The East German Protestant Church for decades had been a refuge for the oppressed. It had no state funding and was constantly harassed by the communist regime. As a result, the church was viewed as related to the *Volk*. However, instead of leaving this relationship intact, the GPC in the East was absorbed into the West and became a part of the petrified institution. The church lost a golden opportunity to allow the church in the East to develop without hierarchical interference. I worked for years via the GCGA with East German pastors. They, along with their families, suffered simply because they were outspoken Christians. I had the privilege of standing with them in mass demonstrations against the brutal East German regime. It

---

26. J. Knoblauch, interview by author, 24 September 2003.
27. Murray, *Post-Christendom*, 197.

is completely understandable that they relished the new circumstances that the fall of the Iron Curtain ushered in. Now, they could look forward to a steady income, an assured pastoral position, and no harassment from the government. It will never be known what might have happened if the GPC-East had continued to develop its independent course coupled with the freedom of democracy. One thing is certain; the unification with the GPC brought many Christian pastors a sense of relief.

The Prominence of Liberal Theology

There was much opposition to the GCGA throughout its history, and just one source of this opposition: church traditions. Two of the most prominent traditions standing in the way of church revival were infant baptism being equated with salvation, and the pastor being viewed as a civil servant. These traditions arose as a direct result of the monopoly the universities have in the liberal training of pastors. If the GPC had held a more conservative and biblical view of theology, most of the problems would become manageable. The problem remains that even questioning these traditions is met with hostility. At this point it must be stated that when referring to German liberal theology, the issues involved are not peripheral. This liberal theology denies the most critical tenets of the Christian faith: the Virgin Birth, the atonement, and the Resurrection. Among conservative German scholars there was a sense that a believing student's faith would be destroyed if not given support from Christian theologians serving as mentors. Student housing was established for this specific purpose. I served in one of these dorms based near Heidelberg. The mentors were well versed in Greek and Hebrew and strived to give the students a conservative view of Scripture. However, after spending much time with the students, I found that they were very wary of church growth and of me as a missionary. I am convinced that it was because of my organization's ties to the charismatic movement.

Germans were raised in this structure so it had become normal, comfortable, and convenient. It was so convenient that it took precedence over Scripture and mission. Tradition was so engrained into the culture that it was perceived as the will of God, although it was actually against the will of God. This led to complacency, shame, and cowardice. Most Germans became ashamed to be outwardly committed to Christ and to love the lost for the sake of Christ. One of the most devastating traditions arising from liberal theology was the election of church board members regardless of their spiritual condition. This led directly to the sabotaging of any evangelistic efforts by a believing pastor. Those on the board opposed to conversion simply voted against these efforts. There were also cases where a segment of a church board wrote letters to the local bishop complaining about pastoral efforts to convert church members.

Traditionalism also gave rise to liberal theology that adhered to the premise that Scripture is not divinely inspired. According to Klaus Eickhoff, the most committed opponents to the GCGA were liberal theologians. The primary issue was not certain theological concerns, but the more basic issue concerning Jesus. Was Jesus Christ the savior and judge of all mankind? Did he have a universal claim on all people or not? If these things were true, then we must obey and seek those who are lost for his sake. Liberal theologians rejected this view of Christ.[28]

The immovable traditional structures of the GPC were never static. It is incorrect to imagine them as simply defensive barriers, such as a wall or fortress, preventing church growth access to the church. These structures, represented and championed by individuals, were active and offensive in their opposition, and vigorously prevented evangelism. The GPC hierarchy actively prevented the gospel from being preached by failing to back pastors who were preaching the gospel. Although the churches were growing, the church superintendents refused to give support to pastors who preached the gospel. This led to non-believing church members holding sway over the evangelistic efforts of the pastor. Instead of encouraging the pastors, the hierarchy sided with the non-Christian elements sitting on church boards and labeled Bible believing pastors as fanatics and fundamentalists.

For example, I have had people stand up during my seminars and say, "Are you saying I am not a Christian?"—Who can tell them that they are not Christians? They were baptized, have been active in the church, and they paid their church taxes. How dare anyone insinuate that they are not Christians! They are not drug addicts, have never stolen or killed anyone, and have a good reputation in the community. They do not view themselves as sinners.—This is the "trickle down effect" of liberal theology. Those anti-gospel forces taught at the university level find their way into the very fabric of the beliefs of the person in the pew. When traditional beliefs are questioned the response is often one of anger and

---

28. Eickhoff, personal communication with author, 19 February 2006.

obstinance. This is why it usually takes several years for Germans to respond to the gospel. It is not only new information, but it goes against everything that they believe. As a result, the missionary is not starting at zero, but at a minus ten.

These anti-gospel structures have faces, names, personalities and centuries-old beliefs that would not succumb without a fight. As a result, these structures were anti-evangelistic or anti-missionary. This label pointed to the fact that opposition was never inert, but always active.

Summary

Infant baptism, the role of the pastor, and non-Christian church board members were indicative of the end result of undermining the authority of the Bible. Any effort by the GCGA to successfully make major changes in the structure of the GPC was impossible. There were small pockets of resistance in a number of parishes. However, these parishes were not the normal GPC parish. They had believing pastors and church boards sympathetic to the church growth movement. For example, the parish where we lived had a believing pastor and board members who understood the need for conversion. The pastor was able to evangelize and emphasize the need of personal conversion after baptism. He had three sons, none of whom were baptized as infants. His reason resonated in the congregation. When they were able to make a decision for Christ, then they could be baptized. There were other GPC pastors who took this stand. The only way they were able to remain pastors was they had the support of the church board and the congregation.

The anti-evangelistic label indicated that the atmosphere regarding evangelism and individual conversion had not changed. Fritz Schwarz realized this years before the GCGA was founded. The church hierarchy was not to blame for the resilience of GPC structures, but rather Christians who tolerated them. According to Klaus Eickhoff, if Christians had loved the lost as Christ loved them, these anti-missionary structures would not be tolerated, but would have been done away with long ago.[29]

In order to change the GPC mentality, there were certain steps that must be taken:

---

29. Eickhoff, *Gemeinde entwickeln*, 303–4.

1. The GPC needed a new theology. This theology must be centered on evangelism, being part and parcel of the universities' programs for educating future pastors.
2. Pastors must be freed from the false security of the current church tax system. Parish churches must have the freedom to fire pastors who are not evangelistic minded.
3. Lay pastors must be allowed to participate in the traditional role of pastor.
4. The local church must be allowed to call its own pastor, and to decide which laity it wants in leadership.
5. The local church must be financially independent, thus refusing the church tax.
6. The local parish church must support the establishment of other churches within its borders to reach those not interested in the traditional church.
7. Church boards must be called on the basis of spiritual gifting. Board members should have the spiritual gift of shepherding.[30]

These steps were not seen as ways to save the *Landeskirche*; rather, they were promoted as an exit out of the traditional institution that warred against evangelism. This was a crucial component of German church growth in Germany. Institutional structures were perceived as ingredients that were actively working against the GCGA. Eickhoff's suggestions mirrored Schwarz's separation of *ekklesia* and institution. Institutional structures must serve the building up of the *ekklesia* if the institution was to have meaning. This was further indication that the situation in the GPC remained unchanged. Eickhoff was repeating the same appeal Schwarz made in the late 1970s.

Reasons for the Decline of the GCGA

There were internal and external realities that throttled the ability of the organization to operate successfully in the harsh religious environment of Germany. It is important to note these factors, some of which were weaknesses, while realizing that they were not the only reason for the

30. Ibid., 307–8.

GCGA's closing. Another significant concern was the GPC's resistance to change throughout the years. The GCGA's leadership felt their time could be better used in individual ministries, therefore they moved on to focus in other areas of service. It is commendable that they avoided the trap of continuing the organization just for the organization's sake.

Internal Weaknesses of the GCGA

It is safe to say that the organization had no intention of "hunkering down" and working within the GPC for the next fifty years just to chip away at the institutional GPC. This was the mentality of the Gnadau Society and the Confessional Movement, and the GCGA wanted no part of that approach. The GCGA adopted the American paradigm of pragmatism that wants results in a matter of years. This grew into one of the GCGA's weaknesses.

Pragmatism

The GCGA faced the question as to whether or not they had emphasized programs (pragmatism) at the expense of dependence on God. Although the organization had strived to change this image and practice, pragmatism remained the chief target of its opponents. However, it was not just the antagonists of the GCGA that highlighted this fault. The members of the organization saw this as one of the primary problems. The issue was not the process of planning to reach a specific goal, but rather the over-emphasis of the planning process as a cure-all for church problems.

The best examples of this were the study trips and the exposure of German pastors to large, growing churches in the United States. Although it was constantly emphasized that German pastors should not try to copy the methods of the Americans, the idea that following certain methodologies would lead to larger German congregations was unavoidable. This led to much disappointment among German pastors, since the North American situation was not compatible with the German parochial system. There was not enough emphasis given to those situations where church growth methods did not function. There were many situations where pastors developed church growth programs and implemented evangelistic models, but failed to produce a growing church.

The GCGA, as well as the CGM, was criticized for ignoring prayer and the work of the Holy Spirit, and replacing them with methodologies. This criticism by the GPC may be answered in the fact that the GCGA combined the adhering to every pragmatic methodology with the working of the Holy Spirit, not leaving it out. The problem was that the GPC used the truth, "the Spirit blows wherever it pleases" (John 3:8) as an excuse not to undertake anything to change the condition of the church. The result of this ongoing debate was the GPC's resentment of the GCGA's pragmatism.

Inconsistent Leadership

Board members did not stay with the GCGA for very long. In part, the reason for this may be explained by personalities constantly seeking new ideas that would excite and invigorate those interested in church renewal. This is illustrated by the constant pursuing of new programs touting formulas for revitalization. Once a new vision ran its course and failed, a new concept needed to be found to re-invigorate those seeking church renewal. The constant coming and going of personnel at the board level resulted in the continual battle to maintain the image of the GCGA.

Pastoring in the GPC came at a high cost. Believing pastors were under immense scrutiny and pressure not to split their church with evangelistic and missionary ministries. It was impossible for most board members to maintain a church, a family, and a presence with the GCGA for an extended period of time. Others felt disconnected from the organization stemming from a lack of regular contact. Still others felt the need to branch out into other ministries and felt they no longer needed the support of the organization. In addition, the majority of American missionaries were gone. The Campaign for Church Growth—one of the original member organizations—disintegrated, leaving a large hole in the GCGA. All of these conditions resulted in inconsistent leadership.

Overemphasis on Numerical Growth

Although the GCGA emphasized that the growth of the church (quantity) was no indication of its spiritual depth (quality), the unmistakable message was that success equaled large numerical growth. However, there was little emphasis on the length of time it may require. Willow

Creek, for example, was over twenty years old when it appeared on the church growth scene in Germany, but this fact was never emphasized. German church growth would have been better served if the amount of time necessary to build a growing church in a given culture had been thoroughly explained. Especially in Germany, where the wheels of progress turn slowly compared to America, realistic models for the situation should have been emphasized. The growth issue was addressed broadly instead of focusing on individual churches.

Charismatic Influence

GCGA ecclesiology became another weakness contributing to the ultimate decline of the movement. Although the understanding of the essence of the church was biblical, the subsequent addition of the charismatic element lent to an uneven and unclear profile of the movement. The GCGA defined the church as a growing organism composed of those who have personally trusted Jesus for forgiveness of sins. With the charismatic emphasis also came the charismatic need of the provocative and contemporary. To keep the movement going, there had to be a constant change of programs ever-promoting the new and exciting, promising the long awaited revival. In 2001 Peter Wagner predicted that there would be a European revival by 2005.[31] The prophecy was false but was never strongly condemned by the GCGA and the strong ties to Wagner made it culpable with other charismatic prophets such as Benny Hinn, John Wimber, and Paul Yonggi Cho.

The Oasis church in Giengen suffered from the charismatic influence soon after its founding. A church leader received a "word of prophecy" that all activities of the church should cease except Sunday worship. Since the church was founded on the seeker service philosophy, this "word of prophecy" suspended all activities related to this end. As a result, the church ceased to exist as a model for seeker-sensitive services within the GPC.

The situation in Giengen revealed the results of dependence on extra-biblical revelation at the expense of previously revealed biblical authority. In this case, an individual claimed to have received direct revelation from God that countered not only this local church's pre-determined purpose, but also the clear biblical mandate to make disciples (Matt 28:

---

31. "Falsche Propheten," 11.

19). The biblical mandate to reach the lost was trumped by the extra-biblical revelation to "cease all activities." Herein lies the extreme danger of the practice of such sign gifts without a biblical foundation, and leads to categorizing such phenomenon as fanaticism. Both the work of the local church and the work of Christ were nullified by one individual's claim to have received a message from God.

This is serious business for the missionary. My work as a missionary involves working with many denominations. I have also seen the danger of the misuse of the charismatic gifts, especially the gift of prophecy. The missionary must be grounded in what the Bible says about the use and misuse of the sign gifts. Make no mistake; no matter the part of the world in which a missionary serves, he or she will be confronted with this dilemma.

The inclusion of Neo-Pentecostalism into the GCGA ecclesiology was not the problem. At issue was the prominent role that the charismatic movement played in German church growth. Pursuant to the GCGA ecclesiology, the church was not the true church unless its saints were practicing the *charisma* as defined by the charismatic movement.

External Loss of a Distinctive Profile

In 1998, Klaus Eickhoff, chairman of the GCGA, delivered an important message to the leadership giving specific direction to the work and explaining the mission that guided them. First, he noted the error in the prevailing notion that the church needs missions. In fact, he argued the opposite: the church exists in order that missions can reach its intended goal. Second, Eickhoff warned the members to be careful about waiting for the next movement to come along before deciding what to do, and reminded them that the reason the organization existed was to bring glory to God. This warning revealed an endemic flaw of the German church growth movement. The GCGA no longer had a precise profile.

The GCGA had evolved into movement characterized not by a particular philosophy, but by the next pragmatic wave originating from the American church. As a result, the charismatic-based ecclesiology had no real foundation from which it could continue to propagate its message. Instead of a clear German-oriented church growth program that had guided its foundations, the organization had evolved into a theological vacuum, waiting for the next infusion of an American movement. This was by far the Achilles heel of the later German church growth movement.

In the beginning it had a clear mandate and methodology: reach Germany with the gospel through the GPC. The gospel was the preeminent fact that brought both salvation and animosity. Church growth programs were a means to an end, with the end being the founding of Bible discussion groups at the local church. This is where people came to faith in Christ. Over the years this goal began to be slowly overshadowed by the need to experience the next new Christian wave originating in North America.

It would have been expedient for the GCGA to return to the propagation of the simple gospel by training Germans to start and lead Bible discussion groups. Training Germans to lead these home-based groups has been the backbone of my evangelistic and church planting ministry. In my estimation it is one of the best ways to reach Germans. Most importantly, leading these informal groups is something that a German Christian easily can do. This should be fundamental missionary practice. Never teach or model anything that only a trained missionary can do. Otherwise, the people will become too dependent on the missionary. This was the major problem with the new trends that came to Germany every few years. They modeled concepts that were not transferable to the life situation of the normal German Christian.

The Future of the GCGA

In October of 2001 the leadership of the GCGA met to discuss where the organization had been and where it was going. The first exercise was reflection on the past twenty years to gain perspective on where they had success and where they had missed the mark. In retrospect, the strength and success of the organization had been countered with weaknesses and failures. The organization had promoted optimism for the church in a climate of pessimism and apathy. They brought new concepts to the German scene and were not afraid to experiment or promote them. A pioneering spirit permeated the organization and they were able to bring like-minded people to the same table. This resulted in church growth thinking for many in the GPC, and the development of concrete plans and goals. The GCGA also built bridges between opposing groups such as evangelicals and charismatics.

However, weak points also accompanied these events. They had failed to be a real catalyst in the GPC and had relied too heavily on "technocratic" thinking and programs. Over the years they had allowed their profile in Germany to weaken and had not strengthened the regional church growth associations. The most critical element that led to the end of the regional associations was the lack of communication by the leadership, which had responsibility for the oversight and management of the regional associations.[32]

The meeting in October led to the conclusion that the individuals within the GCGA leadership had differing points of interest and ministries. For example, there was the house church movement, the city church movement, and the new emphasis on building Christian leadership within the business communities. Church planting maintained its emphasis and interest within the Free Churches. These different aspects brought the GCGA back to where it began. There were once again various ministries vying for acceptance and notoriety in Germany. These different perspectives needed to be brought together to form a united front, which was the original purpose of the GCGA. The decision was made not to disband but to maintain their contact with one another through the medium of the GCGA. It was decided to forge a new vision for the movement with a renewed focus on finding the commonality between all the differing ministries. A team having a clear focus with a new purpose statement was the goal. Re-inventing the GCGA was the next step.

Forging a New GCGA

In 1985, the original GCGA was founded with four organizations: the Prep Course for Church Growth, the Institute for Church Growth, the Association for Church Growth, and the Campaign for Church Growth. After assessment and re-evaluation in 2001, the new GCGA would be the meeting point for five organizations with the same goals, but different methodologies:

1. DAWN: Discipling a Whole Nation promoted church growth concepts with emphasis on church planting.
2. CoachNet: CoachNet provided online consultation for church planters and church leaders.

32. GCGA Archives.

3. Natural Church Development: Developed by Christian Schwarz and still in existence, NCD provides a guide to enable churches to develop eight essential qualities of a healthy church.
4. Kingdom Companies: Initiated by Jörg Knoblauch, this organization promoted companies whose CEOs wished to reach their employees with the gospel.
5. Association for Christian Executives: This association's mission was to provide a platform for church, community, and business leaders to network and learn from one another how to better promote Christian values in their respective spheres of responsibility.[33]

The initiatives of these five groups would be coordinated and networked through the arm of the GCGA. In order to keep the entire country in view, a national strategy would be developed. In addition, the GCGA would take steps to join forces with the Lausanne movement. They would be careful to maintain their own profile and image, but the task was too great for the GCGA alone. Specific steps were planned to clear and clarify the image of the re-tooled association, as well as to contact German representatives of Lausanne. The result would be a new GCGA, with a new image and vision. The entire planning process would culminate in 2003 with another national congress.

The Closure of the GCGA

Wolfgang Simson was to be responsible for promoting the new vision and process forged at the meeting in 2001. It was a severe blow to the GCGA when Simson resigned his position at the GCGA in December of 2002. It was during this same period that the reality of the fall in *Praxis* subscriptions came to the forefront. Serious questions began to be raised concerning how the GCGA could further legitimize its existence.

In May of 2003 the GCGA board met in Berlin. It was during this meeting that serious questions were raised concerning the future of the organization. The key question for each member was his relationship to the GCGA. The consensus was that the association no longer had priority in the various ministry activities of the board members. Other activities were of more interest than keeping the organization together. Klaus Eickhoff also had other interests and was convinced that the GCGA had

33. Ibid.

reached its goal. As a result, on May 30, 2003, eighteen years after its founding, the GCGA board decided to disband, instead of re-inventing the organization.[34]

Organizations have life cycles. They are born, grow and prosper, decline, and eventually outlive their usefulness. Some organizations continue on regardless of their viability and purpose. The GCGA was not in this category. It followed the fate of other church growth organizations such as the North American Society for Church Growth and the European Church Growth Association, both of which no longer exist. The decision to close the GCGA in 2003 did not disappoint or discourage Jörg Knoblauch. He believed that the people involved with the association had grasped the principles and then taken the initiative to start new ministries. The breaking up of the GCGA was not perceived as failure, but as success, with the members continuing on with their own ministries. In their view, the umbrella organization was no longer needed. In 2004 Jörg Knoblauch explained why the GCGA disbanded: "The GCGA has fundamentally fulfilled its mission."[35] He reasoned that church growth was now a common theme in Germany and as a result the organization was no longer needed. Thus, the GCGA had fulfilled its primary mission of introducing the church growth movement to Germany. However, this statement was a pivot from the original intention of the organization, which was to revive the GPC. Revival was to be evident by a decreasing number of those leaving the church. Since this did not happen the organization insinuated that the original goal was the introduction of church growth to Germany. However, the original goal was GPC revival. The *means or methodology* for revival was church growth. The propagation of church growth was not the initial goal.

At the birth of the GCGA there was much enthusiasm and hope about the acceptance of church growth principles in Germany. The church was in trouble. As a result, the founders saw the German church was ready to open up to new ideas, from both inside and outside of Germany. This proved not to be the case. However, the GCGA clearly communicated to the GPC the most important aspect for German church growth. They clarified that real church growth occurs only when men and women come to personal faith in Jesus Christ. Without this firm

---

34. GCGA Archives.
35. "Gemeindeaufbau: Unsere Mission ist erfüllt," 7.

clarity, the German church growth movement could have gone into many various forms and lost any effectiveness.

Discussion Questions

1. Is planting new churches always necessary for contextualizing the gospel? Why or why not?
2. Did the lack of renewal in the GPC point to the failure of the GCGA to contextualize the gospel and church growth? Why or why not?
3. Discuss this statement: "It is easier to plant a new church than to revive an old one."
4. What was the connection between the GCGA's pragmatic approach to church growth and its embracing of the charismatic movement?
5. Why were Free Churches eager to implement new ministry ideas and plant new churches? Why was the GPC reluctant to change its ministry traditions and plant new congregations?
6. Why did Jörg Knoblauch suggest that the GPC was "demonized?" Do you recognize demonic activity in Christian organizations as viable?
7. Discuss Peter Brierley's assessment for the future of institutional or national churches. How does his assessment affect the contextualization process in countries with a national church?

7

Analysis

German Church Growth and Missiology

In the 1960s there was an invasion on the ranch where I grew up in Texas. White birds began to flock to the pastures and meadows where the cows grazed. My grandfather greeted this invasion of birds in the same way he greeted wolves and coyotes or anything strange lurking around his cows. The wolves had long since been eradicated and now for some reason these birds by the hundreds had flocked in, and found a home literally at the feet and even on the backs of the cattle. With a few blasts of his shotgun, these white, long-billed birds were flushed and sent flapping back from wherever they came. However, the next day they were back. My grandfather soon realized that these birds had no intention of leaving.

He learned that these birds were cattle egrets, common all over the South, but just making their way to East Texas. Far from being a pest, these birds were actually good for the cows and indirectly performed a service for the rancher. They flocked to where cattle were because they had learned that cattle meant an easy meal. The birds simply walked among the hooves of the grazing cattle as they scared up grasshoppers and other insects. This made easy pickings for the egrets. They also rode on the backs of the cows picking off ticks and other bloodsuckers. The cattle soon learned to tolerate these hitchhikers.

Ranchers spend thousands of dollars each year battling ticks, chiggers, and other parasites that prey on cattle. Cows are tormented while suffering from skin irritation, blood loss, and weight loss. This costs the rancher when he sells the cattle. The relationship between cow, cattle egret, and rancher is a symbiotic relationship. The cows kick up grasshoppers for the egrets; the egrets pick off annoying ticks that make the cows miserable; and the rancher makes a better profit. They each serve the other for mutual benefit. This is how missions, contextualization, and missiology work together. They form a symbiotic relationship much like the cows, cattle egret, and rancher. Each could survive without the other, but as companions, their lives are made easier.

The Requirements of Missiology

In the last six chapters the history of German Church Growth Association and its mission endeavor has been laid out and scrutinized as a case study in contextualization. This indigenous mission organization wanted to reach Germany with the gospel of Christ in one of the most difficult mission fields; a post-Christian country at the center of a post-Christian continent.

Germans are terribly ashamed of their war-plagued past, but very proud of their contributions to theology and they can boast of beginning the Protestant Reformation and the Protestant missionary movement. The contributions to the church of Martin Luther, Count Zinzindorf, Rudolf Bultmann, Emil Brunner, and Dietrich Bonhoeffer cannot be underestimated. However, this impressive history has also given rise to destructive and heretical theories, such as the historic-critical method, the documentary hypothesis, and redaction criticism. These theories that sought to refute the supernatural elements of the Scriptures contributed to the arrogance and pride of the GPC's refusal to embrace any real renewal efforts.

The point of this case study was to introduce the reader to the process of contextualization with a view to having a deeper understanding and appreciation of missions. This history of contextualization was to reveal the successes and failures of a committed group of Christians, on the front lines and in the trenches, doing missions in a very complicated and sometimes unfriendly environment. Their history has shown that those involved in the GCGA mission were not just writing and talking about reaching Germany, but actually endeavored to do it by putting their lives, reputations, and finances on the line for the sake of Christ. It would be a serious mistake not to study carefully what these German believers did and learn from it. This is where the discipline of missiology begins.

Following each chapter was a series of discussion questions meant to spur further investigation, looking for keys of contextualizing the good news about Jesus. The questions were meant to be an exercise in the discipline of missiology for each chapter. This final chapter deals with developing a missiological mindset and a missiology for the GCGA. This is paramount for those interested in understanding missions practice. The purpose of this case study is to help the reader develop his or her understanding of how missions function and come to a new appreciation of what God is doing in the world through his church.

Thinking missiologically involves a process. First, the ecclesiology of the missionary or mission organization must be clearly defined. This definition leads directly to the second step; contextualization. After enough time has elapsed so that the results of the contextualization model can be determined, missiology reflects on and analyzes the process. The end product should show both positives and negatives of contextualization. Most importantly, missiological findings are necessary, not only for the particular case study, but for missions worldwide.

Step One: The Ecclesiology of the GCGA

Schwarz/Schwarz attempted to construct an ecclesiology in *Theology of Church Growth: An Introduction*. This formed the foundation for the GCGA ecclesiology as well as its subsequent praxis of contextualization. *Theology* defined the true church as the *ekklesia*, constituted from those having personal fellowship with Christ. The *ekklesia* was in contrast to and totally distinct from the institutional church. According to *Theology, ekklesia* was not to withdraw from this institutional framework, but rather to use the institution's resources for the propagation and maintenance of the *ekklesia*.[1]

THE TRUE CHURCH IS A FELLOWSHIP OF BELIEVERS

The foundational element of the GCGA ecclesiology was evangelistic in nature. It affirms that salvation depends on explicit personal faith in Jesus Christ. Church growth occurs when men and women come to a saving knowledge of Jesus Christ and become members of a local church body. This was not only the foundation of the worldwide Church Growth

1. Schwarz and Schwarz, *Theologie des Gemeindeaufbaus*, 44.

Movement but also carried over to the German movement. According to the GCGA, those having a personal faith were members of the *ekklesia*.

The *ekklesia* should reflect the true nature and ideal of the Body of Christ on earth. Inherent in this reflection was belief that faith, fellowship, and service must characterize the church's commitment to continual growth. Faith and fellowship were essential elements that empowered the church for service. Service was defined as missionary or evangelistic outreach to the community.[2] Thus, there was a clear delineation between the *ekklesia* and institution. The institutional church only had meaning insofar as it supported the growth of the *ekklesia*, as it propagated the gospel. The gospel, as enunciated in the New Testament, was an aspect of the church that had pure apostolic origins and must be continued by proclamation. The GCGA understood there was an unbroken line of truth in this regard, beginning with the early church, continuing to the present, and ending only with the Second Coming.[3]

The True Church Experiences Conversion Growth

The second mark of the GCGA ecclesiology was the growing church. It is not enough that a church is a fellowship of believers. According to GCGA ecclesiology the true church must show signs of individuals consistently coming to faith. If this is not occurring then the church is outside the will of God and cannot be called a true church. Thus, this church is not obeying the Word, but acting contrary to it. The church may have Sunday worship, a sermon, and the Lord's Supper, but according to the GCGA it is only an institution.

This characteristic was in direct conflict with the traditional GPC, where growth was measured positively by the number infant baptisms, and negatively by the number of those breaking ties with the church. Although the GCGA did not attack infant baptism, they did reject the notion that it was sufficient for salvation. They maligned the fact that the GPC posed no functioning plan to ensure that the church fulfilled its role to make certain at some point that church members understood their need for an authentic faith and conversion. The GCGA offered methodologies to reach the mass of baptized church members, and it was here

---

2. "Gemeinde wohin?," 15.
3. Eickhoff, *Gemeinde entwickeln*, 69–70.

that they were attacked because they automatically called into question the spiritual condition of the majority of church members.[4]

Although the GCGA was often criticized for its lack of theological reflection or biblical basis for its principles, this was not the case regarding the growth characteristic of the true church. Certainly more could have been done, but the GCGA offered enough biblical evidence for its stance. John 20:21 and Luke 19:10 were the basis for the "sending" where God sent Jesus and, likewise, Jesus sends his followers. The third issue of *Church Growth* dealt directly with Matt 28:19 and the church's role in mission. According to this verse, Jesus sends the church into the entire world to make disciples. This is no option, but rather a clear command from the Lord. The church has no choice but to obey. A local church not involved in carrying out this command has ceased to be a true church.[5]

The Great Commission was the biblical mandate that formed the basis for the GCGA's missiology and was clearly communicated from the beginning of the German church growth movement. The sending was not only emphasized, but the command to make disciples was clearly explained. It is not only the duty of the church to reach lost souls, but to train them to reach others and to be true disciples of Christ. Matthew 28:19 was also the basis for the "growth" in German church growth. Logically, carrying the message to the whole world and making disciples implied a numerically growing movement. Thus, if the church was not making disciples, then the church was not following the Lord's command.

The True Church Exercises Charismatic Gifts

The third characteristic of the true church was a direct result of the growth of the neo-Pentecostal movement. Since this branch of Protestantism was growing at an astounding rate throughout the world, this was proof for the GCGA of its authenticity. Coupled with this was the influence of Peter Wagner, who promoted the charismatic movement in Germany with the blessing of the GCGA. Although the GCGA always had been sympathetic to the movement, it sealed its commitment to charismatic ideology in 1987. At that time it joined forces with the Charismatic Church Renewal Movement and encouraged German evangelicals to cease criticizing those who practiced the sign gifts. The CCRM was actually a small

---

4. Ibid., 91–97.
5. Parrish, "Die Kirche muß evangelisieren," 4.

movement within Germany. Unlike in other countries, the charismatic movement had not made any great gains in the traditional churches. In 1999 there were approximately seventy-five thousand sympathizers of the movement in the GPC, with 3 to 5 percent of the GPC pastors subscribing to the CCRM magazine. In 2005 the number of charismatics from all denominations numbered only around 250,000.[6] Regardless of these relatively small numbers, the GCGA was convinced that since charismatic churches were growing in other countries, this was the missing element in Germany.

GCGA Ecclesiological Summary

GCGA ecclesiology defined: The church is a fellowship of converted and committed believers, gathered into a continually growing fellowship, characterized by the free and complete manifestation of the entire range of the spiritual gifts as defined by the charismatic movement.

Step Two: The Model for Contextualization

Contextualization has to be defined within the current understandings of the term before analyzing the contextualization efforts of the GCGA. The definition of contextualization—and the specifics of how it is employed in missions—has become diluted and confusing over time. In the same way that the traditional meanings of missions, missiology, and evangelism have become convoluted, contextualization has evolved into several different meanings depending upon the user's worldview and understanding of missions.

According to Stephen B. Bevans, there are currently six models or definitions of contextualization:

1. The Translation Model: This model sees the gospel as unchanging. The chief trait of this model is that culture must be understood and respected, because it is used as the chief vehicle for transmitting/contextualizing the ageless gospel to individuals. Culture can have both good and bad qualities. The job of the missionary is to discover those cultural attributes conducive for communicating the gospel.

---

6. Böckel, *Gemeindeaufbau im Kontext*, 298.

2. The Anthropological Model: This model promotes the basic goodness of human beings. The gospel is not unchanging, because it has been translated and polluted by the interests and politics of Western Europe. If the gospel is introduced from the outside, it must concede that the Divine is already manifested within the culture itself. As a result, the true gospel must be discovered in the fabric of the day-to-day life of the target culture. The job of the missionary is to discover the innate presence of God in each person and help the person reach personal fulfillment.

3. The Praxis Model: Liberation theology is most often used to describe this model. The gospel is not so much a message as it is a call for radical social reform. The praxis model demands that missionary activity address the social needs of the oppressed and marginalized. The gospel is not merely to change unfair societal structures, but to eliminate and replace them with those deemed more equitable for the masses. The job of the missionary is to find the sources of social injustice and work toward their change or eradication.

4. The Synthetic Model: This is the "middle of the road" model of contextualization. It strives to synthesize the three models already mentioned. The synthetic model acknowledges that there is the central gospel message as prescribed in the Bible and handed down through tradition. However, it reserves the right to interpret the gospel and tradition in light of the needs of the responding culture. That is, contextualization is achieved when the target culture interprets and responds to the gospel in its own way and then develops its own theological traditions. Thus, with this model culture is on equal footing with the gospel. The job of the missionary is to ensure that the target culture has the last word in how it responds to the gospel.

5. The Transcendental Model: The starting point of this model is not culture, but your own religious experience and your ability to express it. The focus is not on the gospel as found in Scripture, but on your own (transcendent) experience with God. As you learn to authentically express your own experience with others, they in turn discover and express their own encounter with God. This mutual exchange results in both you and your subject growing in

your understanding of the Divine. As this process is repeated and the circle of contacts widens, contextualization automatically takes place within a particular culture. The job of the missionary is to know his or her own belief system and experience with God, and be able to express it to another.

6. The Countercultural Model: This model is not anti-cultural, but takes seriously the fact that all cultures have sinful aspects that need correction. If the gospel truly takes root (becomes contextualized) in a culture, then it will challenge those areas that need transforming. Just as the contextualized gospel confronts the sinfulness of individuals, it must also expose the sinfulness of society and call into judgment those engrained cultural sins that need confronting. The job of the missionary is to work towards the conversion of both culture and individuals.[7]

Contextualization in the Old Testament

Scriptures in both the Old and New Testaments testify to the missionary activities of God. God is a missionary God and the Bible is simply the story of God seeking to reconcile all nations to himself by sending people he has chosen to speak for him. Abraham and Sarah were first chosen to represent him and bring his message of salvation to the world. Contextualization always involves God's *sending* and a missionary *going* in response to God's command. This sending always involves contextualizing his message so that it can be understood and accepted by people to whom the missionary is sent.

God's contextualization process is laid out plainly in the Old Testament. Abraham and Sarah were sent from their home in Mesopotamia to the foreign culture in Canaan to expose the nations to the one true God. They journeyed throughout the land of Canaan building altars and preaching (Gen 12–13). The question is, why Canaan? Why not send them to Anatolia (Turkey), or east to India? Why not simply stay where they were? The sending of Abraham and Sarah to Canaan was strategic in order to contextualize God's message to all the polytheistic peoples of the Ancient Near East. Canaan was picked as the center for which God's message for the whole world would radiate.

---

7. Bevans, *Models of Contextual Theology*, 37–137.

A Case Study in Contextualization

At that time, Canaan was the crossroads of world trade and commerce. All the caravans traveling to Africa from Anatolia and Mesopotamia journeyed through Canaan to avoid the Arabian Desert. This is why this area is referred to as the Fertile Crescent. The mouth of the crescent is empty desert, so commerce traveled the well-worn route through Canaan. In this way all the people of the known world could hear of God as traders picked up the message in Canaan and carried it back home. In this way the world would eventually be "infected" with Abraham's message. What was the message that God wanted to contextualize? What was the message that Abraham preached? In Genesis 14:22, Abraham states his message in a nutshell: "I have raised my hand to the Lord, God Most High, Creator of heaven and earth. . . ." The good news was that there is only one God, the Creator of everything. This message was in vast contrast to the hundreds of national, regional, and personal deities worshipped by those populating the Middle East.

The contextualization process continued with the giving of the law at Mt. Sinai. Many scholars and theologians have claimed that the Law of Moses was simply copied from the laws of the surrounding nations, since most of the laws given to Moses were already in force in the kingdoms of the Ancient Near East. However, there was one drastic difference; the basis of the Law of Moses was the worship of only one God, not a pantheon of gods and goddesses. This meant that proselytes, who were required to follow the Mosaic Law, would find many things in common with what they were accustomed to in their home culture. However, their allegiance would now be to one God.

Contextualization in the New Testament

Jesus was God's most profound act of contextualizing his message to the world. As John writes: "The Word became flesh and lived for a while among us" (1:14). God contextualized himself in the person of Jesus Christ. The question is similar to the question concerning the call of Abraham and Sarah to go to Canaan and preach God's message. The question here is: why was Jesus born at this particular time? The answer given is solidified by the fact that Jesus was born and raised in Canaan. This narrow strip of land between the Mediterranean and the Syrian-Arabian Desert continued to be the route of commerce during the time of Jesus and the Roman occupation. So, we know why this particular piece of real estate was chosen for the birth of the son of God. However, why did God choose this particular time in world history for the coming of the Messiah and the contextualization of his message? Paul wrote to the Galatians: "But when the set time had fully come, God sent his Son . . ." (Gal 4:4). Therefore, the timing of the coming of the son of God was important.

There are three primary contextual reasons that God chose this time to send his son. First was the speed of travel and communication. Rome built fifty thousand miles of primary thoroughfares and two hundred thousand miles of secondary roads throughout its empire to connect its provinces. These highways made travel much easier than at any other time in history. Rome wanted excellent roads to speed the travel of its armies to anywhere in the empire. The faster the army arrived at a certain location, the quicker any insurrection could be dealt with. Many of these roads are still visible today and some continue to be used.

Second was the safety of travel. With the highways came the protection by Roman soldiers, causing thieves to think twice about attacking travelers along these roads. This provided merchants and travelers with confidence that both goods and people could safely move about the empire. It should also be noted that there were many Christian soldiers among the Roman troops who carried the gospel with them throughout the Roman Empire. However, as the Apostle Paul makes clear there still was danger when traveling about the empire: "I have been constantly on the move. I have been in danger from rivers, in danger from bandits . . ." (2 Cor 11:26).

Third, for the first time in history the world was unified, albeit under the heel of Rome. As long as they submitted to Rome, most people could carry on their lives in relative peace. At no other time could the news about the son of God spread so quickly and safely through the known world. Jesus was born at the perfect time in human history for contextualizing God's message. Paul gave proof of the success of contextualization in writing to the church in Rome only thirty years after the Resurrection: "First, I thank my God through Jesus Christ for all of you, because your faith is being reported all over the world" (Rom 1:8).

After the Resurrection his disciples attempted to carry out his command to make disciples of all nations. At first, and most naturally, they spoke to their own culture, the Jews. As the gospel broke into the Gentile cultures the message about Jesus had to be contextualized, so those outside of Judaism could understand who Jesus is. Phrases such as, Messiah, Son of David, or Lamb of God, spoke directly to the messianic expectations of the Jews, and recalled all the redemptive glory of the Passover and blood sacrifices. However, these words had little or no meaning to the Hellenistic Gentile world.

In Acts 11:20 Luke records a change in how Jesus is described, depending upon the audience. Instead of Jesus, the Lamb of God, Jesus the Christ, or Jesus the Messiah, he is now, the Lord Jesus. The followers of Jesus realized that the pagan Greeks would not understand the earlier titles given to Jesus. On the other hand, the Greek word *kyrios* or lord, which was the title given to pagan deities, would communicate what they were saying about Jesus. The Apostle Paul followed the lead of his earlier counterparts who preached to Jews that Jesus was the Messiah (Acts 9:22; 17:3; 18:5). However, he also proclaimed the Lord Jesus to Gentiles (Acts 13:48–49; 16:31; 19:5; 20:21).[8]

Given the controversies surrounding the inclusions of Gentiles into the church, which precipitated the Jerusalem Council, one could speculate that this change in wording to describe Jesus in order to accommodate Gentiles was not without controversy. Timothy Tennent lists three alternatives that faced the Jewish Christians at that time:

1. They could conclude that the gospel message was only meant for the Jewish race. All others were excluded because of national heritage outside the Jewish faith.

2. The Gentiles would have to be taught the intricacies of the Jewish faith and acclimate themselves to the belief, language, and culture of the Jews. This was the Judaizer solution. Only then could they appropriate the forgiveness in Christ that God offered.

3. The messengers of the gospel must enter the world of the Gentiles and communicate the good news about Jesus using the framework of the culture, society, and language of the Gentile world.[9]

The Jerusalem Council adopted option three (Acts 15). The decision of the Council can be summed up by the Lord's brother, James: "It is my judgment, therefore, that we should not make it difficult for the Gentiles who are turning to God" (Acts 15:19). This policy should also guide missionaries today. They should not make it difficult for people to come

---

8. Tennent, *Invitation to World Mission*, 326–29.
9. Ibid.

to Christ, by making them adapt to the Christianity of the missionary's home culture or the missionary's preconceived notions of the Christian faith.

The most profound and extreme example of contextualizing the message about Jesus is found in Acts 17:16–34, when Paul preached in Athens at the Areopagus. His audience was Greek, not Jewish. It is quite astounding that Paul never quoted from the Old Testament, but rather from the texts of two well-know Greek poets, Epimenides and Aratus (17:28). Both of these poets were committed to the worship of the Greek Pantheon, and the verses that Paul quotes are in praise of Zeus! However, Paul uses the verses to show that the true God will one day call all people to judgment.[10]

Contextualization by the GCGA

Option three, above, was the basic premise by the GCGA for contextualizing church growth and the gospel; it should be easy for a German to understand the gospel and accept Jesus Christ as Savior. This is why the GCGA chose to work within the GPC instead of with the Free Churches. Although the attitude toward Free Churches in Germany has changed, when church growth was introduced to the country, most Germans put Free Churches in the same category as Jehovah's Witnesses and Mormons. As the German culture became more open to Free Churches, the GCGA began to work more closely with them. Although the GPC had serious problems often making it difficult for the gospel to be presented, the GCGA used the *Volkskirche* as the conduit to contextualize church growth. This philosophy of contextualization would fall under the Translation Model, since the GCGA's ecclesiology calls for a strict gospel interpretation and the use of the cultural icon of the GPC as the tool for its proliferation.

This automatically excludes the Anthropological Model, because the narrow understanding of the gospel precludes the notion that humans are basically good. The Praxis Model is also rejected since the GCGA defined "the poor and marginalized" as those church members without Christ. The association did not outright reject the idea of social reform. However, the first step in any social reform was first reforming the human heart through a confrontation with the gospel. Also, the GCGA

10. Ibid.

interpreted "service" for the Christian as reaching others with the good news about Jesus.

The GCGA meets the Synthetic Model half way. Like this model, the GCGA held to the traditional and biblical gospel. However, the Association rejected the idea that the German culture be allowed to interpret the gospel. This is perhaps one of the most interesting aspects of the entire contextualization process regarding the different models. The proposed models are based on the premise that the original gospel has been so polluted by Western European colonialism, politics, and theology, that it is no longer viable for those in the rest of the world. This especially holds true for the people in Africa, Asia, and in Central and South America. This is the philosophy from which liberation theology, feminist theology, and black theology springs. Since the text of the New Testament has been interpreted through the Western European lens, it must be re-interpreted through the cultures of indigenous peoples. The GCGA rejected this philosophy and believed that the Bible should be used to interpret culture and not vice versa.

The Transcendental Model is also rejected. The basis for all religious experience is not based on one's experience or inner feelings, but on the Scriptures. Shared feelings are encouraged as long as they are in line with a clear understanding of the nature of the gospel and what it requires. The Counterultural Model would be the second choice for its resemblance to the GCGA's contextual philosophy. The only difference may be a semantic one, where the Counterculture Model lays heavy emphasis on the role of the church in unmasking and actively seeking to change culture when it is evil. The prerequisite is that the church must first be practicing Christian ethics itself, before taking on the ills of society. This is something the GCGA certainly agreed with and promoted. Its emphasis was on the bringing the GPC in line with the New Testament. The Association saw the greatest barrier preventing the church from living out a New Testament faith was its refusal to acknowledge that infant baptism did not equal Christianity. As a result, it was impossible for the church to reflect the Christian lifestyle since the majority of members had not made decisions for Christ.

GCGA Contextualization Summary

The contextual model of the GCGA reflected the characteristics of both the Translational and Countercultural Models. The Translational Model is more weighted because of having to constantly clarify the gospel and the necessity of evangelism. Nevertheless, the GCGA understood the church as the necessary element to bring about cultural change.

Step Three: Missiology

Both the ecclesiology and the contextualization of the GCGA have been defined. In addition, enough time has elapsed in the missions' process to begin focusing on missiology. As with other missions' terms, it is difficult to find a clear definition of missiology and determine exactly how it functions in the real world of missions practice. Most of the definitions ring of academia and give little information on how missiology can practically support missions. The *Evangelical Dictionary of World Mission* defines missiology as the conscious, intentional, ongoing reflection on the doing of mission.[11] Johannes Verkuyl explains that missiology is the study of the salvation activities of the Father, Son, and Holy Spirit throughout the world geared toward bringing the Kingdom of God into existence.[12] These are concise definitions but say little about the practicality of the science for the missionary or the sending agency.

The *Dictionary of Mission* struggles to explain what missiology is and leaves the non-missiologist scratching his or her head:

> The development of the churches and theologies in the Third World, the increasing differentiation between being a Christian and being a church member, the experience of a common faith despite the diversity of Christian traditions, the movement toward the foundation of religious truth outside Christianity through dialogue . . . all these issues present missiology with a variety of tasks for which this branch of theology does not seem to be prepared . . . Nevertheless, some cultural manifestations have not yet been widely considered as objects of missiology: for example, the broad field of art. But in spite of all the very

---

11. Neely, "Missiology," 633.
12. Verkuyl, *Contemporary Missiology*, 5.

relevant individual and special studies, it becomes obvious that a comprehensive concept of missiology is lacking.[13]

Thankfully, Tennent in his *Invitation to World Missions* not only clearly defined missiology, but also explained its role and importance to missions. He described the first instance of missiology being practiced:

> The Jerusalem Council was called in the wake of a missions movement in order to engage in vital, reflective missiology. They did not gather to discuss theology in some abstract way removed from the life of the church. It was fundamentally a discussion over the terms through which the Gentiles would enter into the church and enjoy fellowship with believers who were Jews. Missiology happens *after* the missionary advance: mission happens at "sunrise," missiology at "sunset."[14]

Tennent goes on to explain that missions and missiology must form a symbiotic relationship where one supports and stimulates the other. If there is no dynamic mission taking place, then missiology has no purpose. Missions and missiology must stimulate each other. Missions is activistic; missiology is more reflective. Missiology is an attempt to answer questions and engage the issues that missions have raised on the front lines of the Great Commission. Without missions there would be no questions or issues for the work of the missiologist. On the other hand, if the missiologist is unable to give an adequate assessment of missions, or cannot raise new questions and give adequate answers, then the missionary movement can become ineffective.[15]

The Practice of Missiology

In 1992, I planted a church in Neuhofen, Germany, under the auspices of the German Baptists. The most critical theological issue concerning the new congregation was adult baptism. German Baptists require believer's baptism for church membership, whereas the GPC and the Catholic Church practice infant baptism. Since all new converts would have been baptized as infants, how would the congregation deal with those who objected to being baptized a "second" time? In Germany, undergoing a

---

13. Findeis, "Missiology," 299–303.
14. Tennent, *Invitation to World Missions*, 496–97.
15. Ibid.

second baptism is tantamount to blasphemy and can have negative effects on an individual's immediate family and local community. For example, how do you handle a case where the wife wants to be baptized, but the husband objects? Should the wife then be denied membership in the church? What about those who serve the church faithfully, but hold their infant baptism to be sufficient? Are they to be denied fellowship? These were issues our young church faced. The option of finding another church in the area was not possible. Although Neuhofen had eight thousand people, there were only two churches before the church plant, a Catholic church and a GPC.

Baptism was not only a theological matter, but was also grounded in history. As stated in chapter 4, the Baptists had suffered terribly for their stand on adult baptism and were not about to compromise their belief to accommodate infant baptism. However, there was also the reality that new converts needed love, patience, and fellowship. The new church worked out a plan whereby those who held to their infant baptism could become members. Although another category of membership had to be worked out, it solved the turmoil. There was also a critical decision regarding the teaching of believers' baptism. The doctrine would continue to be taught, but not in a dogmatic way. The church leadership wanted to stay true to the biblical teaching on baptism, but also allow people time to wrestle with the Scripture themselves and make a decision based on conscience and not on outside pressure or group persuasion. Over time many of those holding adamantly to their infant baptism have decided to undergo believers' baptism.

The church leaders at Neuhofen in no way saw their decisions as a practice in missiology. They acted in a way that they believed reflected biblical teachings. They did not call the local missiologist for advice on how to extricate themselves from this dilemma. It is left to missionaries and missiologists to frame their actions into a missiological concept. The missiologist looks at the church plant at Neuhofen and asks, "What does this situation have to offer for church planting in other fields? How do the decisions made by this small group of believers in Germany affect the worldwide missions/church planting effort?"

The true practice of missiology must not stop at the local church but has ramifications for the wider practice of missions. As with the case of the Jerusalem Council and also in Neuhofen, missiological decisions must have implications for the whole church and her missions practice.

The decision at Neuhofen suggests that when it comes to doctrinal issues, allowing new Christians adequate time to study the Scriptures and make decisions for themselves—guided by the Spirit—may be the best method of teaching doctrine. This in no way is a new missiological stance. According to Roland Allen (1868–1947), an Anglican missionary, this practice was introduced by the Apostle Paul. In Allen's view, the Apostle "urged" the churches to follow correct doctrine rather than "threatening" them if they did not do so (1 Cor 1:10; 1 Thess 4:1–2). Contrary to the mission practice of his day and in many cases the present day, Allen believed that requiring new converts to first learn and practice church doctrine before being allowed into the church membership was contrary to Scripture. He believed this practice held these new converts back and made them dependent on the missionary and the European church.[16]

The Process of Missiology and the GCGA

In order to apply missiology to the GCGA we must first understand how it contextualized church growth and the gospel. The first step in this process is to recognize how the association developed and defined its ecclesiology. The historical case study explained why the GCGA chose to establish a new movement instead of joining other organizations already established in Germany. It was the presupposition of this study that the movement's ecclesiology directly influenced how the gospel was contextualized for the German culture. Ecclesiology defines the church, clarifies its purpose, and guides its mission.[17] Therefore, this study is not about ecclesiology, but how ecclesiology influenced contextualization. Now, the process of missiological thinking can begin. This means we must evaluate the GCGA and how it contextualized church growth and subsequently the gospel. In order to do this, the most significant contextualization decisions must be evaluated. One of the most critical areas of contextualization is how the mission organization, in this case the GCGA, responded to mission organizations already present in Germany.

---

16. Allen, *Missionary Methods*, 81–107.

17. Van Engen, *The Growth of the True Church*, 11; Margull, *Hope in Action*, 68–72.

The GCGA and Contemporary Mission Organizations

The charismatic-based ecclesiology of the GCGA had the most profound effect on its relationship to the three major contemporary renewal groups. It solidified the unification with the Charismatic Church Renewal Movement, but ended any possibility of working with the Gnadau Society or the Confessional Movement. Although there was a basic theological conviction from which to work—the necessity of personal conversion for those baptized as infants—both theological and historical barriers remained. Any hope of alliance was damaged when the GCGA formed such a close relationship with the Charismatic Church Renewal Movement. This, along with the ensuing combined GCGA-CCRM congresses emphasizing the necessity of charismatic gifts and church planting, sealed the fate of any coalition with either the Gnadau Society or the Confessional Movement.

Representatives of the GCGA also had reservations concerning cooperation with either of these two groups. It was important for the new movement to maintain its own profile. There was the opinion that those in the Pietistic camp had been active for many years and had not yet brought about any real change. Subordination to one or both of these organizations would have stymied any attempt to incorporate a pragmatic theology required by church growth epistemology. It was the opinion of those in the GCGA that they were viewed as a foreign threat, rather than partners for renewal. The provocative style of journalism characteristic of *Church Growth* only accentuated the notion that church growth was a foreign element. There was also the prevalent belief that both groups were simply too theologically narrow for the work of the GCGA, and would have consistently balked at their pragmatic based methods.

The cooperative barriers between the GCGA, the Confessional Movement, and the Gnadau Society can be formulated under three categories:

1. Church Growth Pragmatism: The idea that somehow the growth of the church was mandatory and could be analyzed, formulated, and planned was not accepted by the Gnadau Society and the Confessional Movement. Church growth theory required that growth must be premeditated. The idea that the church, a spiritual entity, could somehow through managerial technique be manipulated was rejected by both groups.

2. Charismatic Church Growth: The charismatic manifestations were seen by the GCGA as the way to combat the constant criticism of pragmatism. The CCRM's emphasis on the role of the Holy Spirit would counter this criticism. This addition, however, served only to alienate both groups from the GCGA and the CCRM.

3. Archaic Ecclesiological Paradigms: The GCGA understood that the paradigms of the both groups had been ineffective in penetrating the entire country. Their time had passed and a new, fresh approach was necessary. Cooperation with the Confessional Movement and the Gnadau Society would only hinder the work of the GCGA.

Barriers to cooperation with the two prestigious organizations are best illustrated by GCGA's promotion of the evangelical-charismatic debate. The organization called for a theological truce between the two groups for the sake of evangelism. However, as a result of its identification with charismatic theology, the appeals fell short because, according to opponents, there was no neutrality. The reason the GCGA sided with the charismatics was not based on a careful study of the New Testament. It was based solely on the interpretation of charismatic phenomenon: charismatic churches were growing at an astounding rate throughout the world. The conclusion was it must be from God. With this brand of theological interpretation, the GCGA, with its new and controversial American church growth program, found no welcome mat from the Gnadau Society or the Confessional Movement.

The Communication of the Gospel Message

The most important aspect of German church growth was how GCGA associates communicated the gospel and how they trained GPC Christians to reach their fellow church members with the good news about Jesus. The process was simple, but the actual implementation proved challenging.

The evangelistic program was based on starting Bible discussion groups. The first step in the process was personal relationships. Believers who had personal contact with family, acquaintances, and friends who had never made a commitment to Jesus were asked to pray for these people for several weeks. The second step was to invite these people to attend a four to six weeklong Bible discussion group. The group met once a week in the home of the leader of the discussion group. Since it lasted only a few weeks, more people were willing to make this time commitment. During this period certain discussion topics would be introduced to encourage the participants to ask questions. Since the questions were always the same, the leader was prepared with the appropriate Bible text, which answered the question. The questions were:

1. If God loves the world, why is there so much evil?
2. What about other religions; is there really only one way to God?
3. What about those who have never heard about Jesus?

This was the most important element of the discussion group. Instead of the leader answering the questions, the Bible text that answered the question was pointed out. The person who asked the question then read the text out loud and discussion followed. By the end of the series of evenings, all the participants understood the requirements of the gospel message and were encouraged to make a decision for Christ.

This method of evangelism fit perfectly with the needs of the German culture. Germans love discussing interesting topics with a small informal group of acquaintances in a home setting. They do not like dogmatism or authoritarianism. This cultural characteristic permeates all corners of German society and reflects lessons learned from the Hitler era. The Bible discussion group allowed the Scriptures, instead of a leader, to speak. The participants had to argue with the Bible, not with the person leading the discussion. This method also spoke to the spiritual condition of those attending who rarely, if ever, came into contact with the Bible. It allowed the Holy Spirit to speak directly to the individuals through the Scriptures.

The Broad Vision of the GCGA

The mission of the GCGA was defined early. To gain the entire scope of the vision, the goals of the predecessor association that began in 1980 must be considered because they carried over to the daughter association. The basic goal of Church Growth: Association for Church Development in Germany was "to discover ways to bring men and women, who have no personal relationship with Jesus Christ, into fellowship with him and into active service for him. This goal will be reached through regional seminars, local seminars and church consultations, magazines, helpful materials, and study trips."[18] This was to lead to an awakening in the GPC and this goal was carried over to the GCGA in 1985. The organization was to promote evangelistic church growth through the training of pastors and the laity. The avenues to accomplish this were study trips, seminars, literature, and congresses.

Additional GCGA goals were not mentioned in the by-laws but were conceived at a session for long-term planning in 1986. These long-term goals, formulated under the rubric of "visions for German church growth," failed to be realized:

1. The GCGA ministry should result in hundreds of churches in German-speaking Europe being evangelistically active and characterized by powerful ministries, such as healing.
2. The GCGA should encourage the planting of new GPC churches where they do not yet exist. Ordained pastors would lead these churches and integrate them into the GPC.
3. The regional associations would be so numerous that pastors and lay leaders would not have to drive over fifty kilometers to attend a meeting.
4. No one should have to drive over twenty kilometers to attend a growing church.
5. A church growth educational center needs to be established; for example, the Fuller School of World Mission: Germany.
6. Thousands of prayer cells should be started to pray for renewal.[19]

The vision of the GCGA was to bring new life into the GPC, employing church growth principles. Devised methodologies were to implement classic church growth principles. Methods can be considered rungs on the ladder leading to the fulfillment of the mission. The success of some of the methods is easy to determine. For example, there were five fundamental methods employed to promote the church growth message which were easy to assess. These were study trips, literature, seminars, regional associations, and congresses.

---

18. GCGA Archives.
19. Ibid.

Analysis of the Vision Statement

The analysis of the vision statement is divided into two parts. With the exception of "congresses," the first section deals with elements already employed at the time the GCGA was established. These were the "bread and butter" of the organization. The second part analyzes those six long-term goals the GCGA intended to reach. Analyzing these six goals or visions is important because it allows us to clearly see what a spiritually revived Germany would look like according to the GCGA. The initial five elements were:

1. Study Trips: These trips not only brought German pastors and American church growth leaders together, but they also opened the eyes of German church leaders to new possibilities for their churches.

2. Literature: After the publishing of *Theology of Church Growth* and *Dynamic Church*, church growth literature grew at an astounding rate in Germany. This was evidence that church growth theory was recognized on a countrywide scale. In 1979 there were only two books available on church growth and these were translations of American works. By 1990 there were over thirty writings dealing with some aspect of church growth from German authors. In 2003 there were over ninety. Included in this was the church growth magazine, *Church Growth*. The significance of the magazine lay in the fact that it was the voice of the German church growth movement. The development of the magazine was a reflection of the development of the GCGA.

3. Seminars: Hundreds of church growth seminars were held all over Germany throughout the entire history of the GCGA. The seminars sought to contextualize church growth not only for the German culture, but more importantly, for the local church. Coupled with the church analysis, it encouraged church growth concepts to be formulated for the local community.

4. Regional Associations: These also reflected the lifecycle of the GCGA. At the beginning they were few in number but grew until there were regional associations in West Germany, East Germany, Switzerland, and Austria. However, the leadership of the GCGA

5. Congresses: National congresses were considered by the GCGA to be very successful. During the congress years, 1991 to 1995, thousands of church leaders and laity from all German denominations attended these assemblies. These congresses also spawned further congresses dealing with church growth issues. The best example of this was the German Baptist-led Willow Creek Germany, formed in 1996 as a direct result of the congress in 1993.

The additional six goals or visions formulated in 1986 had little success. In fact, the only goal reached was the encouraging of the planting of new churches where they did not exist. And it was argued that it had no success within the GPC—for which the vision was intended. There is no evidence that any of the other goals were met. This does not mean that there were not hundreds of churches practicing evangelism and spiritual gifts as a result of the GCGA's influence. However, given the specific criterion of "powerful" and "including healing," it is impossible to determine the actual fulfillment of the methodology since there is no empirical data available regarding this goal. There were also people praying for renewal in Germany. There was no evidence, however, of thousands of prayer cells begun by the efforts of the GCGA. The establishment of a church growth educational center never occurred in a form similar to the School of World Mission at Fuller.

Analysis of the goals formulated in the by-laws, and those in 1986, is complicated by the fact that the GCGA deviated from a fundamental premise of the worldwide Church Growth Movement: the necessity of empirical statistics. In light of the fact that their ecclesiology demanded empirical conversion growth, the GCGA at no point embarked on an analytical study to determine if this indeed occurred. Such an empirical study would not have been difficult. For example, Gerhard Maier analyzed the results of the study trips in 1992. Since the GCGA supported the ministry of the regional church growth associations that were scattered throughout Germany, it would have been no great task to determine the number of conversions in those churches represented by the pastors attending these regional associations. The organization kept detailed records of the number of subscriptions to *Church Growth* and the number of those who attended the congresses. Therefore, a more detailed analysis of the results of the congresses also could have been attained. A thorough study of only those churches within the reach of the regional associations would have given at least basic data to determine if church growth actually was taking place, and provided concrete information concerning the ramifications of the congresses.

However, on the most crucial aspect of their work there are no records. This is even more peculiar, since the organization consistently used empirical church growth studies from other countries and the growth of the church in Acts to bolster church growth theory. Win Arn spoke directly to this problem:

> Research has always been a critical part of the church growth movement. Dr. McGavran used to say that clear facts about the situation help "remove the fog" and let us see why things are happening or not happening in the spread of the gospel. This is still a wise recommendation. Research can help answer the question, "why?" As churches began to seek to apply the principles of church growth in their situation . . . as some churches grow and add new believers and church members . . . and as churches sought to apply principles of church growth and did not experience the success they had hoped, the question should be asked, "why?" Diligent research would have been helpful at that time, to better understand the results of church growth endeavors.[20]

A study on the number of true conversions in those churches that were directly influenced by the GCGA would have been attainable and invaluable to determine the real impact of church growth in Germany. Another case study that would have greatly helped the church growth cause, as well as greatly enhancing future missionary efforts, would have been a thorough analysis of those churches in East Germany that employed church growth principles. However, there were no efforts to collect this data. Thus, the "fog," mentioned by Arn, remains for the most crucial aspect of German church growth.

The Renewal of the GPC

Underlying every goal, methodology, and program was the ultimate objective of reviving the German Protestant Church. The GCGA had

20. Arn, personal communication with author, 8 September 2004.

always encouraged the Free Churches, and it was the Free Churches that responded early to the church growth message. However, the heart of the German church growth movement was renewal of the GPC. It was the dream of all those dedicated to the GCGA to somehow breathe new life into the *Landeskirche*. This was evident by the fact that every board member was a member of the GPC, and that every chairman was a GPC pastor. The American organization, Campaign for Church Growth (*Aktion Gemeindeaufbau*), was a good example of the intensity of this purpose. The Americans were required to attend and be involved in the *Volkskirche* where they lived. Free Church participation was strongly discouraged for fear that it would send the wrong message to the *Landeskirche* leadership.

It is noteworthy that the specific wording regarding GPC renewal is absent from the founding documents. Only when the history of the organization is scrutinized is the intent to renew the GPC obvious. There is particular reasoning behind the absence of precise wording in the founding documents that would directly point to the renewal motive. Hans Wilhelm explained that if the *renewal* motive had been in print and made public at the initiation of the GCGA, it would have had a negative impact on the ability of the GCGA to build contacts within the GPC. The idea that a new organization was forming to bring life to the dead church of Germany would have been perceived as arrogant and presumptuous.[21]

The GCGA's vision was simple to understand. The conversion of the unbelieving GPC church members and pastors was the goal of renewal. Renewal of the GPC meant a change in philosophy and structure. Renewal would be evident when the majority of churches in Germany became involved in the true conversion of baptized church members. This would be obvious by a decline in the number of those leaving the church. It would be precipitated by a large number of GPC pastors responding to the message of church growth in their respective parishes and subsequently encouraging lay participation in local evangelism—specifically the starting of Bible discussion groups.

The initial issues of *Dynamic Church* and *Church Growth* made it clear that the goal was to reverse the trend of those turning their backs on the church. This is also obvious from the response of those who read the magazines, as well as those who attended the Evangelism Explosion training by Bernd Schlottoff. Both pastors and laity wanted to fill the local church with new converts won from the plethora of the baptized

---

21. Wilhelm, interview by author, 8 February 2008.

unconverted who no longer attended church. This was the source of the fascination with church growth that made it so appealing, not only to the founders of the German movement, but to the many pastors and laity in Germany. However, it became clear that church renewal was not going to happen, at least not in the near future. It was obvious, especially after the Nuremberg Congress in 1991 and the Erlangen Congress in 1992 that the need for the change necessary for renewing the structure of the GPC would remain. It also was evident from the continuing decline of the GPC, and the persistent hostility toward church growth, that the renewal would remain elusive.

However, the GCGA was able to penetrate the GPC with the church growth philosophy. The church was exposed to new ideas from abroad, and this was positive for the *Volkskirche*. Many of the ideas and church forms were rejected outright while others were accepted and contextualized. The GCGA was instrumental in opening up Germany to the outside world with respect to new ideas influencing the dynamics of the church. It contributed to the globalization of Germany regarding global Christianity and forced the GPC to debate church growth theory.

Did the GCGA Fulfill Its Mission?

Knoblauch described the period between 1997 and 2003 as the phase of penetration for church growth in Germany. According to him, it was during these years that the church growth message finally penetrated the German Christian culture, and as a result the GCGA no longer was needed. Evidence of this was that major Christian magazines, like *ideaSpektrum* and *Relax*, regularly reported on growing churches, church growth principles, and practices. As a result of the GCGA pioneering church growth in Germany, there are now many ministries offering help in the area of church growth.

The accuracy of Knoblauch's assessment is validated by the fact that in 1979 when *Dynamic Church* was published, there were four organizations that identified themselves with the ideals and principles of the church growth magazine. In 2003 there were twenty groups that identified themselves as belonging to the church growth movement.[22] This does not mean that the GCGA established these groups; it proves that

---

22. "Adressen von Gruppen", 3; "Gemeindeaufbau praktisch," 34.

the number of organizations identifying themselves with German church growth grew as a direct result of the efforts of the GCGA.

These facts were confirmation to the GCGA leadership that their efforts to introduce church growth to Germany had been a success and were another indicator that their mission had been fulfilled. This led Klaus Eickhoff in the final months of the organization to conclude: "The goal of the GCGA has been reached."[23] Jörg Knoblauch followed with the similar statement in 2004: "For the most part, we have fulfilled our mission."[24]

Missiological Conclusion: Impact of the GCGA on Missions Worldwide

The last step in the missiological process is the implication for world missions. What can be learned from the GCGA? How can the work of this organization be used to encourage or warn the worldwide missionary effort?

Define Ecclesiology Early

This is one lesson that the GCGA learned well. From the beginning the definition of the church is paramount. There can be no deviations or questions. The GCGA defined the church as a membership of converted believers. They meet in a fellowship determined to serve their community by espousing the gospel presented in the New Testament. Feeding the poor, helping addicts, and fighting for the lives of the unborn are important, but nothing is more important than the gospel message. This is crucial in today's climate concerning missions. There continues to be serious debate between those holding to an ecclesiology of the gospel and an ecclesiology of the needy.[25] On one side are those who believe that providing for the needy should be the foremost duty of the church while the other side believes that the gospel message must be paramount. Both of these issues are important. It is the duty of the local church, and not mission agencies, to decide where this balance lies.

---

23. GCGA Archives.
24. "Gemeindeaufbau: Unsere Mission ist erfüllt," 7.
25. Stearns, *The Hole in Our Gospel*, 15–24.

Choose the Method of Contextualization Carefully

The GCGA rejected becoming involved with the Confessional Movement and the Gnadau Society. As a "Monday morning quarterback," this might have been unwise. Both organizations held to the biblical gospel message, but rejected the charismatic persuasion. Perhaps it would have been better to work with one of these two groups. However, the GCGA felt that the Gnadau Society and the Confessional Movement had failed in their renewal efforts and both groups would have rejected the methods of the Church Growth Movement.

The choice of working through the GPC was made based on German historical and cultural needs. This was no mistake. For years American missionaries in Germany had evangelized and planted churches without considering the needs of the German culture. Free Churches were even rejected by American missionaries as capable church planting partners. As a result, the majority of the few churches planted by these missionaries never grew. It still would be unwise for missionaries to work in Germany without spending at least two years serving in the GPC in an area with a believing pastor. This would help the missionary to better understand the authentic German spiritual climate rather than going directly to serve in a German Free Church. If a missionary first began working in a Free Church, he would likely have a highly skewed understanding of the spiritual climate in Germany.

Germany has changed. God has blessed Germany with a church planting movement and with many evangelistically minded churches and organizations. It would be foolish for any foreign missionary to go to Germany as a "pioneer" missionary—that is, to start a work from "scratch." Any missionary wanting to serve in Germany could and should work under the auspices of a German organization.

Missionaries in other cultures must choose the avenue of contextualizing the gospel carefully. This is the missiological lesson learned from the GCGA. However, like the GCGA, they must be willing to pivot and change course if necessary. This means that at yearly intervals a reevaluation is necessary. The key is to find that conduit which is widely culturally acceptable and poses the least barriers for people to come to Christ. Although the avenue may not be totally theologically compatible, it still may be the best route for the entire culture or nation at hand.

In 1979 my wife, two-year-old son, and I went to Poland to work with an American missionary organization serving there. We served under the umbrella of the Catholic Church. This was a radical move at the time and was criticized by many evangelicals. However, this American mission had reached many priests with the gospel, and they were converted. There was a truly evangelistic movement within the Polish Catholic Church. The summer we were there was the same summer Pope John Paul II visited Poland and we saw many Poles put their faith in Christ. On many things we were not theological partners, however, we did agree on the gospel and the need for personal conversion, even for priests. Although controversial, this American mission organization realized that the key to reaching the Polish nation was through the vehicle of the Catholic Church.

Summary

Regarding the renewal of the GPC on a nationwide basis, the GCGA found itself in company with the Confessional Movement and the Gnadau Society. There was no renewal as indicated by the continual withdrawal of thousands from the church. If on the other hand success were measured by the introduction of the CGM to Germany, then the mission was accomplished. This was indicated by the nationwide interest in church growth as a direct result of the GCGA. It was the predominant judgment of those in the GCGA that this indeed was the primary mission.

Since it was impossible to force church growth theory and practice, the most reasonable mission was to introduce it and make it practically available to the GPC. If it was rejected then it was obviously outside the power of the organization to implement it: "We simply made an offer. We presented the church a way to grow. Whoever took the offer took it. Whoever refused it, refused it. That was our attitude."[26] Knoblauch reflected the views of others in the organization; the original idea that the mission of the GCGA was intended to renew the GPC was minimized since renewal failed to materialize on a nationwide basis. It is true that the mission included introducing the CGM to Germany as the *means* of renewal. However, the original goal was a countrywide spiritual revival of the GPC and not just the introduction of church growth. This nationwide focus is seen by the introduction of *Church Growth*, the calculated founding of regional associations, and the national congresses.

26. J. Knoblauch, interview by author, 31 August 2005.

The intention of the GCGA was not just to introduce church growth at the parish level, but also to invoke change in the entire structure of the GPC; the most pivotal point being the orientation of the GPC pastor. This was the key. If the traditional role of the pastor did not change, then church growth theory was impossible to thoroughly implement. Eickhoff concluded: "The traditional orientation of the church around the pastor leads to a barrier that cannot be overcome. As a result, it is impossible to have an evangelizing church."[27] It was at this crucial juncture that the GCGA was not able to make national headway, and subsequently unable to evoke any widespread revival. The function of the *Landeskirche* pastor was so thoroughly entrenched by German convention, and further bolstered by rationalistic theology at the universities, that any thorough revival was rendered impossible.

From the early formation of the GCGA, the *Volkskirche* was always the primary focus. This ideology was also apparent on the American side. Both Roger Bosch and Hans Wilhelm saw the *Landeskirche* as the most culturally relevant avenue for evangelizing Germany. It is important, however, to note that it was the Free Churches who initially and consistently adopted and employed church growth principles. In this respect the GCGA failed to heed one of the most basic elements of the Church Growth Movement: to concentrate on those evoking the strongest response to the gospel.[28]

The GCGA was an important element in the historical development of the German church, for both the GPC and the Free Churches. Although the GCGA was unable to bring revival to the GPC, it was instrumental in opening up Germany to the CGM. Before the founding of the GCGA there was little information concerning the worldwide CGM. Introduction of the Church Growth Movement was positive for Germany, but the majority in the GPC did not welcome this development. However, it forced the GPC to consider the meaning of church growth and to debate the proposal that the true church should experience growth instead of decline. It is on this basis that the GCGA made its most important contribution to church growth and the spread of the gospel in Germany.

The insistence that infant baptism did not guarantee church membership or justification was paramount. Coupled with this was the

---

27. Eickhoff, personal communication with author, 19 February 2006.
28. McGavran, "Church Growth Strategy Continued," 179–85.

constant call for personal conversion. This was especially important during the ensuing years of the movement as church growth theory became known and many misleading definitions of church growth emerged. The movement never altered from this most important element.

The GCGA also contributed to the aid of Christians in one of the darkest periods of Christian history. The East German government was ruthless in its goal to rid the country of Christianity. The regime killed hundreds of people trying to escape and jailed hundreds of dissidents. In the 1980s and 1990s the GCGA supported and encouraged local pastors and their families through both spiritual and financial support. For conservative East German GPC pastors, the GCGA was their link to the West.

Although the GCGA had much success, it was never able to breach the ingrained historical-critical theology, and the religious pluralism of the *Volkskirche*. The universities held a monopoly on theological teaching as well as pastoral training. The GCGA leadership recognized that they had to integrate church growth if it was going to result in church renewal. Church growth had to be accepted as a legitimate method to bring new life to the church. This only happened in isolated cases where the pastor had made a personal decision for Christ.

The GCGA remained a foreign movement in Germany and is an excellent example of an indigenous mission organization facing hundreds of years of liberal theological tradition. This does not mean that the organization failed to get its message across. Church growth was successfully communicated in Germany. However, even though the organization was tolerated, the GCGA was never accepted as a legitimate part of the GPC structure. The reasons for the tension between church growth and the GPC were symptoms of the fundamental problem faced by the GCGA in contextualizing church growth. Its ecclesiology required a truly converted, growing, and charismatic church. These three requirements were confronted with sacramentalism, institutionalism, and liberalism at every turn. In addition, the renewal organizations already at work were extensive. This meant there was no room for a new organization touting a new and exotic ecclesiology from the United States.[29]

The introduction of church growth into Germany offered an unprecedented opportunity for the *Volkskirche* to change course. The GCGA presented the GPC with a biblical model for revival offered in a culturally

29. Schlottoff, interview by author, 14 September 2005.

acceptable form. However, church growth was rejected because of its steadfast refusal to change the requirements of the gospel. The church growth format required baptized church members to have a conversion experience. This requirement was unacceptable to the majority of the GPC leadership since it automatically divided baptized church members into converted and non-converted. The gospel also raised the question of God's ultimate judgment of those without Christ and the GPC leaders rejected God's judgment of sinners. Both John and Paul spoke about religious leaders who reject the gospel message:

> Yet at the same time many even among the leaders believed in him. But because of the Pharisees they would not confess their faith for fear they would be put out of the synagogue; for they loved praise from men more than praise from God. (John 12:42–43)

The Holy Spirit spoke the truth to your forefathers when he said through Isaiah the prophet:

> Go to this people and say, "You will be ever hearing but never understanding; you will be ever seeing but never perceiving." For this people's heart has become calloused; they hardly hear with their ears, and they have closed their eyes. Otherwise they might see with their eyes, hear with their ears, understand with their hearts and turn and I would heal them. (Acts 28:25b–27)

These passages represent a dire situation for the future of the GPC. All is not lost, however, as Germany remains a mission field and must not be written off. There are still opportunities to make disciples in Germany through the *Volkskirche*. Although the majority of the GPC continues to propagate an anti-gospel message resulting from liberal theology, there are organizations within the GPC that preach the gospel. The Gnadau Society and the Confessional Movement, as well as some parish churches, continue to hold to biblical evangelism. Missionaries desiring to reach Germans for Christ should consider the possibilities of working alongside these organizations. God certainly has not forgotten the thousands who call the *Volkskirche* home.

Discussion Questions

1. How did the author determine the "sunrise" and "sunset" of the GCGA? How can the missiologist determine the "sunrise" and the "sunset" of a mission endeavor when the parameters are not clear?

2. How does ecclesiology directly effect contextualization?

3. Which of Bevans' contextualization models can you most identify with? Which models do you find unacceptable?

4. Discuss the similarities between the "Anthropological Model" and the "The Praxis Model."

5. Discuss the symbiotic relationship between mission and missiology and its importance to world missions.

6. How can the work of the GCGA be used to either encourage or warn worldwide missions? Discuss the author's views on pages 210–11.

7. German Christians have practiced their faith in a post-Christian culture for over four decades. Since the United States is now entering a post-Christian cultural phase, should American Christians look to Germany for ideas on how to reach those without Christ? If so, how?

Appendix

For Further Reading

Allen, Roland. *Missionary Methods: St. Paul's or Ours?* Eerdmans: Grand Rapids, MI, reprint 2002. (An Anglican missionary questions his church's missionary methods.)

Bosch, David J. *Witness to the World: The Christian Mission in Theological Perspective.* Wipf & Stock: Eugene, OR, 2006. (A concise history of the theological development of missions.)

Chadwick, Owen. *The Secularization of the European Mind in the 19th Century.* Cambridge University Press: Cambridge, UK, 1975. (Describes the political and philosophical principles giving rise to secularism in Europe.)

Gilliland, Dean S. *Pauline Theology & Mission Practice.* Wipf & Stock: Eugene, OR, 1998. (A comprehensive study of Paul's mission philosophy.)

McLeod, Hugh and Werner Ustorf, eds. *The Decline of Christendom in Western Europe, 1750–2000.* Cambridge University Press: Cambridge, UK, 2004. (Explores the reasons for the decline of Christianity in Europe.)

Murray, Stuart. *Post-Christendom.* Paternoster Press: Waynesboro, GA, 2004. (Murray defines and contrasts Christendom and post-Christendom.)

Ott, Craig and Stephen J. Strauss, eds. *Encountering Theology of Mission: Biblical Foundations, Historical Developments, and Contemporary Issues.* Baker Academic: Grand Rapids, MI, 2010. (A comprehensive and contemporary treatment of the theological basis for missions.)

Appendix

Tennent, Timothy C. *Invitation to World Missions: A Trinitarian Missiology for the Twenty-first Century*. Kregel: Grand Rapids, MI, 2010. (Focuses on the theology of missions, contextualization, and the importance of missiological thinking.)

Glossary

Charismatic Renewal Movement. The German charismatic renewal movement is a branch of Pentecostalism. Charismatics are often referred to as Neo-Pentecostals. Adherents believe the so-called sign gifts of the New Testament continue to be valid. Speaking in tongues, healing, speaking words of knowledge, and prophesying are notable characteristics of the charismatic movement.

Church Day (*Kirchentag*). Church Day is a nationwide church conference organized by the German Protestant Church convening every two years. All organizations having ties to the GPC are invited to attend and use Church Day to propagate their positions. This brings a wide spectrum of groups with religious, political, environmental, and social agendas together.

church growth. Church growth is the discipline that investigates the nature, expansion, planting, multiplication, and function of the church as they relate to the fulfilling of the Great Commission. This involves integrating biblical principles with the insights of contemporary social and behavioral sciences. The defining focus of the church growth movement is evangelism.

culture. Culture refers to the common ideas, feelings, and values that guide community and personal behavior, that organize and regulate what people think about God, the world, and humanity.

documentary hypothesis. This theory denies that Moses wrote the first five books of the Bible. Julius Wellhausen (1844–1918), a German theologian, was its chief proponent. The hypothesis is often called JEPD referring to the sources or editors (Jahwist, Elohist, Priestly, Deuteronomist) who wrote down the oral tradition that formed the Pentateuch.

Glossary

evangelism. Evangelism is communicating the gospel in such a way that individuals understand it and make a decision either to accept it or to reject it. Thus, the task of evangelism is completed only when people have reached this point of decision.

evangelist. An evangelist is a Christian who communicates the gospel within his or her own culture. This definition allows for a distinction between evangelist and missionary.

German Free Churches. Baptist, Methodist, Pentecostal, Evangelical Free, as well as other denominations, do not pay a church income tax. Therefore they are called Free Churches, since they are "free" from paying the church tax.

German Protestant Church/*Volkskirche*/*Landeskirche*. The German Protestant Church (*Evanglische Kirche in Deutschland-EKD*) is made up of twenty Lutheran, Reformed, and United regional churches. Church members pay a yearly church income tax to maintain their memberships.

historical-critical method. The German, Johann Semler (1725–1791), is the father of the historical-critical method of interpreting the Bible. Its premise is that the Bible is not inspired by God, and should be interpreted as any other book. The historical-critical system revolted against the supernatural nature of Scripture.

indigenous. The term stems from biology and indicates plants and animals native to an area. In missions it refers to a group of people who reflect the characteristics of their home culture.

missionary. A missionary communicates the gospel across cultural, geographical, and linguistic borders.

mission. Mission is the Great Commission given by Jesus to his disciples to "go and make disciples of all nations . . . " (Mat 28:19). The church exists to fulfill the Great Commission.

missions. Missions are all activities involved in fulfilling the Great Commission in spite of cultural, geographical, and linguistic barriers.

missiology. Missiology is the study of missions. It includes the theories of missions, the study and teaching of missions, as well as the research, writing, and publication of works on missions. Missiology should ultimately impact the spread of the gospel worldwide.

Pietism. Philipp Jakob Spener (1635–1705) is considered the founder of German Pietism. The goal of Pietism was/is to finish the Reformation, and its inception ranks second only to the Reformation in its impact on Protestantism. It reacted against dead German orthodoxy and called for personal spiritual renewal and the true conversion of individuals. The importance of Pietism is that it resulted in the sending of the first Protestant missionaries.

religious pluralism. Religious pluralism is concerned with comparing the claims of Christianity with those of other religions. It rejects the exclusive claim, which dictates that Jesus Christ is the only way for salvation. Pluralism sees other religions as being just as valid as Christianity in pointing the way to God.

synod. A synod is an assembly of elected church officials that meets at specific times to discuss and make church policy.

Important Events in the Development of the GCGA

1967	Bernd Schlottoff invites the Janz Team to his church
1970	Bernd Schlottoff visits Billy Graham Crusade in Dortmund
1974	Jörg Knoblauch visits growing churches in America
1975	First USA study trip for German pastors
1976	First EE seminar in Germany
1979	Institute for Church Growth founded by Roger Bosch; *Dynamic Church* debuts at Church Day; Fritz Schwarz's *The Manageable Church* vol. 1 published
1980	First Prep Course for Church Growth (EE); *Dynamic Church* becomes *Church Growth*; Church Growth: Association for Church Development in Germany founded
1984	*Theology of Church Growth: An Introduction* published; Charismatic Church Renewal Movement founded
1985	German Church Growth Association founded
1986	Christian Schwarz becomes editor of *Church Growth*
1988	Church growth associations founded in Austria, Switzerland, and East Germany; Wolfram Kopfermann leaves the GPC to start a Free Church
1990	Klaus Eickhoff replaces Bernd Schlottoff as chairman of GCGA
1991	The Congress for Church Renewal in Nuremberg; proclamation of the Nuremberg Manifest calling for Christian unity for the sake of the gospel
1992	The Congress for Church Planting in Erlangen; church planting within the GPC established as a viable but radical option for church renewal; *Church Growth* becomes *Church Growth Plus*
1993	The Vision for Post-Christian Germany Congress in Nuremberg; "seeker services" come to Germany by way of Bill Hybels; the Oasis Church claims to be first GPC church plant in Germany
1995	*Church Growth Plus* becomes *Praxis*; charismatic ecclesiology fully integrated into the GCGA

Important Events in the Development of the GCGA

1996	The first conferences specifically for church planting in the GPC held in Germany and Switzerland
1997	*Praxis* subscriptions plummet; Christopf Schalk replaces Christian Schwarz as editor; Christian Schwarz founds Natural Church Development
1999	GPC Synod in Leipzig calls for renewed emphasis for mission and evangelism, vindicating the message of the GCGA
2000	Research reveals 1,500 Free Churches planted in the past decade—a clear sign that a Free Church planting movement was in progress; regional church growth associations decline
2002	Oliver Schippers becomes business manager of the GCGA in order to stem the losses of *Praxis*
2003	The German Church Growth Association disbands; *Praxis* becomes an insert in *Relax*

Bibliography

"1.500 'neue' evangelische Gemeinden." *idea-Spektrum* 36 (1999) 6.
"4.500 Teilnehmer bei Kongress mit John Wimber." *Gemeindewachstum* 31 (1987) 14–15.
"7.000 Willow Fans in Oberhausen." *Praxis* 73 (1998) 7.
"1980 Missionarisches Jahr und was nun? Rückblick und Ausblick." *Christaktuell*, Februar (1981) 15.
Adler, Gerhard. "Wird die Jesus-Bewegung von Amerika auch nach Europa überspringen?" *Herold: Sonderausgabe*, Februar 1972 2–12.
"Adressen von Gruppen, die sich mit Gemeindewachstum beschäftigen." *Dynamische Gemeinde* 1 (1979) 3.
"AGGA betont Zusammenarbeit." *Gemeindewachstum* 24 (1986) 14.
"Ako Haarbeck: Einladung mit Vorbehalten." *Gemeindewachstum* 34 (1988) 14.
Allen, Roland. *Missionary Methods: St. Paul's or Ours?* Grand Rapids: Eerdmans, 1962.
"Arbeitskreise." *Gemeindewachstum* 18 (1984) 12.
"Arbeitskreise." *Gemeindewachstum* 35 (1988) 25–26.
Balfour, Michael. *West Germany*. New York: Frederick A. Praeger, 1968.
Barth, Karl. "Zwei Vorträge." *Theologische Existenz Heute* 3 (1946) 13–14.
Bäumer, Rudolf. "Die 'Gemeindetage unter dem Wort.'" In *Weg und Zeugnis: Dokumente und Texte der Bekenntnisgemeinschaften zur kirchlichen Zeitgeschichte 1980-1995*, edited by Walter Künneth et al. Bad Liebenzell: Liebenzeller Mission, 1980.
———. "Die Bekenntnisbewegung 'Kein anderes Evangelium' (Gal. 1, 6)." In *Weg und Zeugnis: Dokumente und Texte der Bekenntnisgemeinschaften zur kirchlichen Zeitgeschichte 1980-1995*, edited by Walter Künneth et al. Bad Liebenzell: Liebenzeller Mission, 1998.
———. "Vom ersten zum zweiten Kirchenkampf." In *Weg und Zeugnis: Dokumente und Texte der Bekenntnisgemeinschaften zur kirchlichen Zeitgeschichte*, edited by Walter Künneth et al. Bad Liebenzell: Verlag der Liebenzeller Mission, 1980.
Bekehrung bedeutet Freiheit. Wanne-Eikel Tagesblatt, BGEA microfilm, CN360-Reel 21 (1970).
Bevans, Stephen B. *Models of Contextual Theology*. Mary Knoll, NY: Orbis Books, 2004.
Beyreuther, Erich. *Kirche in Bewegung*. Vol. 7, Studien für Evangelisation und Volksmission. Berlin: Christlicher Zeitschriftverlag, 1968.
"Bilanz einer bisher einmaligen Großevangelisation." *idea-Spektrum* 60 (1981) 1–3.
Birke, Adolf M. *Nation ohne Haus: Deutschland 1945–1961, Die Deutschen und Ihre Nation*. Berlin: Siedler Verlag, 1989.
Böckel, Holger. "Gemeinde für andere: ein US amerikanisches Gemeindemodell und seine Diskussion in Deutschland." *Theologische Beiträge* 29 (1998) 102–3, 298, 456–58.

Bibliography

———. *Gemeindeaufbau im Kontext charismatischer Erneuerung*. Leipzig: Evangelische Verlagsanstalt, 1999.

Bosch, Roger. "Geistesgaben und das Wachstum der Gemeinde." *Gemeindewachstum* 3 (1980) 2.

———. "Gemeindewachstum was ist das?" *Dynamische Gemeinde* 1 (1979) 2.

———. "Research Project Church Growth: Germany 1978." Pasadena: School of World Mission, Fuller Theological Seminary, 1978.

———. "Sekten wachsen schneller." *Dynamische Gemeinde* 1 (1979) 3.

Bramsted, Ernest K. *Germany, the Modern Nations in Historical Perspective*. Englewood Cliffs, New Jersey: Prentice-Hall, 1972.

Brierley, Peter. "Warum institutionelle Kirchen schrumpfen." *Praxis* 79 (1999) 6.

Brüning, Gerhard, and Ingeborg Brüning. "Gemeindeaufbau Methoden contra Heiliger Geist?" Evangeliums-Rundfunk Sendung, 1988.

———. *Die christliche Lehre von der Kirche, vom Glauben und von der Vollendung*. Zürich und Stuttgart: Zwingli-Verlag, 1964.

———. *Die christliche Lehre von Gott*. Zürich: Zwingli-Verlag, 1960.

Büchner, Carlo. "Kein anderes Evangelium." In *Weg und Zeugnis: Bekennende Gemeinschaften im gegenwärtigen Kirchenkampf 1965–1980*, edited by Rudolf Bäumer, et al. Bad Liebenzell: Liebenzeller Mission, 1998.

Bühne, Wolfgang. *Die "Propheten" kommen!* Bielefeld: Christliche Literatur Verbreitung, 1994.

———. *Dritte Welle: Gesunder Aufbruch?* Bielefeld: Christliche Literatur Verbreitung, 1991.

Burkhalter, William Nolan. "A Comparative Analysis of the Missiologies of Roland Allen and Donald A. McGavran." PhD diss., Southern Baptist Theological Seminary, 1984.

Bush, George W. *Decision Points*. Random House: New York, 2010.

"C. Peter Wagner kommt." *Gemeindewachstum* 46 (1991) 10.

Chadwick, Owen. *The Christian Church in the Cold War*. Allen Lake: Penguin, 1992.

Clay, Lucius D. *Decision in Germany*. New York: Double Day, 1950.

Cox, Harvey. *The Secular City*. New York: The Macmillan Company, 1966.

Das "Maschinengewehr Gottes" knattert in Westberlin. Berlin: National-Zeitung, BGEA microfilm CN360-Reels 8, 42,43 (1954).

"Der Bruch." *idea-Dokumentation* 28 (1988) 1–7.

Der Showmaster Gottes. Zürich: Die Weltwoche, BGEA mircrofilm, CN360-Reel 21 (1970).

"Der Willow Creek Leitungskongress in Oberhausen: Geistlischer Tiefgang für Leiter." *Praxis* 92 (2003) 5.

"Deutschland braucht 87.000 lebendige Gemeinden." *Gemeindewachstum* 44 (1991) 7–8, 26–27.

"Die Brüder sind im Kommen." *idea-Spektrum* 13 (1999) 12.

"Die vier grössten Hindernisse." *Gemeindewachstum* 35 (1988) 16–17.

Dr. Billy Graham kommt nach Berlin. Berlin: Die Neue Zeit, BGEA microfilm, CN360-Reels 8,42,43 (1954).

Drechsel, Joachim. *Das Gemeindeverständnis der deutschen Gemeinschaftsbewegung*. Gießen/Basel: Brunnen Verlag, 1984.

Drummond, Andrew L. *German Protestantism since Luther*. London: The Epworth Press, 1951.

"Eickhoff: Nur noch die Kirchensteuer hält die Volkskirche am Leben." *idea-Dokumentation* 100 (1992) 4.

Eickhoff, Klaus. "AGGA Vorsitzender Klaus Eickhoff zum Gemeinde Kongreß." *Gemeindewachstum* 45 (1991) 13.

———. *Gemeinde entwickeln für die Volkskirche der Zukunft.* Göttingen: Vandenhoeck & Ruprecht, 1992.

———. "Heute: Bei wem liegt der Schwarze Peter?" *Gemeindewachstum* 52 (1993) 10.

"EKD: Missionarisch orientierte Christen fühlen sich an den Rand gedrängt." *idea-Dokumentation* 100 (1992) 4.

Elliot, John B. *Hitler and Germany.* New York: McGraw-Hill, 1968.

Evangelisationsfernsehen. Salzburg: Salzburger Volksblatt, BGEA microfilm, CN360-Reel 21 (1969).

"Falsche Propheten: Keine Erweckung in Deutschland." *idea-Spektrum* 15 (2008) 11.

Findeis, Hans-Jürgen. "Missiology." In *Dictionary of Mission.* American Society of Missiology Series 24, edited by Karl Müller et al., 299–303. Maryknoll, NY: Orbis Books, 1998.

Fleisch, Paul. *Die moderne Gemeinschaftsbewegung in Deutschland.* 3rd ed. Vol. 1. Leipzig: H. G. Wallmann, 1912.

Fremde-Heimat-Kirche: Die dritte EKD-Erhebung über Kirchenmitgliedschaft. Edited by Klaus Engelhardt and Hermann von Loewenich. Gütersloh: Gütersloher Verlaghaus, 1997.

Fremde-Heimat-Kirche: Ansichten ihrer Mitglieder. Edited by Studien und Plannungsgruppe der EKD. Hanover, Germany: Studien und Plannungsgruppe der EKD, 1993.

GCGA Archives (German Church Growth Association). Located at Drilbox Georg Knoblauch, Hähnlestr. 24, DE-80537 Giengen an der Brenz, Baden-Württemberg, Germany.

Geldbach, E., and P. Schneider. "Graham, William (Billy) Franklin / Billy Graham Association (BGEA)." In *Evangelisches Lexikon für Theologie und Gemeinde,* edited by Helmut Burkhardt and Uwe Swarat. Wuppertal und Zürich: R. Brockhaus Verlag, 1993.

"Gemeinde Kongress 1995." *Praxis* 61 (1995) 11, 26.

"Gemeinde Kongreß Erlangen: Kontroverses Echo in den Medien." *Gemeindewachstum* 51 (1992) 11.

"Gemeinde wohin? Ein Seminar zum Thema: 'Gemeindeaufbau.'" Gießen: Institut für Gemeindeaufbau, 1986.

"Gemeinde wohin? Ein Seminar zum Thema: 'Gemeindeaufbau' Seminar Notes." Seminar notes, available from author.

"Gemeindeaufbau praktisch: Diese Gruppen können Ihnen weiterhelfen." *Praxis* 93 (2003) 34.

"Gemeindeaufbau: Unsere Mission ist erfüllt." *idea-Spektrum* 7 (2004) 7.

"Gemeindekongreß 1991: 5.000 Christen für Versöhnung." *Gemeindewachstum* 48 (1992) 26.

"Gemeindepflanzung in Deutschland ist tot!" *Praxis* 84 (2001) 7–8.

"Geschichte." *Die Evangelische Allianz in Deutschland* (April 2004). No pages. Online: http://www.ead.de/die-allianz/geschichte/geschichte.html.

Gollwitzer, Helmut. *The Demands of Freedom: Papers by a Christian in West Germany.* Translated by Robert W. Fenn. New York: Harper & Row, 1965.

Greschat, Martin. *Die evangelische Christenheit Und die deutsche Geschichte nach 1945: Weichenstellungen in der Nachkriegszeit*. Stuttgart: Kohlhammer, 2002.

Grosser, Alfred. *The Federal Republic of Germany*. Translated by Nelson Aldrich. New York: Frederick A. Praeger, 1964.

Haarbeck, Ako. "Theologie des Gemeindeaufbaus: Eine kritische Auseinandersetzung mit Fritz und Christian A. Schwarz." In *Diskussion zur "Theologie des Gemeindeaufbaus,"* edited by Rudolf Weth. Neukirchen-Vluyn: Schriftenmissions-Verlag, 1986.

„Hans-Martin Wilhelm: Wir Europäer müssen ganz eigene Wege gehen." *Gemeindewachstum* 29 (1987) 26–27.

Hartrich, Edwin. *The Fourth and Richest Reich: How the Germans Conquered the Postwar World*. New York: Macmillan, 1980.

Heimbucher, Kurt. "Ein missionarischer Unruheherd." *Mitteilungen* 7, 8 (1986).

Hempelmann, Heinzpeter. "Wie kann heute evangelisiert werden? Wie ist heute Gemeindegründung möglich?" *idea-Dokumentation* 1 (1994) 3.

———. "Gemeinde gründen in der Volkskirche." *Materialdienst der EZW* 1 (1993) 23–24.

———. "Vision für ein entkirchlichtes Deutschland: Nürnberger Gemeindekongreß 1993." *Materialdienst der EZW* 12 (1993) 361.

Herbst, Michael. *Missionarischer Gemeindeaufbau in der Volkskirche*. 4th ed. Stuttgart: Calwer Verlag, 1996.

Hollenweger, Walter J. *Enthusiastisches Christentum*. Wuppertal, Zürich: Theologischer Verlag Rolf Brockhaus, Zwingli Verlag, 1969.

Holthaus, Stephan. "Die Berliner Erklärung von 1909." *idea-Dokumentation* 14 (1999) 11.

———. "Die Kassler Bewegung und ihre Folgen." *idea-Dokumentation* 14 (1999) 8–10.

———. "Einleitung." *idea-Dokumentation: 90 Jahre Berliner Erklärung* 14 (1999) 5–6.

———. *Heil-Heilung-Heiligung*. Giessen: Brunnen, 2005.

Hopkins, Bob. *Church Planting: 1. Models for Mission in the Church of England*. 2nd ed. Bramcote, Nottingham: Grove Books, 1992.

"Hubbard's Church Unconstitutional: Germany Prepares to Ban Scientology." *Spiegel Online International* (December 2007). No pages. Online: http://www.spiegel.de/international/germany/hubbard-s-church-unconstitutional-germany-prepares-to-ban-scientology-a-522052.html.

"Im Gespräch: Klaus Engelhardt, Was tun Sie konkret für den Gemeindeaufbau, Herr Landesbischof?" *Gemeindewachstum Plus* 53 (1993) 11–12.

"Im Ton vergriffen oder ins Schwarze getroffen?" *Gemeindewachstum* 34 (1988) 5–6.

Kasdorf, Hans. *Gemeindewachstum als missionarisches Ziel*. Bad Liebenzell: Liebenzeller Mission, 1976.

Kennedy, James D. "The Genesis, Development, and Expansion of Evangelism Explosion International, 1960–1976." PhD diss., New York University, 1978.

———. *Handbuch für Gemeindewachstum*. Edited by Bernd Schlottoff. 2nd ed. Bad Liebenzell: Liebenzeller Mission, 1981.

"Klaus Eickhoff." *Gemeindewachstum* 29 (1987) 23.

Knepper, Claudia. "Konfessionslosigkeit." Evangelische Zentralstelle für Weltanschauungsfragen. No pages. Online: http://www.ekd.de/ezw/Publikationen_2613.php.

Bibliography

Knoblauch, Jörg. "Nicht Eskimos einen Kühlschrank verkaufen wollen." *idea-Dokumentation* 43 (1986) 2.

———. "Wie Stabil ist die Kirche wirklich? oder Die Kirche kommt an 'Management' nicht vorbei." In *Gemeindeaufbau Provokativ*, edited by Bernd Schlottoff. Neukirchen-Vluyn: Schriftenmissions-Verlag, 1989.

———. "Wovon reden wir überhaupt?" In *Gemeinde gründen in der Volkskirche—Modelle der Hoffnung*, edited by Jörg Knoblauch, et. al. Moers: Brendow, 1992.

———, and Roger Bosch. "Gemeindeaufbau welche Erfahrungen gibt es?" Evangeliums-Rundfunk Sendung, 1988.

Knöller, Horst. *10 Kennzeichen der wachsenden Gemeinde*. Heidenheim: Konferenzsekretär für Evangelisation in der methodistischen Gemeinde, 1979.

Kopfermann, Wolfram. *Abschied von einer Illusion*. Mainz-Kastel: Praxis-Verlag, 1990.

Krause, Burghard. "Verheißungsorienterter Gemeindeaufbau in der Volkskirche." In *Gemeindeaufbau Provokativ*, edited by Bernd Schlottoff. Neukirchen-Vluyn: Schriftenmissions-Verlag, 1989.

Kuen, Alfred. *I Will Build My Church*. Translated by Ruby Lindbald. Chicago: Moody Press, 1971.

Lange, Dieter. "Zur Geschichte der Gnadauer Gemeinschaftsbewegung." In *Dem Auftragverpflichtet*, edited by Kurt Heimbucher. Giessen: Brunnen, 1988.

Latourette, Kenneth Scott. *A History of Christianity: Reformation to the Present*. Vol. 2. San Francisco: HarperCollins, 1975.

"Lausanne 1974." Lausanne, Switzerland: BGEA, CN 53, box 1, folder 2, 1974.

Letter from S. Wasserzug to Frank C. Phillips. BGEA microfilm, CN285-Reel 33 (1948).

Letter from Torrey M. Johnson to Harold J. Ockenga. BGEA microfilm, CN285-Reel B33 (1947).

Lindberg, Carter. *The European Reformations*. Oxford: Blackwell Publishers, Reprint 2001.

———. "Programme-Strategien-Visionen: Eine Analyse neuerer Gemeindeaufbaukonzepte." *Pastoraltheologie* 75 (1986) 214–16.

Machel, Edgar. "Brauchen wir neue Gemeinden?" *Praxis* 89 (2002) 6.

Maier, Gerhard. *Gemeindeaufbau als Gemeindewachstum: Eine praktisch-theologische Untersuchung zur Geschichte, Theologie und Praxis der "church growth" Bewegung*. Vol. 22, Erlanger Monographien aus Mission und Ökumene. Erlangen: Ev.-Luth. Mission Erlangen, 1995.

"Management." *Gemeindewachstum* 3 (1981) 7.

Margull, Hans J. *Hope in Action: The Church's Task in the World*. Translated by Eugene Peters. Philadelphia: Muhlenberg Press, 1962.

McGavran, Donald A. "Church Growth Strategy Continued." In *The Conciliar-Evangelical Debate: The Crucial Documents 1964–1976*, edited by Donald A. McGavran. Pasadena: William Carey Library, 1972.

———. "Prof. Donald McGavran im Gespräch." *Gemeindewachstum* 29 (1987) 14.

———. *The Bridges of God*. New York: Friendship Press, 1955.

———. *Understanding Church Growth*. Grand Rapids: Eerdmans, 1970.

———, and Win Arn. *Wachsen oder Welken? Translated by Annerose Goldham, ABCTeam. Witten: Bundes-Verlag, 1978.

"Missionarisches Jahr 1980: Ein Positionspapier." *EPD Dokumentation* 20 (1978) 1.

"Mit Gemeindepflanzungen kirchenferne Menschen erreichen." *idea-Dokumentation* 79 (1998) 7.

Montgomery, Jim. *Eine ganze Nation gewinnen*. Lörrach: Wolfgang Simson Verlag, 1989.
"Müssen die Pietisten 'charismatisch' werden?" *idea-Dokumentation* 6, 7 (1992) 10–11.
Murray, Stuart. *Post-Christendom: Church and Mission in a Strange New World*. Carlisle, Cumbria, UK and Waynesboro, Georgia, USA: Paternoster Press, 2004.
"Natürliche Gemeindeentwicklung boomt weltweit." *Praxis* 74 (1998) 6.
Neely, Alan. "Missiology." In *Evangelical Dictionary of World Mission*, edited by A. Scott Moreau, 633. Baker: Grand Rapids, 2000.
Parrish, Archie. "Die Kirche muß evangelisieren." *Gemeindewachstum* 3 (1980) 4.
"Pfarrer fragen Pfarrer antworten." *Gemeindewachstum* 3 (1980) 7.
Pollack, Detlef. "The Change in Religion and Church in Eastern Germany after 1989: A Research Note." *Sociology of Religion* 63 (2002) 9, 19.
Rainer, Thomas S. "An Assessment of C. Peter Wagner's Theology of Church Growth." PhD. diss., Southern Baptist Theological Seminary, 1988.
Reimer, Hans-Diether. "Die Geistliche Gemeinde-Erneuerung in der Bundesrepublik." *Materialdienst der EZW* 11 (1986) 310–16.
Scharnowski, Reinhold et al. "3 aktuelle Berichte vom 1. Pastoralkolleg in Herne." *Gemeindewachstum* 3 (1980) 5.
Scharpff, Paulus. *Geschichte der Evangelisation*. Gießen und Basel: Brunnen Verlag, 1964.
Schippers, Oliver. "Aufatmen und Praxis fusionieren." *Aufatmen* 98 (2004) 2.
Schlottoff, Bernd. "98 Prozent der Pfarrer wissen nicht, wie man Menschen zu Jesu führt." *Gemeindewachstum* 32 (1988) 7–8.
———. "Eine Gemeinde wächst, aber . . ." *Gemeindewachstum* 5 (1981) 6.
———. "Erfolg Mißerfolg." *Gemeindewachstum* 11 (1982) 11.
———. "Es tut uns leid." *Gemeindewachstum* 35 (1988) 11.
———. "Evangelisches Studienkolleg für Gemeindewachstum in Deutschland." *Gemeindewachstum* 9 (1982) 11.
———. "Keine Angst vor Zeichen und Wundern." *Gemeindewachstum* 30 (1987) 4.
———. "Was steht im Mittelpunkt?" Evangeliums-Rundfunk Sendung, 1988.
Schlottoff, Bernd et al. "Gemeindeaufbau was ist das eigentlich?" Evangeliums-Rundfunk Sendung, 1988.
Schmidt-Schell, Erich. *Meine Gnade reicht für dich*. Lahr-Dinglingen: Verlag der St.-Johannis-Druckerei C. Schweickhardt, 1985.
Schmithals, Walter. *Die Theologie Rudolf Bultmanns*. Tübingen: J. C. B Mohr (Paul Siebeck), 1966.
Schulte, Anton. *Nur ein kleiner Dicker*. Moers: Brendow Verlag, 1982.
"Schulterschluß zwischen Evangelikalen, Charismatikern und Kirchen." *idea-Dokumentation* 103 (1991) 1–2.
Schwark, Christian. *Gottesdienste für Kirchendistanzierte*. Wuppertal: R. Brockhaus, 2006.
Schwarz, Christian A. "Der Praxis Report Nr. 1: Was jeder Mitarbeiter wissen sollte." *Gemeindewachstum* 45 (1991) 23.
———. *Die dritte Reformation: Paradigmenwechsel in der Kirche*. Emmelsbüll: C & P Verlag, 1993.
———. "Editorial." *Praxis* 61 (1995) 2.
———. "GW und der Rambo IV Journalismus." *Gemeindewachstum* 35 (1988) 3.

———. *Natural Church Development*. Translated by Lynn McAdam. Emmelsbüll: C. & P. Verlag, 1996.

———. *Praxis des Gemeindeaufbaus*. Neukirchen-Vluyn: Schriftenmissions-Verlag, 1987.

Schwarz, Fritz. *Ich verweigere mich oder von der Schönheit des Glaubens*. Neukirchen-Vluyn: Schriftenmissions-Verlag, 1985.

———. *Überschaubare Gemeinde: Grundlegendes ein persönliches Wort an Leute in der Kirche*. Vol. 1. Gladbeck: Schriftenmissions-Verlag Gladbeck, 1982.

———, Rainer Sudbrack. *Überschaubare Gemeinde: Die Praxis für Leute, die in der Kirche anpacken wollen*. Vol. 2. Gladbeck: Schriftenmissions-Verlag, 1982.

———. *Unter allen Stühlen: Dialog mit Pedro*. Moers: Brendow Verlag, 1985.

———, Christian A. Schwarz. *Theologie des Gemeindeaufbaus: Ein Versuch*. Neukirchen-Vluyn: Aussaat Verlag, 1985.

Schwesig, Johannes. "Wo Gemeinden wachsen: Zu Besuch bei amerikanischen Gemeinden." *Gemeindewachstum* 4 (1981) 2–3.

Seitz, Manfred. "Wer die Kirche verläßt, hölt sie aus . . ." *idea-Dokumentation* 100 (1992) 3–4.

———. "Missionarische Existenz der Gemeinde in der Volkskirche: Evangelisation und Gemeindeaufbau." *Theologische Beiträge* 13 (1982) 151.

Simson, Wolfgang. "Willow Creek in Deutschland? Nein Danke!" *Praxis* 67 (1996) 35.

Sorg, Theo. *Christus vertrauen Gemeinde erneuern: Beitrag zum missionarischen Gemeindeaufbau in der Volkskirche*. Stuttgart: Calwer Verlag, 1987.

———. *Wie wird die Kirche neu?* Wuppertal: Aussaat Verlag, 1977.

Sproul, R. C. *Lifeviews: Understanding the Ideas that Shape Society Today*. Tappen, New Jersey: Revell, 1986.

Stadelmann, Helge. "Ist zwischen Pietisten und Charismatikern Einheit möglich?" *idea-Dokumentation* 5 (1998) 24.

———. "Nehmt den Bibelfaktor ernster!" *Praxis* 61 (1995) 9.

Stearns, Richard. *The Hole in Our Gospel*. Nashville: Thomas Nelson, 2010.

Stratmann, Hartmut. *Kein anderes Evangelium: Geist und Geschichte der neuen Bekenntnisbewegung*. Hamburg: Furche Verlag, 1970.

Tennent, Timothy C. *Invitation to World Missions*. Grand Rapids: Kregal, 2010.

Thadden, Reinhold von. "The Church Under The Cross." In *Missions Under The Cross*, edited by Norman Goodall. New York: The Friendship Press, 1953.

Tlach, Walter. "Von den wichtigsten Aufgaben der Bekenntnisbewegung in zwanzig Jahren." In *Weg und Zeugnis: Bekennende Gemeinschaften im gegenwärtigen Kirchenkampf 1965–1980*, edited by Rudolf Bäumer et al. Lahr: Verlag der St.-Johannis Druckerei, 1998.

Ulrich, Heinrich-Hermann. *Die Kirche und ihre missionarische Aufgabe*. Vol. 1, Studien für Evangelisation und Volksmission. Berlin: Christlicher Zeitschriftenverlag, 1955.

———. "Evangelism in Germany: An Ecumenical Survey." *World Evangelism Today* 3 (1958) 8–9.

"Umfrage des Emnid-Instituts." Wetzlar: ERF, 1998.

Van Engen, John Edward. *The Growth of the True Church*. Vol. 3, Amsterdam Studies in Theology. Amsterdam: Rodopi, 1981.

Verkuyl, Johannes. *Contemporary Missiology: An Introduction*. Translated and edited by Dale Cooper. Grand Rapids: Eerdmans, 1978.

"Von Pfarrer zu Pfarrer." *Gemeindewachstum* 7 (1981) 3.

Wagner, C. Peter. "Church Growth Movement." In *Evangelical Dictionary of World Mission*, edited by A. Scott Moreau, 199. Baker: Grand Rapids, 2000.

———. *The Third Wave of the Holy Spirit: Encountering the Power of Signs and Wonders*. Ann Arbor, Michigan: Servant Publications, 1988.

———. *Your Church Can Grow*. Glendale: Regal Books, 1976.

———. *Your Church Can Grow: Bible Study Guide*. Pasadena: Fuller Evangelistic Association, 1976.

Wagner, William. *New Move Forward in Europe: Growth Patterns of German Speaking Baptists in Europe*. South Pasadena, California: William Carey Library, 1978.

"War der Ausstieg ein Abstieg?" *idea-Spektrum* 39 (1998) 15–16.

Watts, Michael. *The Dissenters: From the Reformation to the French Revolution*. Oxford: Clarendon Press, 1999.

Wie christlich ist Deutschland? Edited by Wolfgang Simson. Weil am Rhein: DAWN Europa, 1993.

"Wie die AGGA das Wachstum der Gemeinden fördern will." *Konzequenzen: Zeitschrift für die Arbeit in Gemeinde, Diakonie, Ökumene, und Mission* 1 (1987) 6–15.

Wie stabil ist die Kirche? Bestand und Erneuerung. Edited by Helmut Hild. Gelnhausen/Berlin: Burckhardthaus-Verlag, 1974.

"Wie wachsen Gemeinden wieder?" *idea-Spektrum* 43 (1986) 11.

Wilhelm, Hans-Martin. "Church Renewal in Germany: Is It Possible? A Study of the Established Protestant Church." DMin thesis, Fuller Theological Seminary, 1988.

———. "Europe: Should Missionaries Plant Churches in Germany?" *Global Church Growth*, April/May/June (1986) 21–22, 34.

———. "Germany: A Church in Mortal Danger?" *Church Growth Digest*, Spring (1986) 8–12.

Winkler, Eberhard. *Die Gemeinde und ihr Amt*. Vol. 53, Arbeiten zur Theologie. Stuttgart: Calwer Verlag, 1973.

Wirt, Sherwood Eliot. *Billy*. Wheaton: Crossway Books, 1997.

Index

American influence, xv, 4, 12, 16, 32, 33, 37, 40, 44, 51, 57, 62, 78, 84, 126, 153
Anabaptists, 97
Arn, Win, 36, 40, 48, 57, 62, 207
Association for Church Development in Germany, 64, 66, 94
Austria, 2, 21, 94, 132, 151, 161, 164, 205, 223

baptism, 11, 79, 97, 108, 120, 126, 143, 146, 198–99
   infant, 11, 53, 62, 79, 80, 97, 98, 108, 111, 114, 116, 121, 123, 129, 156, 171, 173, 187, 196, 198–99, 213
   Spirit, 69, 120, 146
Baptists, xiii, 7, 45, 198–99, 140, 163,
Barratt, T. B., 120
Barth, Karl, 12, 32
Bäumer, Rudolf, 22
Beatenberg Bible Institute, 13
Berlin Declaration, 27, 121, 124, 134, 136
Bittlinger, Arnold, 26, 122
Bonhoeffer, Dietrich, 185
Bosch, Roger, 32, 37–39, 44, 47, 54, 56, 62, 65, 77, 106, 132, 213, 223
Brethren Church, xiii, 45, 60, 163
Brierley, Peter, 166, 183
Brunner, Emil, 81, 87, 185

Bühne, Wolfgang 134, 135
Bultmann, Rudlolf, 22, 185

Campaign for Church Growth, xiii, 91–92, 96, 126, 127, 176
Campus Crusade for Christ, 32, 38, 75
Catholic Church, xiii, 19, 131, 199, 212
charismatic(s), 25–27, 46, 56–59, 67, 100, 118–126, 129, 132–54, 162, 171, 177–79, 183, 188–89, 201–2, 211, 214
Charismatic Church Renewal Movement (CCRM), 25–27, 52, 100, 118, 122–25, 132–36, 141–42, 188–89, 201–2
Cho, Paul Yonggi, 67, 118, 134, 177
Christenson, Larry, 26
Christlieb, Theodor, 19
Church Day(s), 9, 23, 109, 219
Church Day Under the Word, 23
church growth literature, 37, 48, 77, 101, 128, 145, 157, 160, 168, 205
Church Growth magazine, 32, 37, 47–48, 54, 67–70, 73–74, 100, 107–12, 128, 148–49, 188, 201
Church Growth Movement (CGM), vii, 17, 39, 46–47, 50–52, 60–63, 74, 81, 104–5, 124, 133, 150, 153, 165, 168, 164, 176, 206, 212–13

Index

American, 27, 32, 37, 41, 43, 50, 57, 58, 62, 73, 78, 90, 141, 182, 205
German, xv, 28, 40, 53–54, 59, 71, 95, 100, 125, 153, 156, 159, 160, 168, 179, 183, 188
Church Growth Seminar, 112–17
church planting, xiii, 57, 141, 149, 157, 127, 128, 133, 136–39, 150, 156, 160–63, 183, 199, 201, 204, 206, 211, 223–24
Community Church of Joy (CCJ) 142, 143
Confessional Movement, 21–25, 27, 66, 110, 111, 119, 124, 125, 129, 136, 141, 175, 201, 202, 211, 212, 215
congress(es), 8, 23, 37, 58, 102–3, 158, 160, 162, 181, 201, 204–9, 212, 223
  Church of the Future-the Future of the Church Congress, 142–43
  Congress for Church Planting in the *Volkskirche*, 136–39, 212
  Congress for Renewal and Church Growth, 132–36, 146, 154, 209
  Willow Creek Congress-Vision for Post-Christian Germany, 139–42
conservative theology, 23–24, 74, 153, 163, 169, 171, 214
contextualization, viii, ix, xi, xii, 1, 2, 29, 30, 42, 63, 64, 66, 68, 70–72, 74, 78, 89, 92, 95–98, 101, 102, 106, 132, 150, 169, 185, 186, 189–97, 200, 211, 216
conversion, 16, 20–21, 32, 45, 49, 56, 79, 83, 85, 88, 95, 98, 106, 108, 112, 116, 140, 154, 156, 172–73, 187, 191, 201, 206–8, 212, 215

Dallmeyer, Heinrich, 120
Decision magagzine, 119
Deitenbeck, Paul, 23, 110
Denmark, 128, 153
Discipling a Whole Nation (DAWN), 138, 141, 149–50, 160, 165, 180
documentary hypothesis, 185, 219
Dynamic Church magazine, 32, 37, 43, 47–48, 205, 208–9

East Germany, xiii, 2–14, 17, 30, 41, 59, 63, 143–44, 147, 163, 167, 170, 205, 207
ecclesiology, 16, 18, 20, 21, 25, 29, 57, 62, 71, 82, 86, 95, 111–17, 119, 153, 177–78, 186–89, 195, 197, 200–201, 206, 210, 214, 216, 223
Edel, Eugen, 121
Eickoff, Klaus, 118, 132, 140, 146, 168, 172–73, 178, 181, 210, 223
ekklesia, 85–89, 95, 98, 125, 165, 174, 186–87
Engelhardt, Klaus, 138–76
England (Great Britain), 8, 13, 19, 30, 33, 41, 81, 97, 128, 157, 162
European Church Growth, 128–29
evangelical(s), 13, 46, 100, 121, 124, 133–36, 146, 179, 188, 212
Evangelical Free Church, 13, 163
Evangelism Explosion (EE), 33, 47, 62, 64, 70–76, 82–84, 95, 208, 214,

Fabri, Friedrich, 20
Fallwell, Jerry, 36
Federal Council of Churches of Christ, 8
Fluckiger, Felix, 22
France, 128

Index

Frankfurter Declaration, 24
Free Churches, xiii, 13, 45, 48, 53, 68, 76, 89, 96, 99, 124, 134, 140, 148, 183, 195, 213
Freed, Ralph, 13
Fuller Theological Seminary, vii, xv, 27, 28, 38–39, 41, 51, 54–57, 74, 108, 112, 204, 206

German Baptists, 7, 140, 163, 198, 199
German Christian Society, 118
German Evangelical Alliance, 14, 103, 135, 154
German Protestant Church membership surveys, 17, 93–94, 143–45
German Tent Mission, 15–16, 19
Gibbs, Eddie, 41
Glasser, Arthur, 41
Gnadau Society (Fellowship Movement), 18–21, 24–25, 66, 90, 119, 125, 129, 136, 201–2, 211–12, 215
Gollwitzer, Helmut, 84
Goseberg, Reinhard, 76
Gospel Radio, 104–6, 158
Graham, Billy, 12–16, 33, 58, 135, 154
Great Commission, xii, 44, 48, 61, 74, 95, 107, 149, 188, 198, 219, 220
Great Schism, 131
Gregersen, Dagmar, 120
Griggs, Dennis, 38, 75

Haarbeck, Ako, 109
Haarbeck, Theodor, 20
Hackstein, Jochen, 160
Hansen, Johannes, 109
Heils, Jens, 118
Hempelmann, Heinzpeter, 138
Herbst, Michael, 75
Hinn, Benny, 177

historical-critical method, 166, 214, 220
Hoerscheimann, Werner, 124
Holland, 21, 97, 128
Hopkins, Bob, 157
Hybels, Bill, 139–42, 165, 223
Hyles, Jack, 36, 41

idea-Spektrum magazine, 103–4, 133–34, 160, 209
Institute for Church Growth, 39, 51, 65–66, 126, 132, 180

Janz, Leo, 15
Jehovah's Witnesses, 45, 115, 195
Jesus-People Movement, 26
Jones, Bob, II, 13

Kallestad, Walter, 142
Kasdorf, Hans, 60–61
Kassel Tongues Movement, 120–21, 124, 146
Kauper, Detlef, 118
Kennedy, James, 33, 41, 47, 70, 74
Kingdom Companies, 181
Knoblauch, Jörg, 32, 35–40, 51, 57, 62–63, 66, 103, 132–33, 147, 158, 161, 181–83, 210, 223
Knöller, Horst, 49–50
Kopfermann, Wolfram, 26–27, 100, 119, 122, 123–24, 160, 223
Koslowski, Christian, 160
Krusche, Peter, 123
Kühn, Bernhard, 121

Lausanne Movement, 58, 62, 133, 150
liberal theology, 22, 24, 25, 156, 171, 172, 214, 215
Liebenzell Mission, 16
Lohmann, Ernst, 121
Luther, Martin, 85, 118, 131, 169–70, 185

Index

MacArthur, John, 41
MacDonald, Gordon, 140
Mädel, Peter, 99
Maier, Gerhard, 42, 206
Manageable Church, 34–35, 78–84, 118
Marxism, 9–11, 75, 144
Marxsen, Willi, 22
McGavran, Donald, A., vii, xv, 27, 36, 38, 40–41, 48–57, 61–63, 100, 105, 124, 149, 207
Meincke, Friedrich, 3
Methodists, 7, 5, 140
missiology, xii, 184–216
missionaries, xi, xii, xvi, 1, 14, 28, 30, 53, 91, 92, 96, 126, 167, 176, 194, 199, 211, 215, 221
Montgomery, Jim, 149–50
Moravians, 19
Mormons, 45
Müller, Friedhelm, 118

Natural Church Development, 151–53, 164, 181, 224
New Apostolic Church, 45
New Life Bible School, 15
New Life Mission, 15
Ninety-Five Theses, 85
North American Society for Church Growth, 182
Norway, 120, 128
Nuremberg Manifest, 134, 146, 223

OC International (Overseas Crusades), xiii, 91
Ockenga, Harold J., 13
Office for Evangelism, 14, 16, 26, 58, 65, 89, 96, 99, 103, 109, 126, 129, 132, 138
Office of Education and Religious Affairs, 8
Oncken, Johann G., 19
Orthodox Church, 30, 131

Paul, Johannes, 120
Pentecostalism, 25–27, 119, 121, 134, 219
   Neo-Pentecostalism, 119, 124, 135, 146, 178
Pietism, 18–21, 32, 59, 63, 169
Poland, 2, 3, 30, 211–12
post-Christian Germany, 82, 88, 139, 185, 216, 217
postmoderns, 141
Power Evangelism, 57, 135, 165
Praxis magazine, 148, 159–60, 181, 223, 224
Prep Course for Church Growth, 33, 48, 64–66, 70–76, 108, 126, 180, 223
ProChrist, 135
Promise Keepers, 158, 165

Rambo IV Journalism, 108
Rappard, Carl H., 18–19
redaction criticism, 185
Reformation, 32, 131, 168, 169, 185, 221
regional church growth associations, 70, 77, 128, 163–64, 206, 212
regional church growth conferences, 76–77
Rubanowitsch, Johannes, 121
Russia(n), 2–4, 11, 163

Sanctification-Evangelism Movement, 19, 120
Sauer, Willi, 13
Schalk, Christoph, 159, 224
Scheffbuch, Rolf, 135
Scheffbuch, Winrich, 109–10
Schippers, Oliver, 159, 161, 224
Schlottoff, Bernd, 32–35, 39, 48, 62, 64, 70, 98, 118, 208, 223
Schneider, Peter, 15, 91
Schniewind, Julius, 22

School of World Mission, xv, 27, 38, 51, 54, 57, 112, 204, 206
Schrenk, Elias, 20
Schuller, Robert, 41, 43, 63, 67
Schulte, Anton, 15-16
Schwarz, Christian, 54, 84-88, 97, 107-11, 125, 141, 149, 151-53, 159, 164, 181, 223, 224
Schwarz, Fritz, 32-35, 39, 41, 54, 62-63, 71, 77-82, 84-89, 97, 118-19, 125, 165, 173, 223
Scientology, Church of, 31
secondary (theological) issues, 52, 63, 100, 124-25, 132, 133
Seitz, Johannes, 121
Seitz, Manfred, 137
Simson, Wolfgang, 141, 149-51, 181
Smith, Chuck, 43, 63
Smith, Oswald, 13
Sorg, Theo, 61, 62, 100-101
spiritual gifts, 20, 25, 54, 59, 65, 69, 70, 77, 107, 122, 136, 153, 168, 189, 201, 206
Spittler, Christian F., 18-19
Stauffenberg, Claus Graf Schenk von, 31
Stock, Bernd-Ulrich, 118
student houses, 24
study trips, 8, 23, 39-43, 66, 67, 70, 74, 77, 92, 153, 158, 165, 175, 204-6
Switzerland, 13, 18, 21, 58, 94, 128, 149, 151, 156, 164, 205, 223

taxation (church), 6, 53, 80, 114, 147-48, 163, 166, 168, 172, 174, 220

Teile, Agnes, 120
Tennent, Timothy C., 194, 198
Thielicke, Helmut, 32
Third Wave, 57, 135
Trans World Radio, 15, 104
Trend Churches, 138

unification, 9, 12, 143, 171, 201
universities, 5, 10, 22, 24-25, 80-81, 156, 171, 174, 213-14
Urlsperger, Johann A., 18

Verkuyl, Johannes, 197
Vetter, Jakob, 15, 19
Vorwerk, Bernd, 118

Wagner, C. Peter, 27, 36, 38, 40, 44, 54-56, 62, 84, 133, 135, 151, 153, 165, 177
Warren, Rick, 164
Weth, Rudolf, 110, 124
Wever, Hans-Rudolf, 15
Wichern, Johann H., 19
Wilhelm, Hans-Martin, 28, 91, 127
Willow Creek Community Church (WCCC), 139-42
Wimber, John, 56, 67, 134-35, 165, 177
Winkler, Eberhard, 59, 63
Working Group for Church Growth, 57, 127

Year of Evangelism, 89-91
Young, John, 13
Youth for Christ, 13, 15

Zinzindorf, Count, 185

www.ingramcontent.com/pod-product-compliance
Lightning Source LLC
Chambersburg PA
CBHW071941240426
43669CB00048B/2552